SKIRT STEAK

WOMEN CHEFS ON STANDING THE HEAT AND STAYING IN THE KITCHEN

SKIRT STEAK

WOMEN CHEFS ON STANDING THE HEAT AND STAYING IN THE KITCHEN

CHARLOTTE DRUCKMAN

CHRONICLE BOOKS
SAN FRANCISCO

Library of Congress Cataloging-in-Publication Data available.

ISBN 978-1-4521-0709-7

Manufactured in Canada

Designed by VANESSA DINA
Typesetting by HOWIE SEVERSON

10 9 8 7 6 5 4 3 2 1

Chronicle Books LLC
680 Second Street
San Francisco, California 94107
WWW.CHRONICLEBOOKS.COM

FOR

THE 37 OTHER GRADUATING MEMBERS
OF THE BREARLEY SCHOOL CLASS OF 1993
AND OUR MOTHERS
THE 73 CHEFS WHO TOOK PART IN THIS BOOK
& EVERY WOMAN WHO CONSIDERS HERSELF OR ASPIRES TO BE A CHEF

In spite of all the talk and study about our next years, and all the silent ponderings about what lies within them for our sons [Why only sons? Since I wrote this I have acquired two daughters, and they too shape the pattern's pieces, and the texture of my belief!] it seems plain to us that many things are wrong in the present ones that can be, *must* be changed. Our texture of belief has great holes in it. Our pattern lacks pieces.

—M.F.K. FISHER,
"HOW TO BE SAGE WITHOUT HEMLOCK," 1942

Shoulder to shoulder sweatin' 110 degrees
But I will never faint, I will never faint
They laugh and they expect me to faint but I will never faint
I refuse to lose, I refuse to fall down

—PATTI SMITH, "PISS FACTORY"

WHAT TO EXPECT, A TABLE OF CONTENTS

No opinion has been expressed, you may say, upon the comparative merits of the sexes even as writers. That was done purposely, because, even if the time had come for such a valuation—and it is far more important at the moment to know how much money women had and how many rooms they had to theorize about their capacities—even if the time had come I do not believe that gifts, whether of the mind or character, can be weighed like sugar and butter. . . . All this pitting of sex against sex, of quality against quality; all this claiming of superiority and imputing of inferiority, belong to the private-school stage of human existence where there are "sides" and it is necessary for one side to beat another side.

—VIRGINIA WOOLF[1]

That's original, introducing a book about women with a quote from Virginia Woolf.

Just like you, Virginia knew a cliché when she saw one. If you read her thoughts above, then you know she was decrying a tired practice—comparing men to women—all those years ago, in 1928, when she drafted the two papers that would later be consolidated into *A Room of One's Own*. People have been reading that treatise for decades; people have also continued to, when discussing the matter of women's rights or gals' roles in society, dwell on what differentiates the sexes and how those disparities might handicap one or the other (usually, the Other—as in, the ladies). That tendency has only served to single women out and delineate them as deserving of extra help. Being marked as "special needs" is no way to gain equal footing.

For me, as for Woolf, all this—defining women in opposition to men or as exceptional (meaning, an exception to the rule)—has nothing to do with the price of tea in China. We can opine on women's emotional outbursts, their nurturing qualities, and their ability to multitask until the cows come home. Or we could discuss men's competitive

---

[1] Virginia Woolf, *A Room of One's Own* (Florida: Harcourt, 1929, 1981), 105–106.

nature, physical stamina, and egotism till we're blue in the face. Better yet, since this is a book about the culinary world, we might get into that whole debate about male versus female cooking, and wonder if Hatshepsut's dishes look and taste more girlish than Gilligan's. As my mom would say, *Let's not and say we did.*

A conversation that might be worth entertaining (at least, I know my editor thinks it is—she advised me it was a good idea to introduce myself early on so you'd warm to me) is the one wherein I explain why, with a world full of women fighting for equality, suffering countless injustices under oppressive regimes, struggling for opportunities, or merely deflecting the occasional chauvinist zinger, I narrowed my field of vision to chefs.

The simple, flippant answer would be: Because I'm selfish.

The complicated answer, which you—and this book—deserve, starts with my citing another renowned British author, Martin Amis. A few months ago, I stumbled on something he'd uttered in a 1998 interview.[2] It unnerved me. "But it has to be said," he began, "perhaps with some regret, that the first thing that distinguishes a writer is that he is most alive when alone, most fully alive when alone. A tolerance for solitude isn't anywhere near the full description of what really goes on. The most interesting things happen to you when you're alone."

His is a rather dismal outlook; writers are isolated shut-ins whose only companions are our imaginations and drafting materials. Unwilling to accept this as my lot, I began looking at the writer's life and solitary confinement from a different perspective. Amis dwells on the aloneness of his trade. What he renders melancholy and dramatic is only the by-product of an extraordinary experience. I see it like this: What distinguishes a writer is that she is most alive when writing.[3]

[2] Martin Amis, "The Art of Fiction," an interview with Francesca Riviere in *The Paris Review*, Number 146 (Spring 1998), 133.

[3] If she happens to be alone when this process takes place, so be it. Many people who relish what they do find that the most transcendent moments transpire when one has turned inward. Under that spell, everyone else disappears.

Certain topics, themes, or tangents have a stronger pull than others. I am most alive when writing about what moves me, and that would include one of the following: intelligent, thoughtful, creative souls who are passionate about what they do and express themselves through that medium; food, for example, the Fortunato No. 4 chocolate truffle I tasted yesterday (it is the supplest, most luscious, gentle yet intense burst of pure velvety ganache I have ever had[4]) or a dish that New York City chef Anita Lo just told me she is serving at her restaurant Annisa for New Year's Eve ("a salad of roasted kabocha [squash], lacinato kale, a slow-cooked egg, and Mangalitsa prosciutto[5]"); talented people who aren't getting the recognition they deserve—in a word, underdogs; or, finally, anything that reeks of unfairness (as adolescent as that might sound).

It's not hard to understand how, based on that list, the "plight" of women chefs would appeal. Gender aside, I love talking to chefs about what they do. I've found them less laconic than their reputations would lead us to expect. When you stumble on something that excites them—it could be an ingredient, a delicacy tasted in another country or neighborhood, an idea for a new restaurant concept, an innovative technique, a breakthrough cookbook, or a controversial review—you see the wheels turning, the gleam in their eyes. If a writer lights up when stringing sentences together on a page, a chef comes to life when doing her job—or thinking about it.

I find that contagious. It makes me want to write. And then we have the medium—the grub. Obviously, it's a draw for anyone who gets off on the perfect bite, but there's something bigger than that. Food has become a dominant presence in pop culture. There are television shows devoted to cooking and to eating—there's even an hour-long daily talk show on ABC called *The Chew*, hosted by chefs. Sure, this national "pastime" has its insipid manifestations (Gordon Ramsay's *Hell's Kitchen*

---

[4] It's made by Christopher Curtin of Éclat Chocolate in West Chester, Pennsylvania, and features some strain of rare Peruvian cacao bean previously thought extinct.

[5] Have you tried that cured pork product? You should.

comes to mind when I think of model abysses); it also allows for debates on health, economics, and politics. Food is the metaphorical spoonful of sugar that helps the proverbial "medicine" go down.

As for the overlooked talent and, not so very different, the "unfairness" factor—what some might deem the "medicine" here—once zeroing in on chefs, I could have easily looked at race or sexuality instead of gender. Self-centeredness kicks in. I'm a white, straight girl. That's how I'm going to relate; can't help it. I assess the realm about which I write and I try to put myself in it, and when I do, I spot things that don't add up. If this book could motivate those of another race or sexuality to apply a similar approach to their respective points of view on the culinary or any other arena, that would be some smooth buttercream frosting on the cake.

Why, when we're obsessed, as a culture, with chefs and their output, has that fixation landed on those who are decidedly male? It's as though we have a blind spot. What I've discovered is that it's not all that unusual for a woman to work in a galley kitchen,[6] or—hold on to your hats—be in charge of one. This has not always been the case, and the gender ratio is still heavily weighted toward the penile, but if you think that being a professional restaurant cook is a gig reserved for guys, you're living in the past, 1928, maybe.

When Woolf championed each woman's right to have a room of her own, the one room she wasn't referring to was the kitchen. That was the only chamber of which ladies were already in command. But it was a puppet regime. Today's chefs may joke about being chained to the stove. They merely co-opted the expression from the housewives who were expected to stay on the premises and fret over tasks like putting dinner on the table. That's just what Woolf protested. She was concerned with her sex's lack of access to money and—related—opportunity to engage in intellectual pursuits.

Woolf might be a little flummoxed then to find I've borrowed her words for a book on women who cook. I'd like to think, though, that if

[6] Taking its name from the ships in which it originated, within the culinary world, the galley refers to a professional restaurant kitchen. It is often a small, narrow space, but can also be quite large, depending on the venue.

she realized this, too, is a dialogue about having a room of one's own, she'd be cool with it. The physical context has changed—we've left the residential domain for the grittier workplace and traded the family's Sunday roast for the evening rush of restaurant dinner service—the message has not.

We needn't waste our time bemoaning our (bosomed) troubles, fielding the question "Why are there no women chefs?" or defending our culinary chops. Instead, let's begin with a simple premise: female chefs are the norm.

"Being a woman shouldn't be a novelty; it should just be what it is."
—*Heather Carlucci-Rodriguez*

"Sometimes I get angry at women's organizations like Women Chefs and Restaurateurs and Women's This and Women's That—not *angry*, but I don't relate. I don't look at myself as being special [just because I'm female]. . . . There have been too many conversations about that. It's done. Let's move on."

—*Ana Sortun*

Yes, Ana, let's. First order of business: Figure out which are the questions typically posited to the gals of the galley, skip them, and then raise the ones that aren't asked. For starters, if, in the past, investigations have sought to discover why women leave the industry, I'd suggest we find out how they stay and thrive in it.

Next, instead of presenting individual characters, my strategy was to weave their experiences together and examine the stages of and influences on a chef's career. To that end, I've tried, on these pages, to create a community of people who have two things in common—their profession and their gender. Which of those makes them more alike? That, reader, is yours to decide.

Maybe you'll frown upon what follows as another "Women's This" or "Women's That" production. So be it. I would argue that it's always better to try and fail than to accept the status quo—methodological or otherwise. I'd like to think that's what compelled the women who were skeptical about signing up for this project to take the plunge. Anita Lo (she's the one who ushered in 2012 with kabocha squash), one of my initial inspirations (more on this in chapter 2), expressed as much. "Some female chefs," she acknowledged, "feel that participating in books like this one adds to the problem by underlining the gender difference, by further marginalizing the group—that we can't be just another chef if we're constantly defining ourselves as female chefs. I would agree if I felt we were closer to achieving equality. If you agree that gender is a social construction, then the walls can only be brought down by all of us—by all of us questioning how we add to the problem, by continuing the dialogue."

I'm not sure how much I can do to continue the dialogue beyond these pages. For now, though, I've got twelve chapters, seventy-three trusted cohorts enlisted for the cause, and a laptop[7] of my own.

---

[7] I have named said MacBook Pro *El Lappers*. Mark it down for future reference, please.

CHAPTER 1

What Is a Chef?

Somebody who cooks professionally with a reasonable amount of responsibility, I consider a chef.

—SEEN LIPPERT

[Chef] means a lot of things. It means that I manage a very large group of people; it means I have to be creative and manage a lot of menus that have to be politically correct, economically friendly, and ecologically [conscious] . . . I have to be a psychologist—once in a while, an MD who administers drugs . . . I have to remain cool not only among people in the back, but also people in the front . . . That's what it's all about—being able to juggle.

—MICHELLE BERNSTEIN

I don't call myself a chef . . . the word chef *comes from this long history . . . it doesn't have to be a man or a woman. It implies this sort of brigade system where [there are] higher people and lower people, this whole totem pole situation, and there's one person at the top who's commanding orders. And that's not how I work or how I've ever worked. And so I just prefer to call myself a cook or a restaurant owner or whatever it is. Just the word* chef, *I don't use it to apply to myself. I'm not staunchly against it; I don't correct people when they call me a chef. It's just not the way I think about myself. I think of myself as somebody who cooks professionally.*

—NAOMI POMEROY

Obviously, it's a leader; we all know that. But a real chef can fix any problem that comes up in the course of the day, and that is the cutoff point, that's when a chef is really a chef. You could have a swarm of bugs or something come in and land on every bit of food, you could have a roof fall in, or you could have [food for] a party of eighty people that has to go out—the chef knows how to [handle] these kinds of things. And the other part is, a real chef has a sixth sense about food. He or she can walk through a kitchen and something makes that chef stop at that very moment and look to the left or the right and find something that is off, is wrong. You could say, "Well, how can you do that if you never even looked?"—it's truly a sixth sense. A chef knows when he has to delve into something and get to the bottom of it. A chef is a fixer-upper, somebody who just reads the whole place and knows when he's needed to fix something and help. That never leaves you. You're like that forever . . . but then, on the other hand, to be a chef, hopefully you have talent. It's amazing how many chefs don't really understand food or can't really cook well. They don't know how to season food; they don't know [what] the end result [is]—how something tastes good, how something should be; they don't know how to make it better, which is really sad.

—LYDIA SHIRE

We're cooks and we manage people. It's not an award or an experience. [The word chef is] so misused that, for me, I just like to break it down to its most basic definition, which means "person in charge, managing." That's all it means in French, "chief." It doesn't mean you're on the Food Network or whatever else people think it means. . . . It drives me crazy when everyone in the kitchen calls everyone chef. If we were all chefs, nothing good would get done.

—CLAUDIA FLEMING

A chef is a facilitator as well as a creator. I'm not really sure there's a definition for chef *these days. A chef, now, is someone [who's] a celebrity. Unfortunately, this whole media frenzy in cooking has been a detractor in some ways, too, because it's taken some of the focus on what the real business is of being a* chef *and a restaurateur and turned it into this media scene. But life is always moving forward . . . you have to keep moving with how it's changing.*

—PAM MAZZOLA

A chef is somebody who makes food for people and they pay for it. In some ways, I have an ambivalent feeling about the word chef, *partly because it's so overused now and it has this celebrity chef connotation [and] partly because it really divides the history of people cooking for themselves and the history of people eating out in restaurants. And in some ways, a lot of good could come from merging those things rather than separating them. It has changed, a lot, and one way it's changed is that now, anyone who talks about food for a living could be called a chef; anyone who writes a cookbook could probably be called a chef. There are aprons that are monogrammed that are sold for children that are chef's aprons—it's just become this idea that it's an aspiration; at the same time, it's this attainable aspiration that you can have. I read something [in an airline magazine] . . . it was like, "Create your own signature dish at home with this—whatever—muddler." This idea that we have to have signature dishes coming out of our home kitchens—that part of the word is what is troubling to me.*

—ANDREA REUSING

Don't worry. It's not all going to be a collage of quotes. I'm going to write; I have some thoughts of my own. Although it seems, right now, at the onset of chapter 1, where first impressions are made, like an indolent writer's cop-out to present a compilation of other people's words, there's a strategy here.

I've my reasons for possibly alienating you.

1. Let's put the least appealing, and, perhaps, least relevant first, to get it out of the way. After interviewing seventy-plus chefs and feeling equally vested in and connected to all, the idea of leaving any of them out of the book doesn't sit well. What better way to get a whole bunch in than early on, where you'll find them interspersed throughout these early pages?

2. What is a chef? That was, mostly, the first question I asked each subject. This is, after all, a book about chefs, and I'm a firm believer in defining terms. Shouldn't we know exactly what a chef is before we go on to discuss the rest?

3. Once the first few interviewees answered the question, it became clear that no singular meaning was going to materialize. The term *chef* is one in flux, and the numerous and often contradictory classifications of the word are evidence of a larger, fascinating dialogue about a profession that has changed (and continues to change) so rapidly in ways that are simultaneously bewildering, encouraging, frustrating, challenging, disappointing, inspiring, and disheartening. In fact, this question emerges as *the* question. It's what, regardless of gender, every chef has to grapple with: *What kind of chef do I want to be? What kind of chef can I be?* Once you've answered that, then maybe you need to figure out how your gender is going to come into play.

4. The only way to experience the paralyzing confusion that attempting to answer such a question can induce is to have a slew of myriad responses slung at you. If you are feeling a bit overwhelmed, then I

apologize. You are only experiencing a fraction of what these chefs themselves do, and a dose of what I did during the research process.

Although we might never be able to settle on one definition of the word *chef*—is it a title, a vocation, a synonym for *cook*, an aspiration?—as far as I'm concerned, each of the women who participated in this book is a chef in that she has at some point (at the very least) been in charge of a restaurant kitchen, and thus held the position (whatever that means) of executive chef.[8]

That may be the only constant. Otherwise, here's what we've got: A chef can be an activist, an artist, a craftsperson, a restaurateur, a cook, a bringer-together-of-people, a cookbook writer, a businessperson, a celebrity, a teacher, a mentor, a leader, a shrink, or, even, a superhero.[9]

What has happened (the abridged, grossly simplified version) is this: something that began as a European trade became an American profession and, subsequently, a glamorized lifestyle and entrepreneurial platform. And yet, although it has grown into these phenomena, it has also, in many ways, remained what it once was. In terms of required skill sets, socioeconomic reality, and actual (versus perceived) lifestyle, the what-was-and-still-is and the what-it-has-become are often in direct opposition to one another. The original designation is the most narrowly defined—it emerges out of a French tradition and references a specific, prescribed trajectory that, for most of its existence, has been an experience shared solely by white, apparently straight men. The training and the métier are steeped in repetition and the details of technique, and yet, whereas back in the day final ascension meant overseeing all of that technique, currently, in America, the ultimate goal is often to own numerous eateries, or become one's own marketable brand.

[8] One or two may not have held that title, nominally, but they filled that leadership position.

[9] This last classification was inspired by Lydia Shire's invoking of a sixth sense. As she spoke of a chef who can tell when even the littlest thing in her kitchen is off and, instantly, sniff out the offending peccadillo, an image of Neo—as in, hero of the *Matrix* trilogy—flashed across my mental screen. I imagined Keanu-as-Neo-as-chef (yes, I know we're here to discuss female chefs; no, I didn't envision Trinity in this particular instance), a nimble toque who, as he dodges flying knives and cavalierly tossed flaming brûlée torches, doesn't miss a single beat and can predict a salmon's potential desiccation before the grill cook even fires it.

"We're asked to be too many different things now, and it's hard, because you probably come into this business because you have a talent in a certain area, and then you have to pick up and be all these different things," observes Traci Des Jardins, who's well aware of the pressure placed on ambitious chefs and sees some relief on the horizon. We met at Jardinière in San Francisco, her flagship, and the first of multiple restaurants in which she's involved. I was mildly petrified; Des Jardins is known for only participating in not-for-profit projects. She doesn't contribute to books willy-nilly. And although I wasn't paid a hefty sum to write this and, if I'm lucky, will barely break even on the thing, I couldn't say it was for charity. Word on the street was that she's formidable—as a chef, yes, and as a presence too. Lady doesn't mess around. So there was that.

Also, it was the day before I was scheduled to head home after six weeks of traveling (and interviewing chefs) along the West Coast. I was exhausted, and, for the first time since I can remember, lonesome— missed my friends, my family, my city.[10] I feared my capacity for engaging anyone in conversation had dwindled to the ability to muster a single question: "What's up?" I'm going to assume that either people are easily intimidated, or they haven't spent any time with Des Jardins. As soon as we got going (as in, after the old "How's it hanging?") I asked her "What is a chef?" and the time and chatter flew. She had just returned from shooting the third season of Bravo's *Top Chef Masters*[11] in Los Angeles, which made her more attuned to the many directions in which today's chefs are pulled. You can tell she has given the matter much pondering when she says: "We're going to see more differentiation between the media star-slash-chef who maybe doesn't have the great foundation in cooking, but has that media star quality; we're going to see the chef who only wants to cook and is respected for the fact that they're in their restaurant pretty much every night; we're going to see the chef who's

[10] That would be New York City; I was born and raised on the island of Manhattan.

[11] She went all the way to the finals, along with one Mary Sue Milliken; you'll meet her later.

really good at multiple restaurants and putting together concepts. . . . You want your experience to be good when you go to a restaurant, but what does that mean exactly? If it's really, really good, does it matter [if the chef is the person touching every plate]?"

Des Jardins's vision puts a positive spin on the chef's job description. She imagines a near future when, instead of having to be the whole package, those who carry the mantle (or apron) can specialize. Today, though, if you talk to enough of her peers, you realize that to excel, a 21st-century chef needs to be both a jack of intersecting trades and the master of her craft. Up close, to cite Cher Horowitz in the 1995 film *Clueless*, it's a big old mess.

When I try to break the many facets of chefdom down, my head starts to hurt. The hope is to provide an overview of the basics—chef as manager, as owner, as restaurateur, and as media personality—and then dig deeper into some of those later on.

I guess it makes sense to go back to France first, since that's where the terminology and the title-giving tendencies originate; it's from whence the word *chef* comes and why we're stuck with it. Many of the ladies referenced it and its intended meaning, "chief." That generic synonym for *boss* would appear to be the most straightforward qualifier, but, when you're talking about women chefs, to enter *la patrie* (that's "homeland," a feminine noun) is to find yourself faced with a *casse-tete* (that's "puzzle"; it's masculine). The title and the baggage it totes become anything but applicable. Many a French noun is arbitrarily gendered (as above), but professional monikers usually have both male and feminine forms—like, for an actor, there's *acteur* (m.) and *actrice* (f.). There is no *cheffe*. It's the same word for a boy or girl, and why? Probably because (and you'll note that even now, there are very few female toques in charge) across the Atlantic, professional kitchens were considered male domain—no girls allowed. And you could say that this is a trivial matter—that *chef* is only a word and its meaning and usage can change over time and adapt to modernity. But when we borrowed *chef* from the French, we took more than just a title. We acquired the entire system—kitchen setup included; it became the foundation on which the American restaurant industry[12] was built. Even in our melting pot, that professional pocket has been slower to get with the program or yield to diversity than you'd think (or hope).

"I agree with the French standard, where the chef is the expert. The chef is in charge. Where the definition has changed over the years is that it's not necessarily formal training that puts you in the category of chef any longer. So I consider myself a chef even though I wasn't formally trained in cooking."

—*Johanne Killeen*

"When we think of chefs in a stereotypical way, it's the man with the million badges on his lapels and the big hat, and that's less and less the norm. There's more focus on the artistry of being a chef rather than on the pomp and circumstance of being a chef. I don't know if that's factually true, but that's what I've noticed."

—*Elizabeth Belkind*

"Traditionally, when someone thinks about a chef they probably think about a male who has been indentured in this work since they were quite young—that was the French model. Someone with maybe a big girth and a big mouth and invoking a little bit of fear or terror in their employees and, on the outside, quite a bit of power . . . Since there have been restaurants, there's an element of the chef persona and craft that has been intriguing to the audience, and lots of different things have been thrown at that, especially most recently . . . There's an attention on it that's maybe a little exquisite about the individual, and it's not

---

[12] Obviously, I'm not talking about fast food here. McDonald's is not a restaurant, people. There's a distinction. Let's leave it at that and move along, please.

necessarily about what it is that person is capable of expressing through food. And really, a restaurant is about identifying a reason why you go there, and that reason historically was about an ambient quality that was a reflection of the food, the intent of the chef."

—Amaryll Schwertner

I wonder if this hard-to-sever French connection has something to do with American female chefs being uncomfortable with the "chef" label, which many of them appear to be. It makes sense that anyone who wasn't—by selection or circumstance—affiliated with the traditional toquerie (and if that wasn't a word before, it is now) would shy away from the title. Case in point, we have Jessica Boncutter, who owns a small restaurant in San Francisco's Hayes Valley.[13] Des Jardins suggested I speak to her, and it's just another thing I can add to my list of Reasons to Be Grateful to Traci. "I honestly don't really consider myself a chef," Boncutter told me. The most laid-back of the women I interviewed, she's always laughing, Jessica is. And you find yourself giggling with her. When I played back the tape of that interview, I heard a frequently repeating refrain of cascading *ha-ha-ha-has*, and real ones, from the belly. This rant was no exception: "Yes, I spent my whole life cooking in the kitchen and I know how to do it, and I know how to be a chef, but to me, *chef* almost has a negative connotation. I picture this guy—French guy—with a tall hat, screaming at everybody, throwing pans, and who has severe psychological problems. It's like, 'Save it for your shrink, buddy! Life is already hard enough, we don't need this dysfunctional horribleness in the workplace.' That's what I think of it. When people say, 'I'm a chef,' I have to be honest; my first reaction is an eye roll, mainly just because, to me, chef can equal ego . . . I just want to make good food and create a really warm atmosphere, and I just want to make sure that everyone who comes into my restaurant has a good

---

[13] There—Bar Jules, it's called—I, a person who categorically rejects brunch, had a minor lapse on a Sunday afternoon. I might have licked my plate if I hadn't already soaked up the perfect mess of fried-egg yolk and vegetable-braising liquid with expertly buttered, grilled toast.

time and eats delicious food and enjoys the company that they're with and has great service. It's pretty simple."

Boncutter isn't wanting for ambition; but while others might equate achievement with flouting their prowess, lording over underlings, basking in fame, raking in the chips, or seeing their names in neon lights on eatery signs across the nation, she defines accomplishment on her own terms. "Obviously, I want to be a success in my life, and I want to have a successful career, but all of that stuff that *chef* equals to me is so unimportant in my life . . . I'm sure a lot of those chefs look at me and they think, 'She's not a chef; she's just cooking. She's just a home cook that has a restaurant,' and that's fine. I don't care. That's a different thing. You look at these guys and you chuckle inside a little bit."

I'm chuckling right now. And while I'm feeling lighthearted, I'm going to step outside the guy-girl conversation for a second and note that, if we stick to that original, European classification of *chef*, and consider what it entailed, in terms of necessary training and experience, it remains a baffling position no matter what your gender. The trajectory takes you from a task-oriented line cook[14] to an overseeing executive chef, and there's something almost arbitrary or illogical about that.[15]

[14] *A cook is not a chef.* If we use the more literal, or what I'd call the Strict Constitutionalist appellation of *chef*, then this law is a cut-and-dried one. But here I am spending who-knows-how-many pages trying to make sense of and support a more realistic, modern definition for that word—one that, often confusingly, allows it to be a title, profession, and lifestyle at the same time. And this broader interpretation makes the chef/cook thing a whole lot more confusing. For those who ally themselves with the Frenchies and their galleys, then, sure, there's a big distinction to be made between *chef* and *cook*—both are culinary titles, one is just more advanced than the other, a higher (okay, the highest) rung on a ladder. If you're not one for the hierarchy or the tradition out of which it comes (maybe it seems feudal and unfair; maybe you think it's inherently chauvinistic; maybe you didn't undergo that kind of inculcation; and/or maybe you associate it with a kind of food you don't make), then you might have some hang-ups with both signifiers. On the one hand, you don't feel like *un chef* (Fr.) but you're also aware, as the head of a kitchen with a point of view that you're leading a team to represent, that you are doing a job that's different from your cooks. And if you're a woman in the industry, and you have a problem with the fact that when you say you cook, people assume that means you cook *at home*, then how do you distinguish yourself in that way? Forget having boobs for a second; male chefs have reason to be frustrated with the vocabulary too.

[15] Along the way, it occurred to me that the words *chef* and *cook* had less meaning when pondered objectively than they did when seen through the eyes of whoever was uttering them. A chef's feelings about the terms were more a reflection of how she saw herself than anything else. The best way to approach the *Chef v. Cook* antagonism is Babbo Pastry Chef Gina DePalma's. She suggests that, instead of griping about or getting defensive of the word *chef*, people make an effort to restore the dignity that used to and should be ascribed to the term *cook*.

This I realized after talking to Emily Luchetti, who is the executive pastry chef of two amply sized spots in San Francisco—Farallon and Water Bar. In mapping out her own professional development, she makes some sound points that are indicative of the reality faced by most: "You come into the business because you can be a good cook and you have a technical ability to re-create and you also have a creative ability to make things, and that skill set doesn't necessarily go with the business side. And so, often, over the years I would see that if someone cooks well and does a good job, either on the line on a Saturday night or creating dishes, they make you a manager. Well, [for] managing, the skill set is completely different . . . I've seen so many amazing cooks that never could manage people and so they just burned out and they left, and it was really too bad."

"By definition, a chef has to have their Indians, or they're not a chef. So it's amusing but harmless that you read in the paper 'she's a home chef' or 'he's a chef,' when in fact, it's a person who cooks recipes at home. If you aren't leading others, what are you the chef of? . . . If you come out of professional training and formation in a classical structure like [in] France, there's an unavoidable distinction and awareness; you've got your *chef*, your *cuisiniers*, your *commis*—all the rankings and hierarchies are quite clear and the implications of those roles are clear. Whereas in America, it's more murky. If you hear the word *chef* in America, people think 'person who cooks' more than they think 'person for whom the majority of their mastery may have to do with being a really good manager or inspirer.' Just like in France, it's the *chef d'entreprise* or the *chef d'orchestre*—a chef is the leader of whatever—and leading cooks is tricky, like leading violinists or whatever the case may be. To be an orchestra leader/conductor, I imagine you have to be good at many of the things the people you're leading do, but you don't have to do all of them perfectly. Maybe you're a great violinist and you're decent at some other string instruments, but you're not a reed instrument player and you may not be a brilliant pianist; but you know enough that you can inspire the people of those disciplines. Likewise, in the kitchen, you can be a culinary chef without necessarily being the best pizza maker or best spun sugar constructor, but you probably know something about how sugar works, so you have a respect for what goes into being good at any element of cooking and can bring out the best in other people's culinary skills."

—*Judy Rodgers*

"Being a chef means creating a team . . . A team leader, like I am now, [means] you look at people—the people in your organization—and you say: 'What are their best qualifications? What can I do to make this a better organization and make it so all the desserts are better? How do I bring out the best in everyone who works for me, so the restaurant benefits, everybody has a good working environment, [and] the desserts are great?' And that's a real puzzle, and it's a different kind of creative challenge."

—*Emily Luchetti*

What Luchetti's talking about is the clash between the micro work that one learns and carries out as a cook and the macro nature of what one faces as a *chef* (italicized here to reference the titular definition; it's interchangeable with "executive chef"). If you've had a lick of traditional culinary training, you've spent a lot of time doing repetitive, mechanical, detail-oriented work; for example, deboning fish, chopping mirepoix,[16] nailing a sauce, or searing meat. If you do this for long enough and do it well, you may be promoted to a predominantly managerial position. Nothing you've been doing has prepared you, really, for being able to take in what everyone else, who is executing those menial, precise tasks you once did, is doing and make sure the well-oiled

---

[16] A backbone of French cuisine, this is a combination of diced onions, celery, and carrots that, once sautéed, becomes a base for many stocks, sauces, stews, and the like.

machine stays that way. You go from cog to engineer, and there's no guarantee that your having excelled in the first position ensures you're a good fit for the second. It's mostly a crapshoot—dependent on how you're wired. The ability to do both—master the details and oversee the bigger picture, or act as part of a synchronized team and stand apart as its recognized tone-setter—is a bit like being ambidextrous.

"I run two restaurants and both of them are relatively large . . . so my role is no longer—for better or worse—to stand in the kitchen and chop onions and cook. My role is really to mentor these guys and get them behind my cuisine, get them excited about the food, and get them to cook it the way I want it cooked, to really lead them to understand a philosophy of food, a philosophy of kitchen practices, and a philosophy of work ethic and treating product, and Italy, and Italian cuisine. Sometimes I really miss the day-to-day cooking, and I *am* in my kitchens—I expedite in one or the other restaurant every night I'm at work—but sometimes I really miss that grind of getting in there and cooking for eight hours. Though, sometimes I don't."

—*Missy Robbins*

"I still think *chef* means 'cook.' You don't stop being a cook. It also means 'teacher,' like you're teaching people now that you're a chef. You're responsible for other people and making sure they learn and develop their own talents and strengths."

—*Maura Kilpatrick*

The gulf between little and big pictures widens when you go from being an employee (on the line, or running it) to an owner. Historically, in Europe, the two hats—that of restaurateur and that of chef—were not worn on the same head. As pointed out by Boston's Barbara Lynch, sovereign over eight enterprises, the restaurateurs own the property outright. It's often passed down from one generation to the next. In

France, a (without fail, even throughout most of the 20th century) male chef would be hired to fill that position, and in Italy (if we're generalizing, or getting all "Old Country" about it), the proprietor's (a.k.a. big boss) *nonna* (the grandmother, as embodied by whichever generation of wife, mother, or nana suits) would be in the kitchen. Either way, the business side was the driving force; the cuisine directed by a certain style of technique (instead of an individual's personality or perspective) executed by a hired hand, dexterous as it might be. In the USA, eateries, by and large, are leased, so there's much more fluidity in the operational and financial infrastructure. There's more risk involved, too, of course, which, in a way, fuels the ascendency of the chef as the front person (or at least the owning partner). With a marketable talent at the helm, you have an audience magnet, an obvious story to sell.[17]

That fluidity has provided many female chefs with the dining rooms of their own that the European model (French or Italian) would not. For ladies who wish to run a kitchen, sometimes the best (or only) option is to take proprietary action. Consider this: There's a system that defines and monopolizes a particular arena (i.e., a restaurant kitchen) and doesn't include you. If you want to participate in that zone, you're going to have to go outside that system and, if you can, create a new one. As we all know, in any industry, or really, in regard to any convention, those who don't fit the ideal are forced to follow (or carve) different paths and, by virtue of maneuvering off the usual track, remain outside the matrix. For the professional cooks of this (the Western) world, if you're not welcome in the "standard" space (as embodied by the French fine-dining establishment), you're obliged to take matters into your own hands, which means, probably, going petite (there's the reality of money to consider) and indie (again, with the finances—how much backing can you get if you're a scrappy unknown?).

---

[17] The leasing route also, as Lynch noted, makes it harder to turn a profit, "So to succeed, you need to have more than one [restaurant]," which she does.

That's what a number of gals did, even before it was fashionable (because now, "intimate," chef-driven, and chef-owned spots are in development, under plywood, on every corner). They ditched the formal, large-scale European pomp and circumstance, bucked the system, and rewrote the rules. *Top Chef* alumna (and fan favorite), cookie-baking entrepreneur, and now a cohost of ABC's *The Chew*, Carla Hall witnessed the exodus in Washington, D.C.'s culinary realm, where a number of women "have left to create their own culture." Some skedaddled by choice, others because there wasn't another option. A self-created place was one in which they (and anyone who didn't want to tow *le ligne*[18] or fit the part) could thrive. And a lot of that entailed, deliberately or not, defining themselves in opposition to the "Continental" status quo.

Over in Hayes Valley, where the laughs kept coming, Boncutter talked about the vision she had for her neighborhood spot, and I saw how conscious she was of building something antithetical to the accepted standard. "I appreciate that form of cooking; refined—I don't want to say old-school—but I appreciate that, and I have a big respect for those old French chefs who come from that school of L'Escoffier and all that," she said.[19] "People aren't necessarily impressed by that [old-school approach], I know I'm not. When I go out to dinner and I see something plated like that, with a tiny bit of this and a tiny little bit of that, I mean, it's a great moneymaker, like food cost–wise, because there's just nothing on the plate . . . It's total bullshit."

Boncutter follows in the footsteps of women like Alice Waters, who, forty-one years ago, opened Chez Panisse in Berkeley, Calforina, and not only introduced a new style of fine dining (a more casual,

---

[18] French for "the line." Why not learn a word or two when it makes for a bit of double entendre?

[19] It might be helpful to mention, or not (I mean, isn't that the point? That it shouldn't matter? That a "chef" can be someone who rules the most refined, French-est roost or the casual, less conventional one?), Boncutter did not go straight from tending her home stove to opening Bar Jules. She trained at two modern landmarks: San Francisco's Zuni Café and London's The River Café, both internationally acclaimed spots owned by female toques and known for having launched many a culinary career—Jamie Oliver's for example; he cut his teeth at the latter. Helpful or no, this information lets you know that Boncutter isn't suffering a lack of self-confidence for not having had "legitimate experience."

ingredient-forward one), but also altered the structure of the professional galley when she abolished the hierarchy therein. She got rid of titles and rotated the staff so that her cooks took turns mastering different stations. She was an early example of the modern chef-owner, and she changed the signification (and significance) of the terms used in the back of the house.

In spite of the great respect Chez Panisse enjoys and her position as a major player in the food world, Waters remains intensely connected to the food served at the restaurant, which is unusual when that level of success is achieved. She perpetually insists that she is out and about, at the farmers' markets, on the farms, putting her hands on the produce, and ascertaining that the ingredients meet her high standards. This is a connection that many chefs lose when they expand from having one restaurant to many. The higher you climb, the farther you get from the details.

"I had myself corrected by Jacques Pépin one time when I refused to consider myself a chef, and he said, 'If you are in the kitchen and you are organizing people to produce a meal, you may not be the most accomplished in terms of cooking, but you are, in fact, doing that job, which is the main one in the kitchen, and you can't think of yourself as a cook.' But, for me, a chef has always come with a lot of fanfare and a lot of authority and a lot of experience in the kitchen; and I never went to cooking school, and I've always relied on other people coming in who knew more than I did. And yes, I did dream up menus, and certainly have been a critical taster, and I'm pretty good on the grill, but we work more in a collaboration."

—*Alice Waters*

"I'm pretty simple and not real philosophical about [the word *chef*]. It's just someone who cooks professionally . . . that's basically it. If you get too deep into it . . . I just don't care; I don't care if it's *chef* or *cook*, it's just nonsense to me . . . I understand the hierarchy and realize that *chef* means you've made it to a certain place in the hierarchy . . . But either way, we still just cook professionally; we're all in the same boat."

—*Johanna Ware*

"I find I call myself a *cook* more than a *chef* . . . How I started cooking was something that was just out of not an interest of becoming a chef at all, but becoming someone who just learned how to make things and loved working with my hands . . . [*Chef*] felt like something that was very educated and not so much felt from the heart, and sometimes— because of that idea or maybe by being intimidated by this big machine of the culinary world—I always felt more comfortable just being called a *cook* . . . I'm a little more of [a chef] now because of having three restaurants . . . I'm less cooking on the line all the time, so I feel I'm less of a cook and I'm more of a chef now, by definition. But my heart is still in the simplicity of just wanting to make really good food and make people happy . . . I do [feel the definition is shifting to include that perspective]."

—*Renee Erickson*

A *chef* and a *restaurateur* may not be the same thing (far from it); the former, circa 2012, can become the latter. It doesn't really work the other way around; although, one could ask why, if someone who has professional cooking training can learn how to run a business on the job (or maybe fake it till she makes it), the business savant can't pick up cheffing know-how. We won't go there. This isn't a book about restaurateurs (only chefs who happen to be restaurateurs) and, more important, that kind of question would seriously piss off a whole lot of chefs (especially those with "formal"—ahem, French—training, or at least, extensive galley experience). Plus, I noticed, a few of the girls got a little miffed about the business of the business. In Portland, Oregon (where I now want to move, even if Carrie Brownstein and

Fred Armisen's genius *Portlandia* TV sketch show mocks that sentiment and makes me feel like a sucker for being so easily won over by that city), Sarah Schafer, the executive chef (but not owner) of Irving Street Kitchen, asked, while raging against today's culinary school students and their motivations, "Do you want to be a restaurateur or do you want to be a chef?" I see her point. If you want to be a chef, you may have the opportunity to put your name on a number of outposts, but if all you want to do is open and operate those outposts, you don't really want to be a chef. And if you're happiest when you're in the kitchen, putting out the fires, crafting the menu, and seeing each plate go out, it's probably not a good idea to start building a brasserie chain in your mind. Or, to say it another way, if you love being the CEO of a galley, ask yourself if you want to be the head honcho of numerous joints that contain a galley.

That choice—to plant your flag in various soils—doesn't rile the chefs up as much as the one that entails signing autographs and facing the cameras. It's a hotly contested topic. Finally, we come to the proven crowd-pleaser: glamour. (You're welcome. I like to build to a crescendo; take you from the refreshing, subtle ceviche that tickles your palate to the tender, melting fat and crisp flesh of the pork belly you've been waiting for.) There's an aura of what I call bloodsugarsexmagik[20] around these *pumping-on-your-stereo*[21]-in-surround-sound culinary people, and it's a new acquisition.

In the late '80s, when Seen Lippert (a Chez Panisse vet) was enrolled in the Culinary Institute of America, a "chef was nobody of note . . . someone who produced dinner at the red-leather steak house (where they served steak with sorbet on the same plate, which I never understood) . . . It was a blue-collar profession." Then, in the '90s, the tide turned (the Food Network was founded in 1993). "It has evolved into 'Do I want to go to Harvard or do I want to be a chef?' " observes an

---

[20] It's a Red Hot Chili Peppers reference, in case you're wondering. It's a play on the name of their 1991 album.

[21] Supergrass tune. Check the band's eponymous 1999 album for a peppy listen.

astounded Claudia Fleming.[22] Like the high school outcast–cum-fuckup who, one day, finds herself the front woman for a newly hip indie band, suddenly—and mostly totally unprepared for their fates—chefs are a source of endless admiration and fascination.[23]

The transformation is probably most pronounced for those like Des Jardins, who have been in the industry long enough to know what things were like before chefs or food achieved icon status and who continuously strive to bridge the gap between the kind of chef they once aspired to be and the 21st-century ideal. "In the 1970s, [with] the chefs who worked in restaurants like Lutèce,[24] the pinnacle of the evening was the chef coming out of the kitchen and visiting all the tables, and [the chefs] were there every night. And there's something fabulous about that, and there are so few restaurants that have that anymore."

In the same camp as Des Jardins, you've got one of the first to put in an appearance on the Food Network, Miami-anchored Michelle Bernstein, who seems similarly confounded by the almost surreal bestowal of fame. "We're now walking on red carpets instead of coming into the back entrance." And then, for the blunt delivery, in San Francisco, there's Pam Mazzola's assessment of the situation: "You have to be a social networker to be a chef."

My favorite of these less-than-elated perspectives comes from that straight-shooting pistol known as Mindy Segal. She doesn't "necessarily think the glorification of a chef is the best thing," and construes her lot as being "in the exceeding-expectation business." In her estimation, then, chefs "are not supposed to be famous." Segal has a hybrid

---

[22] Just typing her name makes me hanker for a slice of the legendary chocolate caramel tart she served at Gramercy Tavern in New York City. She sprinkled sea salt on the top. It kicked off a salted caramel craze whose ripple effect we can still taste in truffles, bonbons, ice creams, and plated desserts across the country.

[23] As I type, the following lines of Santigold's "L.E.S. Artistes" have surfaced: "You don't know me/I am an introvert an excavator/I'm duckin' out for now/A face in dodgy elevators/Creep up and suddenly/I found myself an innovator."

[24] Lutèce was a Manhattan institution and bastion of fine French dining from 1961 to 2004. Its chef and eventual sole owner, André Soltner (imported from France himself), is considered an international culinary legend.

space in Chicago called Mindy's Hot Chocolate,[25] so I knew I'd like her going in. After our lengthy (couldn't stop our motormouths, either of us) phone chat, it was a done deal.

No one needs to invoke chocolate (never hurts, though) to convince me that the celebrity thing has its downsides, the most obvious of which is that it doesn't offer the most representative depiction of what life's like for the majority of chefs (who are not on television or writing cookbooks). "There's a glamorization over the last twenty years[26] that has been good for our career, but not always an accurate picture of the reality of what goes on," says Denver, Colorado, representative Jennifer Jasinski.[27]

The biggest concern voiced is that the impressionable youngsters are lead astray by dreams of grandeur, product endorsement deals, and reality-show competitions. They all want to be chefs, or so they think. They want to be the chefs they see on TV, or, sometimes, they just want to be on TV and they think food might be their way in. Two chefs who are fed up with these kids? Presented in order of frustration level: Soa Davies of New York City and Liza Shaw of San Francisco.

The former: "Today, it's much harder to weed out the people who truly love food and cooking from the people who want to do it because they think it's a status career . . . It's a physical job and cooking is manual labor. I don't think so many of the young cooks graduating from culinary school these days understand it . . . Some of these kids

---

[25] "Restaurant. Dessert Bar. Pastries." So reads the website.

[26] As the meticulous and insightful Jane Tunks, my copy editor on this book, fairly pointed out, Jasinksi's "citation of 'twenty years' of glamorization contradicts the citation of 1993, the launch of the Food Network, as the beginning of celeb chefs, that you reference earlier (page 32). On that page you also have the Seen Lippert quote that says in the late '80s, chefs were nothing of note." Point taken, Jane. Before the advent of the Food Network or of the celebrity generated by reality television, there was, in the restaurant world, a prototype for the celeb chef. He was famous in a more insulated—context-specific—way. French legend chef Paul Bocuse is a good example (note the annual international Bocuse d'Or competition held in his honor). Or, for a more modern version, there's Wolfgang Puck, who opened landmark Spago in 1982, published his first cookbook in 1986 (five more would follow), and had three restaurants up and running by 1989. When, in 2000, *Wolfgang Puck* aired on the Food Network, he joined the ranks of today's celebs, like Mario Batali, whose *Molto Mario* series arrived in 1996.

[27] Related: Jasinski recently self-published her first cookbook, *The Perfect Bite*, which, while we're here, I might as well tell you, I like a whole lot.

get out of culinary school with the misconception that they're going to become a sous chef within a year, or they're magically going to fall into a great job straight out of school and then they're going to be on *Top Chef* within five years and become a huge celebrity."

The latter: "We have this problem with these kids . . .who are given all these false promises and they expect to come out of culinary school and (a) be the chef of their own restaurant; (b) have a TV show; (c) write a cookbook right away. And it's so astounding to me, like we get these kids that come right out of culinary school that come stage [intern] in the kitchen and they want to jump up on the oven station. We're like, 'What?! You've never worked in a restaurant before. You can barely cut an onion!' [And they all call themselves] chefs. Makes me fucking crazy."

Less skeptical or wistful (and a smidgen younger), Fōnut queen Waylynn Lucas[28] admits, with optimistic reason, "I'm happy that chefs nowadays are getting this voice and this recognition, and are kind of the new rock stars, because before it was the sort of the thing you did when you were too stupid to go to college . . . But now, it's this very exciting, recognized thing. The fruits of our labor are starting to be recognized, and I do like and appreciate these things, the good that Jamie Oliver is doing now, and the awareness of unhealthy food and the nutrition-starved children in America." Lucas was getting at how chefs can take the attention and pay it forward by aligning themselves with humanitarian causes; they can shift focus away from food trends and on to more pressing concerns.

[28] Hear ye, hear ye. Waylynn Lucas of Los Angeles and I convened at the Urth Caffé on Melrose Avenue while she was the pastry chef at master progressive chef José Andrés's The Bazaar. Conveniently, for me, I was staying at the hotel in which that restaurant resides. Lucas and I, of course, did not meet on those premises, because I wanted her to feel free to speak her mind, which she did and it was a treat. The *real* treat, however, came later that evening, when I returned to my hotel room after seeing a friend's play and found a picnic of baked goods and chocolates had been laid out for me, courtesy of my new pal Waylynn. I felt like Sara Crewe in Frances Hodgson Burnett's *The Little Princess* when the little ragamuffin's neighbor magically makes breakfast feasts appear every morning in her cold, dark, miserable hovel of a room at Miss Minchin's Boarding School. (Right, I wasn't staying in a shithole, so that part doesn't carry.) But I digress. A few months later, Lucas told me she had left the Bazaar (glad it was *after* my visit, so I still could reap those rewards), and was opening a doughnut shop unlike any other. It would not sell doughnuts; it would sell a new invention, unfried fōnuts (like faux doughnuts, get it?). And that it does.

Lucas's advocacy of Oliver's MO puts the sprawling definition (as opposed to the neat and tidy "chief of the kitchen") of *chef* in a positive light. Yes, some of these multi-tentacled forces may fall victim to property hoarding, the blinding lights of fame, or the cushy paychecks gleaned from QVC sales of their cookware, but others can be agents of beneficial change—they might fight to end starvation, raise money for deserving causes, teach people to cook or eat better, or simply present the public with a new, exciting, and delicious style of food or restaurant no one has seen before. A less precise answer to the question "What is a chef?" allows for new models—new types of chefs—to emerge, and that comes with silver linings. We now have the chef as humanitarian and, really, no disrespect to Mr. Oliver, but Alice Waters loaned her name and energy to a cause years before he did when she founded the Edible Schoolyard in 1995 and began lobbying for food education to be added to public school curricula and for gardens to be built on the grounds of those institutions.

There's an alternative breed of chef on the scene, one I dub the chef-farmer (it's not the most accurate, but it'll do for now). This pertains more to a style of cooking and the food-to-table process than to a new role to be tackled. But it also raises the question of what skill set or preparation can be counted as necessary, qualifying, or useful. On a rainy (of course it was) evening in Seattle, at her place the Boat Street Café, Renee Erickson first got me mulling this. "I think everything to do with making food is shifting," she said. "Including myself, many people are untrained in the sense that we haven't gone to culinary school, but we're trained in more exciting ways—we're going to farms, meeting farmers, seeing people butcher pigs—not so much in the classroom setting but in the actual place where the stuff is raised and grown for us to use."

Another resident of the Emerald City, Ericka Burke looks through the same lens as Erickson in trying to claim an alternative understanding of how a chef shapes her craft. "When I was first in the industry, the term *chef* was definitely someone who was trained and very technical and sort of this intimidating figure . . . But I think the industry has changed in terms of [that there are] a lot of self-taught people coming up on the scene that just have deep-rooted core values about food and about gardening and are bringing that to the table. So I don't think that all that education and regiment and technical skills are as sought after . . . as they were back then."

What this "new" strain of chef does isn't so very novel. Getting in touch with one's terroir[29] predates Escoffier.[30] In Europe and beyond, following the seasons and using what your soil has to offer has always been a mainstay of home cooking and haute cuisine. Alice Waters reminded me of this when she quoted something Alain Ducasse[31] had told her. "He said, 'Finding the food is 85 percent of cooking.'" If you go by that recipe, then it should be a prerequisite for any invested culinary professional to be engaged in the sourcing of his or her raw materials. Waters has been a longtime proponent of this practice. "A chef should look at the lettuce and decide how to use it, decide who will work with it." It's that 85 percent of the job that she identified with and latched on to all those years ago in Berkeley. And so we have one more facet

---

[29] This is the French word for "land." Within the realm of gastronomy, it has another application. Integral to the language of winemaking, the term *terroir* refers to the combined environmental factors—soil and climate, for example—responsible for a wine's defining properties and distinct flavor. It has been applied to food and connotes microregionalism. If, for example, a California chef is working with ingredients grown in the Bay Area, then her food could be described as reflecting the terroir of that zone. If another chef grows every product she uses on the farm next to her restaurant, then her food could be described as reflecting an even more specific terroir.

[30] Frenchman (shocker) Auguste Escoffier was born in 1846 and dead come 1935. He was a chef and restaurateur, and the author of *Le Guide Culinaire*, which became the 20th-century bible of French gastronomy and is based on the haute cuisine of the previous century. Escoffier codified that legacy in more "modern" (now, they seem downright fussy and arcane) terms.

[31] For those down-to-earth folks like me who have a copy, *The Food Snob's Dictionary* (by David Kamp and Marion Rosenfeld) "defines" Alain Ducasse thusly: "Streamlined, Bond-villain-ish French chef (born 1956) whose status as arguably the foremost culinary mind of his generation has been compromised by his brash forays into international entrepreneurialism. Making his name in the late 1980s at the Louis XV restaurant in the Hôtel de Paris in Monte Carlo, where his training under the Nouvelle Cuisine stalwarts Michel Guérard and Gaston Lenôtre (see footnote 64, page 61) came to glorious fruition, Ducasse spent the nineties and aughts on an expansionist tear, opening multiple restaurants in France, Japan, and the United States. Though he is the only chef to have simultaneously rated three Michelin stars at restaurants in different countries, his American efforts have suffered from a certain tin-eared, Mentos-commercial Euro-tacky sensibility that doesn't resonate with U.S. diners." (Broadway Books, 2007) NB: I'm enjoying Ducasse's latest U.S. release, *Nature: Simple, Healthy and Good*, the cookbook Rizzoli published in English earlier this year.

of cheffing that we can attribute to Waters, at least here in the United States. At Chez Panisse, she cast off the pretense and put the produce in the spotlight.[32]

Waters lay the groundwork for Erickson, Burke, and their male counterparts to place more emphasis on the products they use than on transforming their ingredients with dazzling techniques. Unfortunately, this approach has, notably, when practiced by women, been painted into an anti-professional corner. If the French masters embody the technical, these ingredient-coddlers are the opposite—they're pegged as untrained or unprofessional, regardless of skill or experience. And once you get to "unprofessional," you're dangerously close to home-cook territory, which, in turn, has long been demarcated as a woman's domain. This kind of association can be both detrimental and misleading, because one's style of cooking should not qualify one's professional status. There are successful chefs who have used peasant food, or their mother's home cooking, or street food as inspiration—some of these have turned it into nearly unrecognizable, wildly innovative fare while others have replicated it with impressive consistency and accuracy. There are also chefs who have done the same with nouvelle cuisine[33]— i.e., transformed or perfectly reproduced it. Meanwhile, there are unsuccessful types of either of these chefs. Many are excellent cooks and lousy leaders (ergo, crappy chefs). Others are excellent leaders and mediocre cooks (so, some would say, great chefs). To decide someone's worth or merit as a chef based on the genre (not caliber) of food her

---

[32] And as much as *les femmes* weren't taken seriously in the French kitchens where Ducasse trained, women were equally disparaged by the purveyors of Northern California. "In the men's world that existed at that time, I had to make myself credible to the producers and everybody else, so I used my best sort of feminine seductive techniques to get people to give me their best tangerines or their perfect rack of lamb," Waters told me. "And I was kind of willing to do just about anything in terms of finding these products, and I think it impressed the suppliers that I would go down there and look at it instead of ordering on the phone. So I was doing things that were just, you know, unprecedented, a little bit, in the way restaurants operated back then."

[33] This time, let's go to the third edition of the *Food Lover's Companion* (edited by Sharon Tyler Herbst) for our definition: "nouvelle cuisine [noo-vehl kwee-ZEEN] A French term meaning 'new cooking,' referring to a culinary style, begun in the early 1970s, that moved away from the rich, heavy style of classic French cuisine toward fresher, lighter food served in smaller portions. The sauces are lighter because they're reduced instead of being thickened with flour. Nouvelle cuisine vegetables are quickly cooked and therefore are tender yet slightly crisp." (Barron's Educational Series, 2011) 417–418.

(or his) kitchen puts out is as ridiculous as labeling that food male or female. Still, in the words of Carly Simon (which I can hear her singing as I type), "It happens every day."

Back in Portlandia, Jenn Louis, another acolyte of the Waters "Produce First"[34] religion, condenses all this drivel into a digestible snack and it's the perfect amuse-bouche for chapter 2: "There's more than one way to do lots of things, and it's all about the process of how you get there . . . If you were to travel in another country, say, Italy, you're going to watch a grandmother in the country cook . . . and she's going to do it this way, which is very different [from the French-based technique taught in culinary school]. The end result I would never challenge because it's going to be so delicious, and if you didn't know her method of getting there, you never would have questioned it either . . . There's more than one way to get to that end result." There's also more than one way to begin.

---

[34] Please note, that initiative does not exist in real life. I've just made it up.

What It Takes

There's something you should know.

I have never worked in a professional kitchen in any capacity.[35] *And I know that I never could.*

Why? In our interview, D.C.'s Ann Cashion mentioned something that hit me, hard. I tried to shake it off, but it stuck. She observed that most of the women who thrived in her kitchens were those who had played team sports, excelled athletically, or possessed physical confidence. "You need that to be on the line," she said. That kind of physical confidence is something I do not possess, and I don't expect to acquire it anytime soon. In grade school, I'd ask my friends to get me out early in dodgeball games, and then I wouldn't rotate back in. When sent to weekly ice-skating classes (the only bright spot found on those Friday afternoons was the granola bar handed out on the van ride home), I spent the entire session gripping the wall.

It wasn't that I had a theoretical fear of falling. Before they laced me up and put me on the rink, I had seen other kids take a spill on the ice now and then and knew it was part of the skating package. And once I'd gotten out there, I'd fallen too. That was the problem. I kept falling, ever and often—more than anyone else. My weak, wobbly ankles weren't holding up. Worse, though, my tumbles seemed nastier than the others'. They'd bounce right back up. Not me. I found it excruciating every

---

[35] Unless you count nonprofit food-service kitchens, which I don't, because those were one-off, short stints in which I chopped celery, packed up meals, ladled out soup, or helped prepare a few large trays of turkey tetrazzini and apple crumble.

time. I came home with golf ball–size bruises and, after landing smack on my coccyx, found it painful to cop a squat or stand up again. My parents insisted I continue participating, although I complained bitterly. My only recourse was to take to the wall and hang on for dear life. I understood this was not for me, this skating business. Now I know why.

My body was aware of its shortcomings well before my logic put two and two together. Between the ages of nineteen and twenty-four, I had managed, in chronological order, to break my kneecap clean in two by slipping on a patch of black ice on the way to an undergrad art history class (I was wearing what my mother would call nonsensible shoes, true); score a herniated disk while riding on the back of a Jet Ski; and, after being run into by someone on a bike, break my femur a few inches below the hip joint. This all seemed a little unusual and prompted me to get myself a bone density test. No shocker, really (except that we don't necessarily realize these things can be diagnosed so early on; they can), I have osteoporosis. It's genetic. My bones are only programmed to get so dense. Break one, it'll heal; it's just not able to reach what's considered the normal mass. Not only that, but a practitioner of ancient Ayurveda once told me that my chart indicates some rare karmic darkness that manifests itself in physical injury. I'm not kidding. The man, who gave me some special chants to sing in order to ward off the evil, claimed that, statistically speaking, if a brick were to fall from a building, mine was the head on which it was most likely to land.

You can see why, then, maybe, the professional kitchen might not be a good place for the likes of me, with my bad juju and tendency to fracture. One of my closest (and maybe not so tactful) friends once noted that Samuel L. Jackson's character in the movie *Unbreakable* reminded her of me (clue: he's the one who personifies the title's opposite condition). Brittle Bones McGee over here needn't be slipping on stock spillage or lifting 100-pound sacks of flour.

As a food writer, I didn't realize how much this handicapped me, until one of the chefs I interviewed asked if I had ever worked in a restaurant kitchen. I felt mildly crap about not doing the method-acting thing and having the actual experience myself. "Mildly crap," in this context, is a euphemism for "total failure." *How can you call yourself a journalist if you don't get in the trenches like a true investigative reporter would? This is worse than publishing a recipe you haven't tested. You're a fake and a phony and I wish I'd never laid eyes on you!*[36] That's more like it.

As the self-loathing abated (a little), and reason returned, I recalled that there are journalists who have already conducted galley experiments and expertly documented them.[37] What I was left with—once I got over my skeletal deficiencies—was the acknowledgment of where so much of my deep awe and respect for chefs comes from.

There are some things we have in common. First, there are the workaholic tendencies (I realized it was 3:20 a.m. when I sat down to edit this chapter). If I wasn't already wired for obsessive-compulsive behavior when facing the task at hand, my schooling instilled that in me. It's some crazy combination of a work ethic and a treadmill approach to homework that did it. One of the teachers at my prep school joked that the reason she gave her students so much reading was to keep them off the streets (not such a dumb idea when you're dealing with New

---

[36] Yes, I purloined that last deprecation from *Grease*. Sandy throws it at Danny.

[37] Should you like some examples, there's Lauren Shockey's *Four Kitchens: My Life Behind the Burner in New York, Hanoi, Tel Aviv, and Paris* and Bill Buford's *Heat: An Amateur's Adventures as Kitchen Slave, Line Cook, Pasta-Maker, and Apprentice to a Dante-Quoting Butcher in Tuscany*.

York City kids). We couldn't slack off if we'd tried. Nothing was more embarrassing than getting a bad grade or, even worse, not completing a task.

Then, which keeps the workhorse at a full gallop, there's an innate need for my toil to be tied to something I'm passionate about. Indifference is the one thing that makes me lose my professional mojo. It's a boundless curiosity for food that's responsible for my uncanny (and mostly useless) memory for menus I've seen and plates I've ordered (I'll usually remember what the other people at my table ate too). It's a love of tasting and pondering each bite that has armed me with something of a sharp palate, and rendered me a strong improviser in my home kitchen. My fixation on all that's edible (and on restaurants) is certainly part of what makes me enjoy talking to chefs and writing about what they produce. An interest in self-expression is something else that draws me to these people.

These traits—the discipline and drive, the fascination with food, and the desire to communicate through a medium (words or ingredients)—are what allow me to relate to these chefs. But this idea that they are physically capable of enduring so much floors me. They're my caped crusaders. Within my profession (typing in front of a blue screen or getting all Barbara Walters on cheese makers doesn't offer much by way of a physical challenge) or in terms of what my DNA has to contribute (I couldn't land an assignment to track climbers on Mount Everest even if I wanted to), there is no equivalent accomplishment I can ever hope to own.

When Ann Cashion or any chef mentioned how athleticism or having participated in a team sport made her better equipped to handle life in the galley, she reminded me that there are some very real limitations that can hinder one's success in this field. Few of us non-chefs are aware of what's required, and how many of those nonnegotiables might be the deal breakers that keep us out of those kitchens.

What those of us who can't (or won't) put ourselves in the galley, or who think they might like to get into the cheffing game, can do to imagine the conditions is ask the real McCoys to tell us themselves. It's the next best thing to being there.

Here, then, in their own words, are some things you should know about what it takes to make it:

"It's not about staying up, drinking, and eating worms. Being a chef isn't about bravado; it's about being consistent."

—*Pam Mazzola*

"Cooking is a little bit like carpentry. You're building a plate, and you have novice carpenters who just start out and all they do is cut planks of wood, and that's like the cooks who are put on garde-manger[38] and do *mise en place*[39] all day. And then you graduate and you do finished carpentry, which is when you're actually getting to shape something a little bit. And then you have your master carpenters who can build beautiful pieces of almost art. And you have to be dedicated the whole way through in order to reach that status of master carpenter or chef."

—*Soa Davies*

---

[38] Both the name for the kitchen station at which cold dishes are prepped and kept cool and a person who is assigned to that area (the *chef garde-manger* would be the one in charge).

[39] Let's take this one to the *Larousse Gastronomique*, self-proclaimed (and rightly so) as "The World's Greatest Cookery Encyclopedia." *Mise en place*, ahem (clearing my throat to signify authority): "The French term for all the operations carried out in a restaurant prior to serving the meal. In a restaurant dining room this constitutes laying the tables; in the kitchen it means setting out the ingredients and utensils required for the preparation of the dishes on the menu. The apprentice or assistant is generally in charge of preparing the vegetables, bouquets garnis, chopped onions, parsley, etc., while the initial preparation of stocks, fumets, sauces, and compound butter and the preparation of meat and game, consommés, soups, and desserts is the responsibility of the appropriate cook or section chef." (Mandarin, 1990), 815.

"Advice to emerging chefs: If you're doing it for money or fame, there are better, easier things you can do . . . In this life, if you don't love what you're doing, it's not worth it."

—*Johanne Killeen*

"You're only making $10 an hour starting out. Can't just be 'I like making cookies at home.' It has to be something you're passionate about and love doing."

—*Karen DeMasco*

"It's not an easy career choice. You don't make that much money, you have to work your ass off physically. If you want to have kids, that's a really tough question you have to ask yourself, because it's really hard to run a business and have children."

—*Jessica Boncutter*

"The strong survive, and that is more true in kitchens than probably [anywhere, except] in the military maybe. It takes a very strong will. It takes a very strong physicality [and] a strong mind to be able to work the hours and get pummeled physically in the way that you do and, also, depending on who your boss is, mentally. The thing that I always tell people is, 'We don't make enough money to not be learning something every day.' You need to make it worthwhile for the cooks who you're employing, because I would love to be able to pay all of my cooks $20 an hour, but you simply can't do that. And I don't think that anybody really gets in it for the money. That's kind of a fact. You need to make it fulfilling in other ways, whether it's teaching or experiential."

—*Liza Shaw*

"If it wasn't for the discipline of dance, I don't think I would have survived . . . In a kitchen full of boys, I'd cut myself on the meat slicer, and the bets were, Michelle won't come back to work for days . . . So I picked myself up and went back. A lot of people lost a lot of money that night. There's no way I could work sixteen hours a day, not sleep much. I was in school and working two jobs . . . I'm sure the only reason I did it, and stayed awake and alive, was because of years of very serious dance training."

—*Michelle Bernstein*

"You have to love it. You have to love it with every ounce of your being to do it, and to sacrifice so much and to do the long hours and to be in that stressful, chaotic environment. If you don't truly genuinely love it, if it's not a part of your soul, you won't make it. And I wouldn't have gotten to a place where I am as a chef. I would have thrown in the towel a long time ago . . . I get really, really mad about it. I've given up everything to become a chef and do what I do. I've given up holidays; I've given up family; I've given up the birth of my best friend's child. I've given up all of these things to be this chef and to know and live food, and to be able to, now, somewhat, create freely."

—*Waylynn Lucas*

"I pretty routinely try to talk people out of it. You really have to be made of different stuff. I love what I do. Would I choose to do it again? I'm not so sure, because it's really hard work. And that's not why I wouldn't choose to do it again—I love hard work. Do I necessarily love working weekends or holidays or not having insurance? . . . The fact that I missed somebody's communion or shower or somebody's wedding . . . Those are regrets I have . . . This is a real sacrifice."

—*Claudia Fleming*

"I don't want women to think they can't do it . . . There's a lot of fighting that we had to do to get as far as we did, a lot of pushing, a lot of life you had to give up in order to have the same chance. I can remember family members' funerals or weddings or birthdays that I had to miss, because I had to get it done . . . Now I look back and it's just like, 'Wow, I really did that.' . . . All the relationships that you lose because of it—all the weird incestuous relationships you gain because of it."

—*Sarah Schafer*

"It's all about commitment. To be a chef, you sacrifice a lot, so the more committed you are, the further you'll get in your career. And, the other thing is, you have to be humble, because you have to always realize that what you have here today can be gone within a second tomorrow. So if you get that huge ego, forget it . . . someone always wants to bring you down. So long as you stay on the course, and you don't get off track, and you're focused and committed, you'll be successful."

—*Heather Bertinetti*

"Maybe a lot of people get the wrong impression and think that a chef position is such a glamorous, fun, exciting thing, which it is . . . But it's also miserable sometimes. It's a lot of pressure, and hard to sleep at night when you actually do get the hours to sleep. If you're truly passionate about what you do, you never stop thinking about other people's perception of what you do, how your food is portrayed, and how it's received by your customers and your peers too. I feel a lot of peer pressure . . . maybe it's . . . partially related to being a woman in the industry and being surrounded by other male chefs . . . I always feel this kind of pressure to keep up with the pack."

—*Melissa Perello*

"If you're not confident—whether you're a man or a woman—then you can let people second-guess and push you around . . . People will find those cracks and exploit them."

—*Jennifer Jasinski*

"Any chef, male or female, [it] doesn't matter, you have to have your own definition of success that's defined by you—not defined by the media, not defined by your cooks, not defined by any chef you've ever worked for—your own definition of success, because if you don't have that, you're always a failure."

—*Shuna Lydon*

CHAPTER 2

An Education

Culinary school's not necessary, no . . . It's an opportunity and it's a jumping-off point . . . Most of the people I know are self-taught. Would I have ended up in school if I didn't have to come up with an excuse for my parents? I don't think so. And I tell people that all the time, they're like, "Oh, I want to end my career because I love to cook, but I don't want to go to culinary school," and I tell them, "Get yourself a job first, and if you really want to be there, then go to school, but don't waste your money." It's a waste of money otherwise.

—HEATHER CARLUCCI-RODRIGUEZ

On December 15, 2010, I learned that I'd actually be writing a book called *Skirt Steak*, based on a proposal I'd submitted. I was given less than a year (nine months) in which to do the research and get the words out. Immediate action was required, and I had no idea what to expect. The only previous book I'd worked on was Anita Lo's cookbook,[40] which was an entirely different project—there weren't many constructive comparisons to be made. One of my early moves was to e-mail Anita to tell her the news, ask her to participate (that would be at least one chef down—and a great one at that), and see if there was anyone she'd like to recommend or help me get in touch with. She generously provided me with a list that would be considered impressive by anyone's standards. On that roster was Heather Carlucci-Rodriguez, whom I very much wanted to talk to for a number of reasons, the most pressing (and selfish) of which had nothing to do with the book. Carlucci-Rodriguez, a pastry chef who three times received three stars[41] from the *New York*

---

[40] It's titled *Cooking Without Borders*, should you wish to track it down.

[41] While I've got you, might as well note that the *New York Times* tends to be the unspoken, understood star-giver (unless otherwise specified). Any chef in NYC (and across the nation) will say it's the one with the power to make or break you. To receive three stars from that publication is most impressive. Four is the maximum (and

cont'd

Times, had opted to leave *choux* and *pâte brisée* behind and open a tiny operation for Indian cuisine in a narrow, corridor-like storefront on Greenwich Avenue. Lassi, as it was called (and yes, it served some memorable versions of that yogurt-based drink), was one of my favorite neighborhood go-tos—I would pop in for the rice pudding of the day (if any was left; it sold out quickly) and often called the shop for a dinner of the best eggplant curry and a *ghobi* (cauliflower) *paratha* with *bondi raita* and extra chutney. Sadly (devastating, really), Lassi had closed. What I wanted—needed—to know was when would Lassi return. (This was not a question of *if*; a Lassi-free world was not one I was prepared to accept.)

She was my first interview. We met in the West Village (not so far from where Lassi once stood) on the first Monday of January (the third). Freezing, we trekked from our original destination, a charming—in that bare-bones way—coffee shop called Doma, which was overrun with grad students, aspiring screenwriters, and klatching neighborhood types, to equally (if not more) shabby and loud Grounded on Jane Street, where we managed to find two stools. Carlucci-Rodriguez, it turned out, had resurfaced, back on the pastry side, at a new restaurant called Print; she works there with her husband, the executive (non-pastry) chef. She hadn't given up on Lassi,[42] and, as soon as that had been confirmed, we moved to the truly important (also fascinating and highly entertaining) stuff. For more than two hours, as she reminisced about her (mostly) former days as a rabble-rouser, we sat there at Grounded with our tea getting cold. I cackled out loud, and at many points during the chitchat, I thought, *I have the best job ever.*

Did I ask too many questions in the earlier stages of the interviewing process? Sure did. Enjoyed every minute of it too. I had a lot to learn about my subjects and their work; I also had to figure

the elusive prize) bestowed by the publication; as of 2011, only six of New York City's restaurants could claim that many.

[42] There's a cookbook concept in the works and, in January 2012, Carlucci-Rodriguez shared the following scoop via e-mail, "It won't be until spring, but I am looking at spaces for the new Lassi!!!!" *!!!!* indeed.

out what kind of information mattered and how to get it. That day, with Carlucci-Rodriguez, I was a walking clean slate. Seventy-three interviews later, when I looked back over my notes, I noticed, at this, the book's (and my own) very beginning, we started with her very beginning—her education. And we spent a lot of time on it. After that first interview, the trend continued. Getting schooled was a topic dwelled on in most of my conversations. For as many different ways as there are to learn, there are an equal number of opinions on those options. There is the most obvious, culinary school, and from there, the matters of geography (will you study at home or abroad?) and of timing (is it better to go immediately, or after having faced life in a restaurant kitchen?). Or you might skip school altogether and seek an extracurricular style of training, which brings another set of alternatives to consider.

"Culinary school, who needs it?" quipped my fellow native New Yorker Beth Aretsky. I've been asking myself this too. One of the conclusions I've drawn is that perhaps those who need it, or benefit from it, today aren't the ones chasing restaurant positions. Now that the job of chef can comprise so many things and, as already noted, is considered as much a lifestyle as a trade, I suspect that you find aspirational sorts who go to school for reasons that are more abstract than simply wanting to cook professionally. The career opportunities available to those interested in food-related exploits have opened up—journalists, authors, small-batch enterprises (those who bake baklavas in a shared commercial kitchen space and sell them locally, for example). This translates to a wider client base for schools to tap. In an effort to appeal to these interests, it's likely that institutions have veered away from the craft they initially taught their students and are placing more emphasis on offering a varied, well-rounded set of curricula—to be all things to all people. On the one hand, the 'Tutes[43] are encouraging more ladies to join the culinary workforce, and some of those non-restaurant jobs are

[43] When I went to graduate school (for art history, bygones) at a place called the Institute of Fine Arts, we affectionately (on a good day), referred to it as the 'Tute. I'm carrying the phraseology forward.

those that have historically drawn women—cookbook writing, teaching, and, yes, catering too. On the other, these campuses have become a less effective training ground for anyone whose intent is to hone her cooking skills and prepare for a life in the galley (on the line and, eventually, in charge of it). Where does that leave women (or anyone, really) who want to be chefs?

Hungarian-born and now living in San Francisco, Amaryll Schwertner didn't go to culinary school and doesn't regret it. You'll find her adored Boulette's Larder at one end of the gourmet food hall inside the Ferry Building. She lovingly prepares locally grown, organic ingredients (so Northern Cali, I know). It's some of the finest to-go fare anywhere, but you can also sit yourself at one of the communal tables and peer into the open kitchen, or watch the world outside drift by. She touched on an angle my suspicious, oft-cynical mind had already begun to ponder: the profit-focused machinations of culinary schools.[44] Now that it's cool to be a chef, the potential customer base has exploded. There's a concern (mine and others', Schwertner's among them) that these institutions of learning are more concerned with making money by building a brand and appealing to paying enrollees than with attracting the cream of the talent crop. "Here [in the United States], there's an industry of cooking schools, and the cooking schools are sponsored by corporations; it's quite expensive and [there are] no criteria to get in to most of them, and none to get out. So people come

---

[44] Mark Wilson's article "Should You Go to Culinary School? (Maybe, but Probably Not)" in the third issue of the magazine *Lucky Peach* (Spring 2012) debriefs readers on the financing of culinary schools—both the for-profit and nonprofit models. ("The difference," he explains, "loosely, is that a nonprofit reinvests any financial surplus back into the organization . . . while a for-profit pays this cash out to its investors.") "Two of the most popular culinary schools in the United States," he writes, "are for-profit institutions owned by Fortune-1000 companies. Paris Le Cordon Bleu is a famed cooking school in its own right; the U.S. franchise is licensed by Career Education Corporation, which accounts for 22 percent of all U.S. culinary school enrollment. The Art Institutes are owned by Education Management Corporation—41 percent of which is owned by Goldman Sachs. For these corporations, culinary schools are a gateway into federal aid dollars. Yet despite federal regulation, the schools hold all the pricing power." That's some racket they've got going. Looks like the government might finally be catching on, though. As Wilson reports: "Low graduation rates among students at for-profit culinary schools, however, are beginning to receive a great deal of scrutiny from the Department of Education. In November of 2011, Career Education admitted to advertising inflated job-placement rates. Out of forty-nine of its schools that were subjected to an internal audit, only thirteen had actually achieved their advertised numbers." The upshot: Le Cordon Bleu is cracking down on its admissions policy in an attempt to improve its disappointing stats.

out with a fair degree of debt,[45] and then they assume, immediately, that they're going to be high [earners], never once considering that they really don't even know which end of the knife to pick up let alone how to taste something; and where it comes from; and what it means; and how to look at an animal and break it down, even if you've never done it before; how to keep your knives in a particular kind of order [and] what that knife feels [like] in your hand. The beginning is when you set foot in a restaurant, and you apply yourself to the rigors of it and you suffer." Hello, schadenfreude, my old friend.

In truth, there's no official "beginning," no right formula here. Plus, times have changed, and with them, the institutions involved. In any of the last four decades, there are success stories that include a chapter in culinary school, and there are those that don't.

I've never been one for statistics, but gather that a numerical survey of the landscape might provide those who appreciate such phenomena with a sense of where things have been and might be going in terms of how many ladies are dipping their toes in the school pool. And because it is considered the best in the land, I went straight to the CIA[46] to see whom it accepts. According to a study published in 2008,[47] the

---

[45] A quick virtual trip to the FAQ page of the Culinary Institute of America's website led me to this helpful summary: "The 2010–2011 tuition cost is $24,360, but the actual cost to attend depends on your individual financial situation—and everyone's different." Every year's different too. If you look at the "Tuition and Fees for 2011–2012 New York Campus" chart (also on the website), you see that the baseline tuition, per semester (for the freshman and sophomore years), was $12,495 and that once additional costs have been tallied (supplies, board, and extraneous fees) that could climb as high as $15,885 for one's first semester. In that Wilson piece (see prior footnote), he cites the going rate, collectively speaking, as falling anywhere between $20,000 and $30,000 per annum.

[46] The Culinary Institute of America was established in 1946 by attorney Frances Roth (a lady!) from Connecticut. Her cofounder was Katherine Angell, the wife of Yale University's president (at the time). The New Haven Restaurant Institute (that was its initial name, and, yes, it was located in that town) was, as per the CIA's website "the first and only school of its kind in the United States. Specifically created to train returning World War II veterans in the culinary arts, the institute enrolled fifty students and employed a faculty consisting of a chef, a baker, and a dietitian." A year later, it became the Restaurant Institute of America, and in 1951, it was given its current banner. Relocation (to Hyde Park, New York) took place in 1972. As per Wilson's *Lucky Peach* write-up (again, please see footnote 44, facing page), like your "typical private university" (as opposed to a trade or a vocational school), the CIA falls into the nonprofit category. Its "overall graduation rate is an astonishing 85 percent, exceeding the national average for all nonprofit four-year colleges." Its stricter application standards might be why, the writer surmises.

[47] This was an internal study intended for the CIA's own use and not for the general public. Thanks to Jeff Levine, the school's communications manager, for sharing it with me and allowing me to reference it here.

percentage of female students enrolled at the CIA—in all programs,[48] combined—was 21.3 percent in 1980, 21.4 percent in 1990, and as of 2007, had increased to 41.2 percent. If we break this down and focus on the AOS track (Associate Degree Program), we see that gals who majored in CA (the standard, Culinary Arts) composed 21 percent of that specific student body in 1995 and 30 percent in 2007, while those who went for B&P (Baking and Pastry, added in 1990) made up 59 percent of their program in 1995 and a whopping 80 percent in 2007,[49] which seems to indicate that there are still more women lining up to take on bread-baking and dessert-making than signing up to master the duties of a chef de cuisine.[50] However, across the board (savory and sweet), with each passing year, a greater number of women join the cooking school ranks. So while most chefs will tell you that institutions have decreased the quality of their classroom offerings and are more concerned with making money and, to that end, attracting paying students, said hallowed halls of higher culinary learning steadily continue to draw more of the ladies.[51]

In 2012, wannabe chefs, especially the females, have options they didn't have when, between 1966 and 1971, the CIA wasn't accepting women into the "regular program."[52] If you were a woman who wanted

[48]   When taking in the stats shown for the whole enchilada, note that up until 1995, the population includes all AOS (Associate Degree Program) students (Culinary Arts + Baking and Pastry). The year 1993 saw the launch of the BPS (the four-year bachelor's degree program). So from 1995 onward, those stats take into account not just all AOS students, but also those BPS students too. According to the study, "(1) Every year except '96, the BPS program had a higher percentage of women than the AOS program; and (2) from 1996 to 2006, the percentage of women in the BPS program and overall increased every year."

[49]   Levine added that in 2010, the total percentage of women on campus—there are now three CIA satellites across the country—was 45.1 percent, and, as for how many are going for that AOS in Culinary Arts, it's 33 percent. Although those numbers climb slowly but continuously, it's Baking and Pastry where women are most active and outnumber the men by greater leaps and bounds with each passing year. In 2000, that program was expanded, which also accounts for the rising total of females matriculated at the CIA (in 1995 it was 23.5 percent and had shot up to 31.9 percent by 2000), and, possibly, for the boost to that specific B&P tally (in 1998, 64 percent of B&P majors were women; in 2000, 73 percent).

[50]   The chef de cuisine is the head of the kitchen, the top dog (unless there's an executive chef, who's the top, top dog); the one in charge of all the cooks.

[51]   In case you're curious (I was), school enrollment has grown steadily since the beginning. It increased by almost 50 percent between 2000, when it was at 1,931 students, and 2008, when that number reached 2,828.

[52]   Chicks were "welcome in the special summer course," reads the 1969 catalog. "The reason is that with so few girls applying, it is uneconomical for the Institute to provide the special facilities, washrooms, etc., required."

to get beyond chopping onions, you were mostly SOL.[53] Not only was school an unlikely possibility, but the idea that you could get your education or prove yourself in restaurant kitchens was equally unfathomable. So what was the scholastic life like back in the day when, presumably, a culinary degree still meant something (and before all the womenfolk started acquiring one)?

Let's ask the legendary firecracker Lydia Shire, who, forty years ago, when a permanent position as onion-chopper wasn't even an option, bet all her chips on school. Smart move.[54] "We were divorced—my husband fell in love with his secretary [and] I didn't know what the word *alimony* meant or anything—and all I knew was that I had to go out and get a job. And really, the only thing I liked to do was cook. And so I went to Maison Robert in Boston . . . [I'd] made a beautiful seven-layer cake. It was in the summer and I had to order an air-conditioned cab to transport it. This was back in 1970 and there weren't that many of them [air-conditioned cabs] in Boston at the time—and I brought this beautiful seven-layer cake, very thin layers with a real French buttercream [to the restaurant], and, needless to say, they gave me the job. So I opened Maison Robert as the salad girl[55] . . . I hated opening oysters . . . I wanted to cook. I decided the only way they would take me seriously is if I went to cooking school. So I hocked my diamond ring and I went to Le Cordon Bleu in London." Her salad days behind her, Shire returned to Maison Robert and was promoted to line cook. By 1974, she was running the kitchen.

Fast-forward to the 1980s when Seen Lippert was at the CIA and one out of every eight students was a woman: "It was a wealth of

---

[53] Shit Out of Luck.

[54] I can't keep count of the number of restaurants Shire has cooked at, consulted for, or fronted. At present, she has her hand in two spots. I interviewed her in Boston, at Scampo, which she owns and where, she informed me with bursting pride, her son had just started working. She won a James Beard Award in 1992 for Best Chef: Northeast, and the accolades kept coming. One of my favorite fun facts: In 2001, she did something wickedly ballsy and took over Boston's staid Locke-Ober restaurant; for 97 years, that place wouldn't let women into its dining room. She wasn't having it. Well played, Lydia.

[55] "Salad girl" would be a reference to what would now, in a more politically correct world, be termed the garde-manger.

information," and she "loved the rare book library." Also, though, she remarked, "It's a machine," and "felt like a long workout every day." Was it rough being there with boobs? What do you think? She had it extra hard and was "treated differently because I was one of few attractive women."[56]

In addition to being one of few women and one of even fewer lovely-to-look-at women, Lippert was an anomaly because she was made a group leader, rare for a female CIA student at the time. Regardless of gender, as captain of the team, you're expected to stay on top of the syllabus and keep your colleagues organized. Lippert had to prepare them for the next day's class and make sure everyone pulled his or her weight. "You sort of assume the role of working slave," she told me. "You take shit if anything goes wrong."[57] You can imagine her taking a ton of shit, then, since she already had those other two burdens to bear (the possession of a vagina and beauty). It was brutal, she admits, but the instructors "were no worse than my worst gymnastics coach." She laughingly describes, "one jaundiced Italian chef, whose skin and teeth were yellow and ate three heads of garlic a day, would yell at me, right up in my face!" She continues: "A lot of them [teachers] were waiting for me to cave." Lippert, let the record show, graduated with the highest GPA in the school, ever (at that time; the year was 1987, and the stat close to 4.0), and went on to spend eleven years at Chez Panisse.

Big Apple talent Amanda Freitag, whom you may recognize from her judging stint on the Food Network competition show *Chopped*, graduated from that same alma mater a few years later. By then, the

---

[56] That is a fact, by the way. Lippert is one of the most elegant and refined-looking women you'll ever meet, and when discussing how her looks affected the way she was treated, it wasn't with one iota of arrogance. She was simply reporting the way it was.

[57] I asked Levine (communications manager, CIA) if the leadership program has remained in place. "The system still exists," he responded via e-mail. "Basically, the students are chosen by their peers (classmates) to serve as the liaison between students and the faculty member for each course. For instance, the group leader meets with the chef of the next course a few days before the course begins, and he/she will let the rest of the class know what will be expected of them and how to be prepared for the first day of class."

ratio of male to female students, according to her, was 5-to-1,[58] and she was completely overwhelmed. Students would be broken up into four sections, each with sixteen to eighteen people and a group leader (which she, like Lippert, took a turn as). Freitag was the only woman in her group but, apparently, wasn't given much trouble from her peers. "I learned probably more at the CIA from the people who were my co-students than the instructors, because it was such an incredible mix, from eighteen-year-olds to fifty-five-year-olds . . . I learned a lot, I partied a lot, you know—I was very young; I wish I had taken better notes." Ah, the memories. "I also encountered a lot of European chefs [who] . . . were challenging me quite often," she reflects, singling out the notably large German chef who taught her skills development class. "I was chopping vegetables and he was asking me why I was doing this; why did I want to be a chef, why not be a secretary, why not go to law school, and he was truly, truly challenging me, but he was actually quite serious. And it was discouraging at times, but I did well and I excelled so I kept going." Thank the lord she did, because otherwise, the world would be bereft of an astounding char-grilled octopus dish (there's salty feta scattered throughout that deliciousness) and a host of other things (a certain Meyer lemony, roasted, crisp-skinned chicken, for one).

"Upon graduation," she notes, "I had the lucky foresight of knowing that wasn't it; I wasn't ready. And there was nobody that said anything else, like, 'You're not ready. You have the basics now.' And, at the time, when you come out of culinary school you were either going to be a sous chef, which was a high-ranking position, a chef, or a certified master chef, which I don't even think anybody has even heard of anymore. I was on the road to getting to become a chef, which took starting at prep or garde-manger and working myself up through all those positions, which I figured would be my career life. So I started thinking,

[58] Freitag's memory checks out as per the stats shared by Levine. In 1980, the percentage of women enrolled at the CIA was 21.3 percent and it was practically the same in 1990 (21.4 percent). The year 1995 shows a minor increase to 23.5 percent. And by 2000, it's up to 31.9 percent (still less than one-third of the student body).

'Now that culinary school is finished, I'm just starting.' So I worked in a lot of random places."

Not everyone who attended school in the '80s or '90s concurs that it was worth the hassle. Or harassment. Beth Aretsky is more acerbic than most about the whole thing because, as she shares, "I was tortured at the CIA[59] . . . I don't know [if other women had the same experience]. If they did, maybe they left. I, for whatever reason, chose to stick it out and call it out." Listening to her also helped me understand, curriculum-wise, how the day-to-day operations play out at the school. Better than that, though, she had me on the floor, in stitches, regaling me with the tale of "this kid named Stephen Zimmerman," a student she was paired with in a pastry class. He repeatedly "hit me in the tit with a palette knife," she recalls. No martyr, Aretsky retaliated by lying to him about what the homework was. He would always leave class after lunch and never bother to stick around to hear the next day's assignment, which would introduce students to another technique. So she would tell him it was something "he really sucked at making, like crème anglaise. He couldn't make crème anglaise because he'd always curdle [the eggs] . . . He'd come in the morning and say, 'What do we have to do?' I'd say, 'You gotta make crème anglaise.' So he's making crème anglaise and I'm doing what I'm supposed to be doing. And the teacher says to him, 'What are you doing making crème anglaise?' And he [Zimmerman] goes, 'Well, that's what we're supposed to be doing.' And the chef looks at me and I look at him, and he says, 'Why is he making crème anglaise?' and I say, 'I don't know. I thought you told me crème anglaise.' You know, I pretended like I was stupid . . . meanwhile he [Zimmerman] made scrambled eggs."

That was just the beginning. More palette-knifing ensues, and Aretsky is "just waiting for my moment." One day, she and Zimmerman are standing in front of the ice cream machine (that day's lesson, as

[59] Class of 1990.

you can tell, was devoted to one of my most favorite things ever), which is one of those behemoth industrial jobs with a portal door that opens so you can scoop out the finished product. As she's scooping, all she can see is what's below the portal door. ("Well, we all know what's below the portal door.") That's when she makes her move. "I just hauled off and socked him, right in the nut sack . . . He dropped to the floor. He's calling me all kinds of names. I said, 'You started it; I'm ending it.' " When her clueless instructor wants to know what gives, she replied, "He hit me in the tit with a palette knife, so I punched him in the balls." No response from the teacher. Zimmerman never touches her again.

You could say Aretsky learned a valuable lesson over there at the finest cooking school in the land: In the kitchen, anything goes, and it's each pair of tits or balls for itself. She also realized that revenge is a dish best served cold, while making ice cream.

A handful of the more seasoned chefs I interviewed preferred to learn their lessons in France. Based in Cambridge, Massachusetts, Ana Sortun talked about her time at La Varenne (attended by a few others), an institution founded by a Brit named Anne Willan more than 35 years ago in Paris.[60] The crucial takeaway, for Sortun, was the value placed on ingredients and seasonality. It's really only in the last decade that she has seen anything that resembles this attitude in the United States. "I would go to the farmers' market and shop, and it was normal," she remembers fondly. "It wasn't like, [Gasps] 'I went to the farmers' market and shopped!' It was like, 'I went to the farmers' market and shopped like everybody else does in France,' you know? You shop and then you come back and [look at] the recipe that you're studying; if those ingredients aren't acceptable to the chef, [you] tear up the recipe and improvise. I have never seen a cooking school here work that way. I have seen the shittiest green beans being used out of season just so that they could demonstrate a technique, and why they can't substitute

[60] Willan relocated École de Cuisine La Varenne (that's its full name, although everyone refers to it as "La Varenne") to Burgundy, France, from 1991 to 2007.

something else for those green beans is beyond me. I don't get what they're teaching people. Are they teaching people just the technique of how to follow a recipe, or are they actually teaching people about what the most important part about food is, the ingredients?"

Although La Varenne was the most mentioned *école* in the country of glorious green beans, other notable *choix*[61] include the Ritz Escoffier (est. 1988) and, the OG,[62] Le Cordon Bleu (est. 1895), both based in Paris. Anita Lo studied *chez* the former from 1989 to 1990 and found it direly sexist. In one instance, she outshone her classmates and impressed her instructor (a chef) with a langoustine and asparagus crepe in her final exam, before, that is, he knew who had made it. So much did he enjoy this perfect pancake that he asked the students who was responsible for it. When Lo stepped forward, he walked out of the room in disbelief and frustration. Such slaps in the face are what gave her access to a tony kitchen—that of David Bouley, one of few chefs to receive four stars from the *New York Times* (in 1990, for his now closed Tribeca restaurant Bouley, where Lo labored)—when she returned to Manhattan.

Nancy Silverton took the opposite route. She signed up for a restaurant gig before studying in France. The environment in which she procured that practical training was just as significant as her doing so prior to hitting the books. Her career began about forty years ago in a San Francisco Bay Area eatery[63] where a self-taught chef led college-educated employees and everyone worked from cookbooks. It was *not*, she notes distinctly, a "kitchen dominated by a European staff, because

---

[61] For your convenience, *école* means "school" (singular) and *choix*, "choices" (both singular and plural form), in that overseas tongue; see, it's just as my fifth-grade primer's title promised, *French Is Fun!*

[62] Original gangster. I'm embarrassed (for you) if you were unaware what that meant. Paris is where the school was founded and remains the epicenter of its many international spin-offs. If your short-term memory is intact, you'll recall that Lydia Shire attended the London outpost. If you're reading these footnotes, then you're also hip to the fact that Career Education Corporation backs the U.S. franchise (see footnote 44, page 52). Do you know which American female trailblazing treasure matriculated at Le Cordon Bleu in Paris? Julia Child, in 1955. My editor asked me why I did not refer to her in the above discussion. It was deliberate. Julia Child was not a chef in the way that it has been defined in this book—she was not a restaurant chef. She was an incredible cook, teacher, cookbook author, and television personality. There is a difference. If you find this confusing, you may revisit the 14th footnote, page 24.

[63] 464 Magnolia.

that's certainly the old way, and I started the new way." This, she claims, makes a difference. "Having that be the experience [in which] you get your foundation . . . also lets you know that you don't have to put up with some of the more oppressive kitchens . . . I've heard some horror stories from other women about their need to prove themselves, and how they went home every night and cried. But I have no stories like that."

Not having those stories to tell probably made it easier for her to deal with her next move. After that apprenticeship in Marin, she went to Le Cordon Bleu in London (holla, Lydia!), which, she notes, was rigid "because it was a school, and that was their job." Silverton remained unfazed by the rigidity because she knew better; she'd been exposed to the "new way" and understood that she didn't have to accept the old. Guided by that initial, positive brush with kitchen life in Northern California, when she returned to that world, she consistently went to well-respected establishments that had a similar ethos. She moved to Michael's in Santa Monica, where she worked under Jonathan Waxman and discovered dessert. Eye on the pastry prize, she reentered the classroom, this time in France, at Lenôtre,[64] to sharpen her skills. There, in Plaisir, west of Paris, she had two things going against her: "one, being American, and two, being a female." Still, though, as she admits, "I paid money to go that school . . . they're not going to turn me away." And, again, she knew she wasn't stuck in such a *plaisir*[65]-free world forever. As we've seen before with those who put up with the crap—Freitag, Lippert, and Lo, for starters—no pain, no gain. Silverton's investment was a wise one. Subsequently, Wolfgang Puck offered her the post of head pastry chef at Spago when he opened in 1982. Silverton ended up with the best of both worlds, because she

---

[64] Gaston-Albert-Celestin Lenôtre (1920 to 2009) was the revered French pastry chef responsible for the culinary empire that contains restaurant, catering, and retail branches, and this school he opened in 1971 to train others in his craft.

[65] Ironically, *plaisir* is the French noun for "pleasure."

had that sane, humane grounding to buffer the harshness of European instruction and, at the same time, she was able to access that classical, technical training overseas.

There are other chefs who believe that some kind of trial by fire in the BOH[66] should precede academic shelter.[67] San Francisco treat-maker and pastry chef Elisabeth "Liz" Prueitt of the Tartine empire (there's the original, eponymous bakery-cum-café,[68] ambitious Bar Tartine with its Eastern and Central European influences, and, housed in the front of that restaurant, a bakery annex that specializes in open-faced Danish sandwiches known as *smørrebrød*) is one of them. Prueitt was twenty-eight by the time she got to culinary school—a good ten years older than the men (they composed the majority of her classmates). She reckoned "she wasn't going to learn enough and quickly in other people's kitchens." Still, she continues, "I tell people to go work in Europe or New York in a hard kitchen *before* school." This kind of work needn't be restricted to the restaurant kitchen, although limiting oneself to that environment has its benefits.

Top Chef breakout star Carla Hall, who often doesn't get the recognition she deserves as a chef, struggles in part, perhaps, because of her less "acceptable"[69] trajectory. Post-graduation (Howard University, where she majored in accounting), she spent her days as a CPA for Price Waterhouse and then went to Europe to do some modeling—you know, your usual chef's résumé. Back in Washington, D.C., she started making lunches she peddled around town to lure the midday working hungry.

---

[66] Back of house, a.k.a. the restaurant kitchen or galley. The FOH or front of house would be the dining room(s) and, when applicable, bar(s).

[67] Possible point of interest: The CIA insists (and always has) that prospective undergraduate students have six months of restaurant work behind them before applying. Throughout the course of Mark Wilson's research (see footnote 44, page 52, again), this was the only school he found that had such a requirement.

[68] Whenever I'm in San Francisco, one of the first (if not *the* first) thing I do is make a beeline for 600 Guerrero Street and get in line for a few slices of loaf cake—I recommend you try one of each flavor available—a brownie, a lemon bar, a brown butter shortbread cookie, and a container of the brioche bread pudding. All are Prueitt productions.

[69] Why less "acceptable"? *Um, duh, because she decided to go bottom-feeder.* (The writer typed, facetiously, to connote the general disdain that members of the professional culinary community seem to have for those who cater. The aforementioned writer continues to type thusly because she realizes that hotel chefs have also been subjected to discrimination by their peers. So, too, chefs at sea.)

She did that for five years and then, at thirty, enrolled in culinary school, and not for any lack of confidence in her talent or the quality of her experience; she wanted to master the theory behind the craft for efficiency's sake. She loved L'Academie de Cuisine in nearby Bethesda, Maryland, where she studied alongside many career changers and people who were there to "throw better dinner parties," and went on to become— after toiling away in a few positions—a chef at one and then another hotel kitchen. After all of that, she started her own catering business.

Hall's conscious move away from restaurants to a line of culinary work that, because it's perceived as less prestigious, important, or glam, is a sector of the industry women are often pushed toward, reminds me of something that Carlucci-Rodriguez discussed. She posited that playing by the rules could actually enable one to build a more subversive career. It's not what you expect to hear; we associate the chefs who don't do what they're supposed to as the ones engaging in subversion. This makes a compelling and unexpected argument for women to go to culinary school. You can go your own way and develop an unconventional style out of necessity (e.g., cater because you can't score a restaurant gig; cook the food you grew up with because you don't have the opportunity to study another cuisine or classical techniques), or do the same thing based on (culinarily) educated decision-making. Let's take her example: She obtains a degree in pastry, continues her education in France, masters her craft, and then, years later, after shining at New York City's top spots, starts from scratch, and, with no background in Indian cuisine, decides to open a tiny, neighborhood takeout shop specializing in the Northern region of that country's home cooking.

Was it the education she received at the Restaurant School in Philadelphia that allowed Carlucci-Rodriguez to take that leap of faith with Lassi? Not necessarily. The confidence that education gave her is what makes the difference; it's the one thing that most of the women who went to culinary school have in common. Once a pastry chef at Bouley and now the proprietor of a New York City baking empire known as Amy's Bread, Amy Scherber convinced me of my hypothesis when she credited the New York Restaurant School with teaching her how to move around, store provisions in, and speak the language of a professional kitchen. Having this knowledge before working in a kitchen bolsters one's confidence when he or she first joins the line of a galley (or ditches the galley for uncharted territory), most alumnae I've talked to agree. Another thing they share, however, is a lack of faith in today's graduates and programs.

Cathy Whims, of Portland, Oregon's regional Italian favorite Nostrana and, which I am itching to try, Oven & Shaker, the pizza joint she opened last year,[70] complains that the grads she interviews for entry-level line cook positions (the appropriate slot for a bright-eyed, bushy-tailed, just-out-of-school newbie) are inexperienced and have received no hands-on training in whatever classrooms they came from. Could they really all be that clueless? Doubtful. There has got to be a fundamental problem with the educations these "kids" are (or are not) receiving. It points to a slippage in academic standards and rubric. More than that, though, there is a vast discrepancy between the fast-track success graduates expect to have when they're set loose on the workforce and the nearly Dickensian reality faced in the galley. "Culinary school doesn't prepare them for what kind of job they have," Whims says. "Even if they enter at a higher rung, they're not going to make enough money. Culinary school is doing a real disservice by promising a career that isn't sustainable."

These academies may be (and who could blame them) capitalizing on the national food fetish, but they don't appear to be doing much innovating on the culinary arts front. By and large, it would seem that

---

[70] I see she has a *bianca* or white—my preference—pie on the menu with buffalo mozzarella, a black-truffled *sottocenere* cheese, and fried sage; gotta have it. And let me tell you something else about Whims. She wasn't in Portland when I got there, so we had to stage a phone chat. A few months later, she came to New York City for the James Beard Awards (she was nominated for Best Chef: Northwest), and we met at the communal bar table of the Breslin (in the Ace Hotel), where April Bloomfield is the presiding chef and everyone stops by for lamb burgers and "thrice-cooked fries" (although, I do love whatever current striped bass preparation she's whipping up). We, however, were there on an off-hour, so it was a coffee occasion. Whims brought me homemade salami that was superb. So thoughtful, that one. Thank you.

they are teaching the same instructional lessons, anchored in the French tradition, to a less selectively culled (and more scattered in focus) pool. In America, circa 2012, we have kitchens like those haute ones that were, for so long, held up as the benchmark, but then, we have lots of other kinds of restaurants that are getting the same amount of attention and praise, if not more. Our schools haven't caught up with that diversity. Maybe it's too much to ask that they might; it could very well be an impossible task to teach so many people in so many ways. Still, I'm left wondering why, if for every galley there's a unique apprenticeship, there can't be some attempt at a scholastically commensurate scenario—either each school distinguishes itself to fit a niche or else makes a concerted effort to expose students to the varied range of BOH settings.

For now, a better way to have that exposure would be to test-drive a number of different kitchens, which is exactly what Whims and Aretsky endorse. "I've talked so many cooks out of culinary school," the former proudly owns up. "My advice is, cook first. See if you want it. It's hard work—you work when everyone has off, long hours; it's physically demanding and you're lucky to find a place that has insurance—why would you sign up without seeing what it's like?" She promotes learning by doing, and by tasting—she encourages students (those in the classroom or the kitchen) to eat out at other restaurants. Waylynn Lucas prescribes that, plus. Nothing's more valuable, she opines, than being in the galley. "That's the biggest learning tool there is. You get to watch and listen to the conversations, and look, and read the recipes," she of the soak-it-up-like-a-sponge mentality says. "And use the time on your own to read cookbooks and know what's going on out there and know chefs' names." Aretsky's right behind 'em, and would like to pass the following along to the youth of America. "Don't waste your money. Stage, if you can." (That message was sponsored by the Partnership for Staging, naturally.[71])

---

[71] Okay, team, huddle up. From here on out, when you see the word *stage*, it probably won't have anything to do with the platform that hams (show-offs, not the cured hind leg of a pig) like to perform on. I'm about to elaborate. Patience, please.

Stage[72] is another French noun—*pardonnez-moi*—that, in the motherland, can refer to vocational training of any kind, or to a studies-related internship. Within the cheffing world, it's the second definition that counts. Whether you're an amateur, self-taught, degree-holder, or experienced line cook, the stage is always an option, if the kitchen of your choice will have you. It is a finite period during that you work—for free—in the galley and learn as much as you can. It is also an opportunity for the chef for whom you're staging (there it is in verb form) to see what you're made of, and, possibly, offer you a long-standing internship or a paid position. An alternative educational outlet, it's a way to try out multiple cuisines, techniques, kitchen setups, and geographic locales.

Thirty years after setting out, Amaryll Schwertner still believes apprenticing offers something important: "the beauty of repetition." She champions "the old-school method [in which] you apprentice with someone," which, she observes, still exists, but fears is no longer prevalent, particularly in the United States.

Traci Des Jardins went abroad for her staging. Her mentor (and, lucky her, first boss) Joachim Splichal was a German-born chef who repatriated to France, where he trained. After doing time in some of France's most renowned kitchens, he went to Los Angeles, which is where he remained and, in 1983, hired Des Jardins, whom he told to bypass culinary school and to follow the old-fashioned method of his European youth, apprenticeship. She counts herself among few American women of her generation who had that experience in France—working in significant (i.e., Michelin-starred[73]) restaurants

---

[72] Pronounced "stahzje."

[73] You know our Zagat restaurant guides here in the United States? They're the poor man's (we're talking destitute) Michelin. Kind of, because although they're of similar size and hue, Zagat is crowd-sourced, while Michelin's rankings are determined by a group of designated inspectors. Also, Michelin is a French entity, and it's a lot older to boot. The first Michelin guide was published by the brothers André and Edouard Michelin for motorists in 1900 to help them navigate the country's crappy roads (makes sense, the boys manufactured tires after all). This little gratis booklet contained information about hotels and their dining establishments, and by 1920 when the duo began selling the guides for profit, they noticed how popular the gastronomic coverage in their publication was. That's when they recruited their anonymous raters and developed a set of criteria for the latter to consider while surveying. In 1926 the now famous (and rigorous) star system, as we

there from the late '70s through the early '90s. She mentioned visionaries like one of Freitag's mentors, Diane Forley, and Cali girls Mary Sue Milliken, Susan Feniger, and Loretta Keller. For Des Jardins, being in that environment—she was in some of the world's best establishments, in the presence of Michelin masters like Michel and Pierre Troisgros[74] and Alain Ducasse—was invaluable, and something that wasn't possible in this country.[75] "I miss the pristine order of those kinds of kitchens, and the luxuriousness of it," she told me. "It's not the same as restaurants here . . . We were usually a brigade of twenty-five that were serving one hundred people for lunch and one hundred people for dinner, and it was that fixed. That's a pretty dramatic ratio, and that was only the kitchen. The front of the house was probably an equal brigade, so you had fifty people working to serve one hundred . . . It's just a totally different world." It's the world that best prepared her for becoming the multi-restaurant-owning top chef she is today. But, as she said, it depends on how you learn. This way happened to work for her. She can't speak for anyone else.

know it, was born. At first, hotel restaurants that met the standards were given one star; later, in 1931, they added the second and third stars to separate the really handsome boys from the even more handsome men. The following year, restaurants were given their own chapter, which, in 1933 was officially titled "La Table." Come 1936, the Michelin crew took time out to define what the stars meant. I'll simplify it for you. If you get one star, you're pleased, very; two stars, you might start dancing a jig or singing in the street; three stars, you can die happy (and should consider calling it quits while you're ahead). It's a big deal, the world over. Chefs have been known to suicide over the potential loss of a star. Now serving (or plaguing) more than twenty countries, Michelin brought its lethal (to unstable chefs) guide to New York in 2006, and now, even as you read this, maybe, its inspectors are sipping champers in that city, plus Chicago and San Francisco.

[74] Back to the *Larousse Gastronomique*: "Troisgros (Jean *and* Pierre): French cooks and restaurateurs in Roanne (Loire). Jean (1926 to 1983) and Pierre (born 1928) were born in Chalon-sur-Saône, the sons of Jean-Baptiste Troisgros, a café owner who later became proprietor of the small station hotel at Roanne, where his sister and his wife were in charge of the kitchen. The two brothers were sent to Lucas-Carton in Paris for their apprenticeships, then to Fernand Point in Vienna. In 1954, they began to practice their trade in the family hotel, then took over the management; from that point on, their progress was continuous (one star in the Michelin guide in 1955, two in 1965, three in 1968).

"Their cookery was inspired by recipes handed down from past generations, sometimes almost peasant in their character: for example, pigeons *à la gouse d'ail en chemise*, snails *en poêlon* with green butter, and foie gras fried with spinach. But they also brought family dishes to a peak of perfection, notably their famous escalope of salmon with sorrel and their *mosaïque* of vegetables stuffed with truffles. Pierre proved to be the meat specialist, whereas Jean was a wine connoisseur. Together they created rib of beef *au fleurie* and *à la moelle*, accompanied by a gratin of potatoes *à la forézienne* (without cheese), aiguillettes of mallard with St. George's mushroom, or, in a more modern vein, scallops *en croûte* with Nantes butter, and *salade riche* (foie gras, lobster, and truffle)." Admit it, you love the *Larousse Gastronomique*.

[75] To clarify: Gaining access to these rarefied kitchens was *not* possible because those French chefs were more inclined to hire women. They're not. Remember, we're talking about staging.

Judy Rodgers of San Francisco landmark Zuni Café was—without any intentionality behind it—the trailblazer of European kitchen-storming. As an exchange student in high school, she went over to France in 1973 when it wasn't the norm (for culinary hopefuls, male or female)—well before Des Jardins and a few years earlier than Feniger or Milliken. She was, as luck would have it, assigned to the Troisgros family and spent her days hanging out in the Roanne restaurant's kitchen. That's where she found her métier. Then, as a professional, when everyone else (among her cooking peers) was discovering France, Rodgers decided to explore neglected Italy. Yes, her education was singular in her own day, but what's truly crazy to wrap your head around is that it's a trajectory that couldn't be replicated today. "I can't imagine my story being possible now, or even ten or fifteen years ago," she admitted. "When I landed at Troisgros in '73, I might have been the one of six Americans who could name the great three-star chefs of France. Big frickin' deal; but a lot of people could two years later, because Paul Bocuse[76] had been on the cover of *Newsweek* magazine."[77] And, as she also acknowledged, Italy's far from untapped by chefs now.

Is this shift such a bad thing for those who would have liked to trod Rodgers's path? Ask her and she'll tell you that today, so much of what shaped her as a chef and made her stand out is barely relevant in a world where exposure to ingredients or culinary styles is no longer dependent on travel. Having trained in a particular skill in Italy or in

---

[76] It's *Larousse Gastronomique* time again. "Bocuse (Paul): French cook (born Collonges-au-Mont-d'Or, 1926). He comes from a line of restaurateurs and cooks established on the banks of the Saône since 1765. Michel Bocuse opened a café in an old Collonges mill, which was taken over by his son Philibert. Philibert's son Nicolas bought the nearby Hôtel de l'Abbaye and ran it with his three sons, Jean-Noël, Nicolas, and Georges. Georges bought the Hotel-restaurant du Pont, also in Collognes.

"Georges's son, Paul, was first apprenticed to Fernand Point and then to Lucas-Carton and Lapérousse in Paris. He began working in 1942 in a restaurant in Lyon and in 1959 saved the small family restaurant in Collonges from ruin and made it into a gastronomic mecca. Attached to the tradition and cuisine of Lyon, he renewed the great classics without entering into the excesses of *nouvelle cuisine*. His family nickname was 'primat des gueules' ('primate of the palate'). With his forceful personality, he became the ambassador of French gastronomy throughout the world, giving conferences and cookery classes, especially in Japan. He published *La Cuisine de Marché* in 1980 and *Bocuse dans Votre Cuisine* in 1982. His creations include black truffle soup, lobster Meursault, and a chocolate gâteau that has become a specialty." (See also footnote 33, page 38.)

[77] He appeared on the cover of *Newsweek* magazine in 1975. It was the August 11 issue, and the related story titled "Food The New Wave." Thank you, Judy Rodgers, for fact-checking and clarifying that.

New York is of equal merit when it comes to getting hired, she said, as long as you're exposed to the same flavors and technique, and you're passionate. According to this founding parent of Californian and, to some extent, New American cuisine, "The mere fact of setting foot on the Piazza del Duomo [in Florence] is not going to distinguish you from the rest of the applicants. Honestly, there are so many restaurants now that are serious and trying hard, [there are] never going to be enough great cooks . . . If you're hardworking and talented, you're not going to have trouble finding a job. So the mere fact of having spent time somewhere exotic or at a restaurant in Italy is not going to get you a job."

And somewhere, a soufflé has just fallen. Or, at least, that's what it felt like when Rodgers relayed that last opinion. It struck me, initially, as disheartening—no need to pack your bags and see and cook the world. But then I realized that this was my problem (namely, relentless idealism), and it wasn't so much disheartening as it was, simply, unromantic. Rodgers wasn't discrediting these adventures; she was recognizing that we live in a world where they're not necessary. More than anywhere else, I think this holds true in America, where the diversity of restaurants is so great. If you go to France to do an apprenticeship, you're going to find uniformity in terms of the infrastructure of the enterprises and their style of or approach to food. And if you want to learn how to work in that rigorous, time-honored, fine dining–driven way, that country probably is the best place to do it. In Italy, you will find some of that, but you will mostly see a predominance of small restaurants helmed by the proprietor's mother—you will learn a tradition, a culture, a way to shape pasta. But you can find chefs in America, like Rodgers or Des Jardins who, having done those things, can teach them to you too. If you're a woman, there's an added upshot to staging in the U.S. of A.; we have more women chefs than you'd ever find in France, and we have both conventional and unconventional restaurant models to study and try on for size.

The European apprenticeships of Schwertner's, Rodgers's, or Des Jardins's memory may not be easy to come by in the United States (we do have a few comparable bastions to hit up—Des Jardins named Napa Valley's French Laundry and New York City's Per Se and Eleven Madison Park), but I disagree that stages aren't to be had. Most of the chefs I've interviewed for this book have talked about being open to (professionally) hungry beginners who have the nerve and prescience to inquire about an unpaid learning stint. Many of those same chefs have also remarked that they don't discriminate against those applicants who didn't go to culinary school. (Some might discriminate against those who did, though.)[78] And they encourage degree holders to stage too. Stephanie Izard, the force behind Chicago's restaurant Girl & the Goat,[79] urges graduates to stage in as many different types of kitchens as possible. "It's just like buying your knife," she says, "see which one feels right to you."

Another Chicagoan, Mindy Segal, envisions an entirely new kind of didactic program that operates through apprenticeships and re-creates that European experience on home turf. Her "great idea for culinary school was to accept apprenticeships—a couple of restaurants would be involved, city to city. The yearlong program, as she imagines it, would ask applicants to write an essay and, if admitted, to spend three months with various local specialists. She'd teach pastry, someone else would take charcuterie, and another expert, fish, for example. It would be similar to the European method, so that, she explains, "when you're done, you'd have a list of restaurants you could work with, or we would send you to Europe." Segal thinks of this "chef's alliance" as an investment in the restaurant industry's future and as an extension of what she tries to provide her employees now. "I worked

---

[78] For example, Stephanie Izard, whom you're about to meet, said that the fact that she gets "girls from culinary school into stage" and thinks "they're not going to make it" makes her want to open a culinary school where you have to cook to get in. Genius.

[79] Last year, Izard released her first cookbook, *Girl in the Kitchen*. I liked it so much I gave a copy to my mother, who can't stop cooking out of or talking about it. Because of this book, she has added sambal paste to her pantry and found ways to put something she always hated—honey—to delicious use. "Her ingredients just work perfectly," says Mom.

with chefs who taught me business and how to conduct myself. They allowed me to bring my creativity out my own way . . . I do that here with my staff."

Until Segal's dream is realized, the answer, it appears, if you are skipping school, is to go trick-or-treating for a series of stages. Or if free labor isn't a luxury you can afford to provide, you can also dive in and seek proper (paid and permanent) employment.

Proof that OTJ[80] erudition can be just the ticket, Southie[81] girl made good Barbara Lynch caught the cooking bug in home ec class (who knew that outdated course could be so empowering?) and worked her way through the best of Boston's kitchens. Then she traveled to Italy to gain an understanding of that country's food from the local women there.[82] Now in her late forties, she owns five restaurants, plus a bar, catering operation, and cookbook shop in her hometown. "I just couldn't accomplish anything in school," admits the thriving chef (and businesswoman), who doesn't hold a cooking or high school diploma. "In culinary school, you learn certain things, and I think you learn some discipline, some critical things in terms of health department and food science, hopefully—but it's too fast. I don't think you can actually learn a craft in two years. I don't think you can learn, really, how to cook in two months . . . [There are] all these things that happen on a day-to-day basis, that helped me to get to where I am, and yes, it was an education, but it was the process of creating the food, the instant gratification of a customer, the team-building, the style of food I was doing." And that was only half of it, because although Lynch had found her voice and figured out how to run a kitchen, she still had to sort out the business

---

[80] Who didn't know that's shorthand for "on the job"? So disappointed.

[81] South Boston, from whence the nickname "Southie" derives, was, during Lynch's childhood, one of the country's poorest, most at-risk neighborhoods. At thirteen, she snagged her first culinary job preparing meals for a rectory of priests. Cooking, she'll tell you, is what got her away from selling drugs (which she did) and serving as a bookie for her teachers (did that too). You can read more about her childhood in her marvelous 2009 cookbook *Stir*.

[82] At a relatively young age, Lynch trained under some of Boston's best known chefs, including Todd English. Then, in the '90s, she left for Italy to study that country's cuisine with the local women who have been cooking it as their mothers did for generations. Upon her return to Boston, she was made an executive chef, and then, in '98, opened the first of her many spaces.

end of opening restaurants. That is not, from what I've heard tell, anything that culinary schools have found a way (or inclination) to communicate. "I didn't have that confidence in myself that I knew how to run a business." She continues, "so I did depend on management, business managers, in the first five, six years. And then once I got confident in the style of food I was cooking, I started to take on more of the business part of it. But I don't recommend that you try to do it all at once."

Across the continent, in Portland, Oregon, with no formal training whatsoe'er, Naomi Pomeroy, of magical, it's-a-dinner-party-every-night Beast,[83] taught herself how to be a chef and run a business at the catering company, underground supper club, and three restaurant projects she started with her then husband. She familiarized herself with the technical aspects of the trade by hiring people who were more practiced or better trained than she. That's how she learned to cook *professionally* (literal def). She had no problem doing that, with admitting what she didn't know and being the boss of those who knew more. The staff all went to culinary school and had worked for notables like Vitaly Paley, Traci Des Jardins, Bobby Flay, and Alice Waters. She learned from their technique and, by not organizing her kitchen in the traditional, hierarchical way, she was able to give them room to develop their own styles.

For being an autodidact and not marching to the beat of the academic or even usual apprentice-circuit drum, Pomeroy found her distinct point of view without having to battle the negative aspect of influence. What I mean by that is, she wasn't put through the same paces as everyone else, so when she approaches her craft, she isn't drawing from the proverbial textbook or lesson plan. For the visionaries of this world who see things the rest of us don't, there's something to be said for not pursuing a standardized education or staying under the wing

---

[83] I vividly remember the tartness of the viscous pomegranate gastrique and the appropriately fatty, gamy duck breast it was served with at Beast on the night of March 4, 2011, when I dined there. Equally unforgettable, the Meyer lemon chocolate sauce that accompanied a heavenly lemon tartlette topped with a cloud of bruléed meringue.

of a sole chef (or, possibly, any number of chefs at all). Women, you might say, have been able to take advantage of this as the result of being discriminated against (as in, not wanted in the norm-defining backs of house). They were, for so long—and are even still, sometimes—not part of the dough to which cookie cutters were applied.

Selected by design or not, atypical training can lead to originality (and recognition for that), but it can also have undermining repercussions, more so for women, who are, from the outset, less likely to be taken seriously. In New York City (the East Village, to be precise), Amanda Cohen has mixed feelings about avoiding the established path to glory. She steered clear of the French format and, get ready for the real plot twist, honed in on vegetables,[84] perhaps the least "sexy," most "female"[85] of ingredients. "I graduated from cooking school and I was like, at twenty-five, 'I'm going to open my first restaurant.' Well, it really did take me twelve years after that to get anywhere near opening my restaurant, and for a long time, it was just, 'What job can I take? What job is interesting? . . . What's the next step?' . . . There [were] so many years [when] the next step wasn't a step up; it was just linear. It was a different restaurant, same job." Cohen, who defeated the odds and opened her own, profitable vegetable venue, wonders, nonetheless, if skipping out on the culinary Ivy Leaguer's predicted journey might have been a mistake. "It's funny," she remarks, "because the advice I want to give to people is go work in those five-star kitchens. Go get that pedigree, because not having the pedigree more than anything else has, I think, changed the way people look at my business. I think, maybe, if I had come out of a Daniel Boulud kitchen or a Jean-Georges

---

[84] Her Dirt Candy is a tiny space with big-ass, animal-free flavors. Omnivores are welcome and encouraged (by me) to go. I brought my parents—all of us meat eaters and one of us (Dad) a firm believer that vegetables do not dinner make—and we were floored. It started with the snacktastic jalapeño hush puppies improved (as though they needed it) by a maple butter that melts on contact with the fried poppers, and it ended with our being stuffed but unable to put down our spoons in the face of a creamy popcorn-infused pudding garnished with crunchy, light, salted-caramel popped kernels.

[85] See Shire's "salad girl" title (footnote 55, page 55) and understand that, on the more highfalutin brigades, whatever women were welcome were immediately shuttled off to that, the garde-manger station.

[Vongerichten][86] kitchen, people would have been like, 'Yeah, his sous chef Amanda is opening a restaurant,' I would have gotten a whole different series of press."

My first reaction to that whole get-the-pedigree comment was: Boulud and Vongerichten aren't exactly known for welcoming the ladies into the back of the house. The latter has definitely employed a female sous or two; the former has, of late, placed women in executive pastry chef slots[87] for the first time, and one sous chef, Florence Murard[88] at New York's Café Boulud, is the first savory-directed girl to get that far in any of his fourteen restaurants. It was considered breaking news (*major!*) when, in 2008, Boulud appointed Maite Montenegro (a woman) the maître'd of his sacred flagship Daniel. BFD, right? Well, in France, you see, it is (and Boulud is French), but that's not even the kitchen—that's out front in the dining room. If he put a girl in charge back there, I can hardly imagine how giant a stink would be made. It's a little easier to have regrets like Cohen's now, when there are more opportunities for women in such kitchens, but there still aren't a ton, and, when Cohen was dreaming about opening her own place by twenty-five, there were a paltry few.

She isn't the only success with pangs of this nature. Ann Cashion, whose career began almost fifteen years before Cohen's, spent time at professional stoves abroad—in France and Italy—during the late '70s before, eventually—in 1995—opening her own restaurant in Washington, D.C. She is one of only two women to receive a James Beard Award for Best Chef in her region (Mid-Atlantic: 2004), and after selling her first spot, she launched a second. It was astonishing to hear someone with all of these accomplishments say that, on looking back,

---

[86] Both Daniel Boulud and Jean-Georges Vongerichten are internationally acclaimed French chefs based in New York City. They have numerous restaurants in Manhattan and satellites beyond. The takeaway: These guys are culinary giants.

[87] As of 2012, there are three executive pastry chefs in Boulud's domain (and they're all based in New York City); they are, by name, Ghaya Oliveira, who stepped up in 2007 (Boulud Sud, Bar Boulud), Mymi Eberhardt in 2009 (DBGB Kitchen and Bar, plus, as of 2011, Épicerie Boulud), and Ashley Brauze in 2010 (db Bistro Moderne).

[88] Murad started as sous chef at New York's Café Boulud in February 2011.

she would have tried to get the male kitchen experience she didn't have. And when she says "male," she means kitchens dominated by men, which tends to implicate (keeping the timing in mind) the same kinds of kitchens Cohen might like to have sous-ed in. In Raleigh, North Carolina, Andrea Reusing, another chef with her own place, Lantern, and, as of 2011, a James Beard Award winner, shared some of those had-I-to-do-it-over pangs. "I wish I had the experience of having worked in high-level kitchens. [There are] things that you learn in those situations that you never—that you literally can't—learn anywhere else."

Part of the incentive to put oneself in another man's (or woman's) galley, especially one of repute, is to find a respected (or worthy of respect), practiced teacher. This is where, in an ideal situation, the bulk of an on-the-job education should come from. The more influence this sage wields within the industry (see facing page, Boulud and Vongerichten), the more he or she can do to promote a mentee's career, and that's a factor for women to consider. If there are fewer of us, and we tend not to be given the same attention or reverence as our male peers, then it's imperative that we help each other get ahead. Those with clout must be that much more diligent about taking care of those to whom they can pass the torch. It's certainly one way that female chefs who are frustrated with the status quo (whether in schools or galleys) can make a difference.

Pastry chef Shuna Lydon might be the model mentor or, at least, one strain of exemplary guide. She's tough and she's not one for TLC, but if I had to pick an adviser, she'd be mine. She relates how she found her method (calling?) in 1997 at, appropriately (while we're shooting for perfection or regretting a missed taste of the four-star life), the French Laundry. "I think that [there are] mentorships everywhere, and I think that someone seeking something formal means they're sitting at home waiting for an invitation in the mail. And I say get off your fucking ass and just cook, because Eric [Ziebold, the then chef de cuisine at 'the Laundry'] always used to say to the cook who's looking for Thomas

[Keller] to say, 'Do it this way; no, no, try it that way,' they're going to die waiting for that, because Thomas teaches by your watching him. So if you're paying attention, you can learn a lot in that kitchen, and if you're asleep at the wheel, you might as well go work at Denny's, because you're not going to learn."

At that citadel of "Oysters and Pearls,"[89] Lydon apprehended (among many other things) the *Art of Mentorship* (what she should title her book on the subject if ever she writes one, which she ought to). "The way that this education system of crafts is built is that the person who's above you, who's teaching you, who's the master, who's apprenticing you, is watching you very carefully and meting out your learning . . . I'm responsible for my cooks, so if I give them too much and they fail, that's my failure; and if don't give them enough, and they fail, that's my failure." Watch and learn, tadpoles. If that's not how you do it, IHOP is down the road.

Sarah Kirnon, like Lydon, is a testament to the difference that finding an engaged boss can make. After paying some unnecessary dues in a few English hotels where she reported to chefs who worship the European way of doing things, "have no respect for women, and don't even acknowledge people of color," the British-born Afro-Caribbean chef took what she imagined as a less-than-ideal position as a sous chef at the private dining room of the Emporio Armani boutique on Brompton Road in London. "It was not where I wanted to be, but they had a female executive chef," she says. And then, to Kirnon's surprise and future-shaping good fortune, "she made me realize I could be somebody in this business, because she was cooking who she was. She took some time out and let me be an active boss of the kitchen." This is what made Kirnon stay chez Armani; she soldiered through and, subsequently, got promoted from one station to the next, until there was no higher she could climb. "Guidance is everything," she learned.

---

[89] The French Laundry's signature dish, it's officially (check the cookbook) described as a "sabayon of pearl tapioca with Malpeque oysters and caviar," and it's heaven.

School, staging, on-the-job training, self-starting, or mentorship, no matter which strategy you settle on, Lydon insists that persistence is the constant variable for anyone who truly wants to learn her craft. "The education that we get in the kitchen is not onefold, it's not two-fold; it's multifold," she pontificates. "It's hands-on experience; it's reading on your days off; it's eating in other restaurants. Nowadays, it's blogs, it's TV, it's all this other stuff . . . So if no one in the kitchen is paying attention to you, go to the library and read one author's books . . . If all those cooks in my kitchen are waiting for a fucking golden egg in their paycheck, the invitation that says come and butcher the pig, you better fuck off, because it's not going to be like that." If you don't have or can't find a Shuna, can't get yourself to school or tap in to a supportive network, you still have only yourself to blame if you don't figure shit out. If Lydon has anything to teach you, it's this: The best educations are those that are hard-won and, frequently, the ones we give ourselves. Be aggressive.

CHAPTER 3

In the Man Cave

Most of my experience is really unpleasant. That's why I'm called the Grill Bitch, and a food and beverage server in corporate America.

—BETH ARETSKY

I'm not sure how many of you have written a book proposal. It doesn't matter, really, because as the narrator here, I'm supposed to assume you, the readers, don't know much of anything going in. (Sorry, guys. It's protocol.) One thing you need to do in order to prove the worth of your to-be-penned prose is to provide some sample material of the thing. (Right, you get it: You must write what hasn't been written so that someone will allow you to write the real thing.) For this number you're currently reading (or leafing through), I submitted an Introduction.

Between the moment the green light was given and the day I sat down to type this here manuscript, something had changed; not my intentions or the topic. I now have seventy some-odd extra voices in my head that weren't there before. That original fragment I drafted represented only two personalities—mine and, by proxy, that of a certain trash-talking line cook. She was a character presented to the world by Anthony Bourdain in his this-is-what-all-other-food-memoirs-will-now-be-judged-against *Kitchen Confidential*. I had taken my paperback copy of that seminal screed off the shelf for inspiration. It was less for its content and more for its tone, which, to me, seemed quintessentially masculine. He was writing about what's perceived as male subject matter and, while some pens are venomous, his was loaded with testosterone. As I revisited some of my favorite bits and pieces of the text, I stumbled on one of few women Bourdain mentions, his "long-time associate" Beth, the self-dubbed "Grill Bitch." He admires her because "she refused to behave differently than her male coworkers: she'd change in the same locker area, dropping her pants right along-side them. She was as sexually aggressive, and as vocal about it as her fellow cooks."[90] His depiction of her, although full of adoration, is pretty one-dimensional, and the hardened, ballsy chef with boobs has become her own cliché. I wondered what the hell happened to Beth? Wasn't that my goal—to find these women and get their stories? I'll always love *Kitchen Confidential*, but if we care to know what it's like for the girls on the line, wouldn't it, as I asked in that initial, scrapped intro, be better to let these Grill Bitches speak for themselves?

Beth Arestky isn't too hard to locate, it turns out. Insert "Grill Bitch" and "Beth" into the Google search prompter and you'll find her website, Grillbitch.com. In the "About Us" section, you'll get this little tidbit: "Welcome to the Grill Bitch. As manager for celebrity chef Anthony Bourdain, Beth (the Grill Bitch) is currently producing T-shirts with exclusive rights to Anthony's logo and slogan." It's in need of an update; more on that in a second.

As soon as I knew the dream was a reality—that I'd be writing this book (careful what you wish for), maybe even before I got in touch with Anita Lo, I e-mailed this Grill Bitch to see if she'd let me inter-view her. I held my breath, made a wish, and hit "send." Two hours later, she replied: "Count me in 100 percent!!!" She added that she had been hoping to write something like this herself but was too busy, and offered to put me in touch with friends of hers she thought might want to contribute too. When I saw her response, I got goose bumps, for real. (I mean, I have really low blood pressure and am often cold and getting the chills, but it was winter and the heat was blasting full throttle in my apartment.) There was some welling up, and I think I maybe spoke to

---

[90] Anthony Bourdain, *Kitchen Confidential: Adventures in the Culinary Underbelly* (New York, NY: HarperCollins, 2007), 58.

my dog, because who else could I share that kind of news with instanta-
neously? It probably sounded like, "I'm writing a book! I'm really writing a book!"

A few weeks later, Aretsky and I sat down to a late-night Skype
session. We'd tried to do an in-person interview, but it was blizzard season in NYC and she's a working mother of two (she's also the primary
breadwinner of her household at present). Two hours of uproarious
laughter (plus a mild dose of solemnity) ensued. Aretsky, who still takes
no crap, hasn't had it easy. She had outgrown her Bourdainian days as
a line cook and ended up as the executive chef at Butterfield 81, one
of my parents' former Upper East Side canteens and a place I'd supped
at with them. Her father and proprietor of that spot, Ken Aretsky, is a
prominent restaurateur in this town and has had his hand in a number
of successful establishments, some quite well known (he ran the iconic
'21' Club in Midtown and now owns an institution supported by the
1 percent, Patroon on East Forty-Sixth Street). Beth graduated from the
CIA and had cooked at a few of her dad's spots as well as places like
the Union Square Café.[91] When he put her in charge of his kitchen on
East Eighty-First Street, it was because she was ready for it. Attaining
that top position was her apotheosis; the reason she'd gone to culinary
school in the first place. "I thought I'd be a chef in a restaurant, and I'd
have my own restaurant and that would be it. You know, maybe I'd be
written up in the *New York Times*."

That's when everything went to shit, when her wish came true.
In 1996, two months after it opened, Ruth Reichl reviewed the joint
and gave it one star, which, if you go by that paper of record's clarification, qualifies a location as "good." "It may be the perfect East Side
bistro," she wrote, and later concluded: "It is easy to see why people
keep going back to Butterfield 81."[92] According to Beth Aretsky, "If
you read the review, it reads like a two-star review,[93] at least, but she

---

[91] See footnote 95, page 83 for more intel on the USC, as we locals call it.

[92] Ruth Reichl, Restaurant Review: Restaurants, the *New York Times*, May 31, 1996.

[93] That would be "very good," as per the *New York Times*.

gave us a one . . . But you know what, I was green; I was fresh out of the gate. And to get one star? Hey, I got one, I didn't get none." Though crestfallen, she probably could have dealt with it had it not been for her boss. "My dad," she said, "I'll never forget, my father said, 'How am I going to look at my customers again?' . . . He made me feel really bad, like it was my fault." Any daughter who has a father she worships would feel her heart break just to hear this (I do, and mine did), so it's probably not surprising that Aretsky didn't stay on at that restaurant. She went to another (not one of her dad's; it was Carola's, opened by a German woman of the same name and operated by an all-female staff), and then accepted a chef de cuisine position at a prominent catering company called Chef & Co. She left that post to be a private chef, then took on the task of being Bourdain's executive assistant, and, when it started, a PA (production assistant) on his television show (*No Reservations*). When, recently, after years of collaboration, the two parted ways, with her family to support, Aretsky quit the kitchen and turned to corporate America, a long way from where she was on Eighty-First Street back in 1996.

We talked about everything. What I was most interested in were her days in the back of house. What had made her assume the "Grill Bitch" title?

"I would say, being a woman on the line . . . I started back in the day before [the term] *sexual harassment* was ever coined, okay? So I was sexually harassed before anyone ever knew that word existed; I think that's where the Grill Bitch evolved from, in a self-defense mechanism manner. I always felt that you can either deal with the guys, or you can't. So if they said something really disgusting that they thought was going to make me cringe, well, I wasn't going to. I'm going to make them cringe from what my retort was going to be. I never would squirm."

What kinds of comebacks was she slinging? Here's one from her pre-CIA days as a prep cook (well before she arrived at Butterfield 81):

"When he [her dad] said, come and work at the '21' Club, I said 'Sure! That'll be great. I'll live in the city, I'll work, I'll get paid—it'll be great.' So I went to work with him as prep; you know, I worked with the saucier,[94] who was named Abdul, and I worked with the grill guy, whose name I don't remember. But, Abdul, I'll never forget, because he cornered me in the walk-in [cooler] one day, and he knew who I was . . . And Abdul cornered me in the walk-in and said, 'Tell your father I want to fuck the shit out of you,' and I was like eighteen at the time. And I said, 'Really? Well, how many camels are you going to give him?' So that's kind of where it all evolved. I was always quick to snap back with an answer. But I learned there that you really need to have some *cojones* if you want to be in the kitchen with mostly guys."

Are things much different for women in today's kitchens than they were in the '90s, when Beth was tousling with Abdul? For answers I went to Chicago's Stephanie Izard, who was the first and, for now, last female to take the *Top Chef* title. To her consternation, she is usually singled out more for that than for winning *Top Chef*. Her clear synopsis of what goes on behind many a dining room curtain: "I hope you have thick skin. There's a lot of offensive stuff said in the kitchen . . . that's what seems to trip most women up . . . That and the fact that you won't be able to do everything physically . . . There's a sexual harassment suit waiting to happen every five minutes."

Pastry chef Waylynn Lucas has no problem giving it back as hard as she gets it and, like Aretsky, sees that particular skill as being integral to survival in the field. "It takes a tough person, and, especially, an even tougher woman, to spend day after day in a kitchen . . . I love it, and I have the mouth of a sailor and a bad attitude. But I'm an intelligent woman on top of it all, and I know how to dish it right back at 'em, and dish it right back at 'em in a way that puts them in their place . . . I get the biggest joy

---

[94] Just below the sous chef on the totem pole, traditionally, the saucier holds the top cook rank on the professional line and is responsible for, as you may have guessed, things like sauces—also stews and hot hors d'oeuvres. This is all part of the French order outlined by Georges Auguste Escoffier. You'll learn more about it later on in this chapter (skip to footnote 99, page 87, now if you can't stand the suspense).

out of that. Because it's like, 'Oh you can dish it out, but you can't take it?' You know, nothing shuts up a man quicker than being called out by a woman in front of his peers. And that has gotten me a lot of respect . . . I work hard, and I don't mess around, and I don't tolerate BS."

No two broads, no matter how combative or Zen, go about securing their standing the same way. New York pastry chef Heather Bertinetti muses: "Every woman acts differently in the kitchen. Like, for me, for instance, I understand that the men made the system, right? I get that. And I get that I need to play along with the game. So I'll play along and I'll say 'yes' and I'll go along and I'll smile. But if you step on my toes and you're barking at me, I'll bite back."

She has given this a lot of thought, apparently. "The only way I'm going to survive is if I know I can go toe-to-toe with those men. And I'm going to stand my ground and I'm going to stick up for myself and I'm going to make my mark, *my mark* on *them*, not going to let them make a mark on me, right? It's like training a dog and you're fighting for dominance."

Someone else, a hero in her own right, witnessed firsthand how brutal the back of house could be in New York City's fine-dining league. Sarah Schafer was the first female sous chef in Danny Meyer's empire (the Union Square Hospitality Group[95]), which includes heavies like Eleven Madison Park and Gramercy Tavern, where she worked. Within those mostly male temples, any success she had was met with hostility and, often, cruelty. When she arrived at Gramercy after three months of trailing[96] in different restaurants around town, Schafer was shocked when Tom Colicchio (1998—back in the day, people) offered

---

[95] When Danny Meyer opened his first spot, the Union Square Café in 1985, he established a model for upscale casual dining in New York City and, some might say, beyond. His emphasis on using seasonal ingredients from the Union Square Greenmarket was part of it, sure, but the real game-changer was the attention paid to service—to killing customers with friendly, welcoming kindness without being too officious about it. That attitude set the tone for the rest of his eateries, including his quality-forward "fast-food" chain of Shake Shacks, and became a template for other restaurateurs.

[96] Trailing is a lot like staging, just less interactive. Think of it as shadowing. It's a way for prospective cooks to see how a galley operates and, possibly, to land an externship or, even, a job. It involves being assigned to a cook and following him/her throughout the course of his/her shift. You may be asked to lend a hand and put to work. Or not.

her a job as a line cook. This was unheard of; incoming young bucks would start out as "tavern cooks" and focus on food for the restaurant's more casual front room, the Tavern. Eventually, they'd be promoted to serve the main dining room as line cooks. Not Schafer. She was put on the appetizer station. A man who applied for a job right after she did was granted, like everyone else, the "tavern cook" title and directed all of his anger at Schafer, whom, he believed, stole his place (because how could she have been chosen on merit, right?). On comes the sabotage. He managed to turn off her stove and burned her with fish stock. And when one is assaulted with a pot of boiling liquid, what does one do? Schafer was advised not to go to the hospital, but, instead, to get a bucket of ice and spend the rest of that evening's service with her injured foot in the bucket. Did she? Sure. And then, once the kitchen had shut down for the night, she was able to go to the hospital. What other choice did she have? "I guess it's a horrible thing to say, but I didn't want to seem like a woman in their eyes," she admits. "I just wanted to be there to cook and be respected for that."

Six months later, her grin-and-bear-it pain tolerance landed her that sous position. But even at that level, the "different" treatment prevailed. At the meetings she attended, she would be asked to leave at moments, she presumes, when the agenda turned to "bawdy sex stuff." She stuck it out and eventually left for San Francisco, where she ran a number of restaurants, including those of Doug Washington and brothers Steven and Mitchell Rosenthal. When that team stormed Portland, Oregon, to launch Irving Street Kitchen in 2010, Schafer moved north to lead the charge.

After getting burned, it would be easy to resort to retaliation, but, according to Traci Des Jardins, the way to endure and ascend is not to look back at the people behind you in the race; don't get bogged down in the meanness. Keep on running, and understand that you might need to be selfish—worrying about someone else's setback is not productive. She put this as candidly as anyone could: "Do you have to fight your way to the top? Is it a battle? Is it cutthroat? Yeah, it's like, people ask, 'Do you have to be cutthroat?' In a way you do. You don't have to sabotage other people, but you have to be willing to step over the bodies . . . People will usually self-destruct. But, you know, in the French environment, in the kitchens that I grew up in, it was dog-eat-dog; if you weren't rising to the top, you were going to the bottom." When she shared this, I admit, my skin may have prickled.

This culinary sport is rough stuff. That's a fact. Amanda Cohen contends that the competition is steeper for the girls who want to participate. It's as though the entire male gender is seeded while the ladies, all unranked, have to duke it out to score a single entry slot in the tourney bracket. "When you go in as a woman, your competition is the other woman working in that kitchen." Chills the blood, that. "And I think if you're a man, you walk into a kitchen and you're like, 'I'm going to do the best job here. Who's the best chef at this restaurant? I'm going to compete with [him].' If you're a woman . . . there's only room for one, if you're lucky, two [of you].' In other words, in an industry in which support is essential, women are actually being encouraged to undercut each other. Cohen, of course, gets how detrimental and ridiculous this mentality is; still, she can't completely free herself from that destructive conditioning. "That might not be true. But that's how you feel. 'Okay, it doesn't even matter who the best cook is here; I'm going to be compared to this woman. And she might be horrible and she might be great, but *that's* my competition.' "

I'd like to tell you that Cohen's take on all this is extreme and not representative. Call her paranoid, but then be prepared to categorize a whole slew of female cooks under that heading. In Chapel Hill, North Carolina, Andrea Reusing acknowledges that adversarial tendency in her peers' reluctance to give advice. "There is that feeling [that] if you call a male *chef*, they're flattered. And a woman chef isn't always flattered for whatever reason . . . Maybe there is that kind of weird competition that . . . there's gonna only be one female nominee this year or one female on the cover of Best New Chef [97] . . . You want to be *the* Woman . . . because there is only one space, whereas men get to have that kind of brotherhood." At this point in our Skype marathon, I interjected with Cohen's view from *Cutthroat Island*.[98] Reusing sympathized and suggested it might stem from a diminished self-worth that is generated and, perversely, encouraged by the collective (white) male force field surrounding mainstream kitchen culture. "Because," she explained, "it's kind of that feeling that it benefits men to be able to be in this brotherhood and to pit you against each other." She went a step further to suggest that the situation (the dominance of the Caucasian fraternity and negative effects it can have on outsiders' confidence) would be the same for an African American (male or female). She dubbed it "that classic kind of divide," and, vis-à-vis women, remarked on its by-product, the low self-esteem that derives from being perceived (and then seeing yourself) as "the other." "You are the woman," says Reusing with the nutshell sum-up. "That's what your identity is."

I don't think we need to discuss why this is so disturbing. What we need is an antidote, and, on a heartening note, Cohen has made a small but meaningful inroad. To counteract the isolation (and low tally) of chicks on stations that the kill-or-be-killed inclination exacerbates, Cohen invited a number of established lady chefs to her restaurant (that would be the elegantly scrappy Dirt Candy, about which I hungrily reminisced in the previous chapter—see footnote 84, page 73) one night along with a few kitchen guppies, girls too. She locked the door and made dinner for all of them (one hopes she served them those hush puppies). The point was for them to inspire each other, ask and answer questions, have a good time, and feel like they were part of a community. When I spoke, afterward, with some of the attendees, they told me how much the evening had inspired them. It wasn't all

---

[97] *Food & Wine* magazine's annual Best New Chef issue.

[98] Appropriately, the plot of this referenced 1995 film is centered on a lady pirate's (she's played by Geena Davis) fight to beat other swashbucklers to a hidden island where booty awaits.

pass-the-candle-and-talk-about-our-feelings; it was easy and empowering, and it filled them with pride for their industry and for being women in it.

Sometimes support comes in less pleasant packages, as Shuna Lydon learned when a female line cook once boiled things down (figuratively) for her. "Just know this," she shared with Lydon, "you're going to work twice as hard for half the respect." The budding pastry chef accepted it and kept on going. "I know I operate in a system that wants to keep me down," she acknowledges, without a trace of bitterness. She explains that some combination of an understanding of capitalism and an appreciation of her mother's radicalism—the pastry chef's mom was an outspoken radical feminist—makes her understand why a kitchen needs to be structured in the traditional way, with an alpha in command. She took that one step beyond in a way that implicates women not simply as the designated non-alphas, but as biologically ineligible for galley duty. Due to the intense physical nature of the life in these quarters, if women are defined by their role as babymakers, they become verboten entities in the hot-pot zone. If the kitchen is a mini-society, and a "typical" one, they're coming from a place where they've been trained to be mothers, and men to be soldiers (and, yes, thanks to Escoffier, there's an army-like rank and file in these societal microcosms[99]). Why, in that reality, would a woman choose an

---

[99] I'm going to get this out of the way now, and, if you don't mind, I'm going to quote myself in order to do so. Here, serving the same purpose I did in that context, a brief summary included in the article I wrote for *Gastronomica: The Journal of Food and Culture*, titled "Why Are There No Great Women Chefs?" Vol. 10, No. 1 (Winter 2010), 24–31: "Serious restaurant kitchens are organized according to the brigade system. The military terminology is not accidental. Although it traces back to the fourteenth century, Georges Auguste Escoffier is often cited as the chef who brought the system out of the barracks and into the restaurant industry at the end of the nineteenth century. At the top of the pecking order is the chef de cuisine, who acts like a drill sergeant to keep his staff in line, by whatever means necessary. The system is extremely hierarchical; underlings and newcomers are often subjected to hazing." Escoffier separated the kitchen into five stations, or *parties*, each responsible for a different element of preparation (cold dishes; cooked vegetables and starches; roasted, grilled, or fried items; sauces and soups; and pastry). In addition to chef de cuisine, positions include a few now-familiar titles—there's the sous chef (the second in command), the *chef de partie* (in charge of a specific section of the galley), and then we get to the more generic titles of cook (*cuisinier*), junior cook (*commis*), apprentice (*apprenti*), and dishwasher (*plongeur*). The saucier, as noted (footnote 94, page 82), gets a lot of respect—he handles sauces and finishes "serious" protein dishes (the big meat and fish numbers). There's the roast cook (*rôtisseur*) who oversees those who roast, broil, or fry, like the grill cook (*grillardin*; see also, Grill Bitch) or fry cook (*friturier*). Don't forget the salad girl, I mean, garde-manger. There are others, too, but I think you get the idea and nowadays, you don't see too many kitchens big enough to house all these worker bees. If you'd like a taste of what the soup cook (*potager*) or the vegetable cook (*legumier*)

cont'd

atmosphere that hard? Lydon asks. "You can't have a baby if you're working nineteen hours a day in a kitchen," she said. At the heart of this polemic lies a painful truth—whether or not you choose to have a baby is beside the point. Choice is an illusion. In this filiopietistic gastronomic gemeinschaft[100] Lydon calls home, the following mantra, phrased by chef Carrie Nahabedian, is an oxymoron: "You're a cook first; you're a woman second." Nope. You're a woman first, and you are only that. Cook at home, sweetheart.

Bertinetti seemed like she could be an acolyte of Lydon, so I decided to run the latter's theory by the younger pastry chef. She agreed with the premise that, within the confines of the traditional brigade system,[101] there's no place for women, behaviorally speaking, at least. She does, however, feel that "not enough women have really stood up and made a place." All told, Bertinetti was ready to vote Lydon in the next election. "That's exactly right, though," she affirmed. "What she said makes total sense. The most hurtful thing ever said to me in a kitchen— it wasn't the name-calling—it was 'Why do you need a boyfriend? Why do you need to be in a relationship? You shouldn't be talking about marriage, you should focus on your career,' right? And I want to say, 'Well, why are you able to be married, and you're able to have a family, and you're still calling yourself this big great [male] chef?' Right? Why? I mean it's ridiculous. 'What makes it okay for you and not okay for me?'" If you subscribe to the notion that women are ultimately meant to be incubators, then of course, for us, parenthood and career are considered mutually exclusive; our career is parenting, duh.

I can appreciate such syllogisms, up to a point. They only make sense within a limited realm, one which continues to shrink, at least in

---

contributes, say, pick up a copy of Escoffier's *Le Guide Culinaire*, in which their stock (no pun intended) recipes are codified. First published in 1903, in French (duh), it has hence been translated into our tongue; the most recent edition came out in 2011. It's titled *Escoffier* and was edited by H. L. Cracknell and R. J. Kaufmann. We good?

[100] Ah, where would I be without Old Trusty, *The Thinker's Thesaurus*? Where would you be? In a happier place, I'm sure. Did you know *filiopietistic* is a synonym for *old-fashioned*, with an implied note of excessive reverence? I did not. *Gemeinschaft* is borrowed from German; it's another moniker for society, which I already used. I don't like word repetition. Apologies for the inconvenience and thank you, Peter E. Meltzer.

[101] In case you were dozing off, check the footnote before last (99, page 87).

this country, where men's and women's functions have become so much more loosely defined (and so have the designations of what is "male" or "female"); and one where the kind of restaurants Lydon is referencing has become drastically less prevalent. As Jessica Boncutter observes, "It's a transitional period for food in America; for women and men. The roles of men are changing; women don't need men. No one knows what role women will have." The line between casual and fine dining has been blurred; smaller venues have opened to greater acclaim, and different (often uncategorizable) genres of cuisine are gaining traction among "serious" diners, critics, and award arbiters. In these new-style establishments, you'll often find backs of houses with unusual, less-hierarchal arrangements and reduced staffs. If these places and their respective kitchens can exist, then Lydon's justification of the original system isn't quite as buyable—perhaps it's the ideal structure for those crumbling palaces, but that's quite a specific context. I mentioned this loophole to Lydon, and she agreed there might be something in it.

Lydon went on to talk about something that I suspect is a more universal issue, as it relates to how women can operate in a male-dominated kitchen of any kind. Progress—or whatever people want to call it (those ass-backward types might use a different name for it)—aside, women are expected, by your average not-so-enlightened (and sometimes, even the most enlightened fall back on this basic behavior) person, to be softer than men: nurturing, maternal, more submissive, or what have you. In a galley full of testosterone, it's easy to lean on that conceit. But that kind of puts a girl, as Lydon said, "between a rock and a hard place," because, "when a woman is not macho, she's not acting out of character, but in a kitchen, everyone has to walk around with more confidence than they possess to get the job done." Along these Lydon-esque lines, I gleaned that if I, the female I am, act the way you (the general populous; not those with radical feminist moms, for example) want me to in life (like a gentle caregiver), I'm a failure in the professional kitchen. And if I act the way you want me to in the kitchen, then I'm a failure as a (female) human being. Or as Waylynn Lucas wraps it up and ties it in a nice bow: "So we're good enough to stay at home and cook all your meals and raise your children, but when it comes to us wanting to cook meals on a professional level, you won't give us the same credit, or you won't give us the time of day." Not unrelated, Lucas also mentioned that her ex-boyfriend, who's a chef and, for the most part, loved that his girlfriend was too, had been known to whine, "Why can't you just be a girl?"

That's about as much women's studies as I'm willing to subject anyone (including myself) to, and, I should note, mine is a hackneyed version at best; I never took a class in that collegiate department, and even Lydon will tell you it wasn't her major. Let's remember, too, with some optimism, that times have changed. Lydon, who remains a firm believer of the brigaderie[102] and, despite its historical exclusion of women, the French halls of fine dining that emblematize that rigid setup, noted that there are still cities where women are forbidden in the professional kitchen. That used to be the case throughout France and, according to her, that has really only begun to shift in the last decade.

In America, progress came earlier and more swiftly. Since Karen DeMasco's[103] career kicked off, there are "definitely more women in the kitchen. Working conditions are better . . . I started working in the kitchen where everyone worked six days; you got paid a salary, nobody ever offered health insurance. Now it's totally different. Now you get paid for every hour that you're here; you get overtime pay. Everyone's working five days a week; you get insurance. It's just a much more realistic, livable situation. And also, when I started, if you worked six months at a restaurant, you put in your time there; you could move on. It was very common. And now I've had cooks for over two years . . . It's just a

---

[102] I made that word up; I think it flies. You could go with brigadery, but I like the nod to the French.

[103] Hers might be my favorite lemon tart. You can order one of your very own at Locanda Verde, where she's the pastry chef. She was previously pastry chef at Tom Colicchio's Craft, which explains the title of her cookbook, *The Craft of Baking* (Clarkson Potter, 2009), a must-have for anyone with even the remotest interest in preparing tart-related phenomena.

lot more livable. And now I think that the minimum you're expected to stay in a job is a year; the bare minimum. It's just a much more stable environment."

Stability's up, that's good news, and the number of women cooking in restaurants has increased markedly. Numerically, though, it's still a man's world. That said, while Miles[104] lingers in many a galley, there are male chefs (and cooks) who aren't tolerating (or enjoying) that kind of douchery on their watches. Aretsky's lot is probably less common than it was in her day. For those young gals who are currently on the lines of these unfriendly (to team estrogen) spots, instead of I-will-cut-you[105] retorts, selective oblivion is the better ploy.

Christina Tosi, the thirty-year-old New Yorker[106] who oversees the hot-as-Hades Momofuku galaxy's pastry operations (including the ever-growing number of its local Milk Bar bakeries) brushes the dame-dissing jabs away like dirt off her shoulder,[107] if she notices them at all. She drily observes, "It's not my battle. I didn't fight it to get one way or the other . . . I don't feel like it affects my experience at all . . . Also, you live in NYC, your feelings are going to get hurt so many times, and if you're just counting, like putting ticks every time somebody says something mean to you or whatever, you probably shouldn't leave your apartment in the morning, 'cause you're gonna get pushed on the subway and someone might call you a nasty name or say something creepy to you as you walk home at night. I guess you could call it because you're a woman, but then you're losing sight of the bigger picture."

---

[104] A mostly unsavory character I knew in college coined a wonderful expression, "Miles of Cock," to describe a situation (often pertaining to a bar or party) in which the room held an unusually large ratio of men to women. Lots of times, it was how he identified a gay venue, but sometimes it was just a guy-heavy straight scene. He'd regale us with tales of an ill-spent evening (wherein he shadily left a girlfriend at home to troll for other company), and say he had stopped by a lounge where he saw Miles. And we would know what this meant. Now, I apply it to any premises on which there's an onslaught of boys.

[105] That's the name of my old buddy Puppy Thompson's (her alias) wickedly funny blog Illcutyou.blogspot.com.

[106] Born in Springfield, Virginia . . . As a native of the Big Apple, I'm never sure at what point a transplant becomes a New Yorker. When in doubt, clarify, I say.

[107] Did you catch the Jay-Z reference there? "Dirt Off Your Shoulder" remains one of my favorite tracks. It's from *The Black Album* (2003), if you're looking for it.

Alex Guarnaschelli, whose name you probably recognize from the Food Network (she hosts a couple of cooking shows, is, like Amanda Freitag, a judge on *Chopped*, and, last year, competed on *The Next Iron Chef: Super Chefs*) heads up the kitchens at two of Manhattan's slickest spots—Butter and The Darby.[108] She didn't have to feign ignorance of whatever gendered power-wielding was going on around her as she toiled away in the French (in France and again in New York) trenches. Her only agenda was "trying to keep my head above water." She hadn't the ability to pull back and look at the structure in which she was installed, because "I was too busy learning how to cook and treat ingredients. I didn't have the presence of mind to think about what kind of system I was in. I was trying to survive; trying not to burn myself, not to lop my finger off. I think I was too young to contemplate what system I was part of. I just didn't want to make a mistake." In no way does she wish she'd had that presence of mind. She counsels against it. "I think it's best to park your gender at the door," she says. "Bring your attitude and park your gender."

I interviewed Mary Sue Milliken at one of her restaurants, Border Grill in downtown Los Angeles, the day after she returned from shooting her near-victorious season of *Top Chef Masters*.[109] She has been in the game since the late '70s, when there was a starker disparity between the number of men and women in the kitchen and the way they were treated. She would agree with Tosi's strategy (the tune-it-out tactic) and advise the rest of their generation to follow suit. "I think [there are] two parts to being trailblazers in a male-dominated field," she noted while looking back on her own career. "One part is that you're better off spending your energy being the best you can be than spending your energy being angry because you're not getting a fair shake; because, if you spend your energy doing that, you don't have that much to spare.

---

[108] It's also worth noting (what some daughters only dream of) that Alex's mom, Maria Guarnaschelli, is one of the industry's best-known cookbook editors.

[109] She and her longtime pal Traci Des Jardins both made it to the final round, when they lost to Floyd Cardoz of Manhattan's North End Grill, which opened in early 2012.

You have to be better than every man around you if you want to excel. You know, all kinds of crappy boys that we worked with in the kitchens would be making more money, getting raises, getting promotions, and the only way we would get that was if we worked circles around them, literally . . . But I think part of keeping your head in the sand about that is just a self-preservation thing; if you let yourself acknowledge it too much, it takes away from your reserves—your energy reserves—to just keep on overachieving." It's thanks to the contributions of Milliken and her peers that Tosi and her contemporaries have less to be phased by.

Although it's relatively easier to be a female in the professional kitchen circa 2012, most women still aren't comfortable expressing their physical femininity in that zone. There are a number of reasons for this. As already touched on, women cooks have frequently had to choose between the lesser of evils to get along in a galley—acting like a man (renouncing all vestiges of femaleness) or becoming invisible (you might associate this with Milliken's head-in-the-sand tactic). Obviously, getting tarted up for a steamy night on the line is not going to accomplish either of those goals (you'd be far from invisible, and you'd be a walking poster girl for your sex). There's a more practical justification for leaving your vanity at home—safety. Milliken explains: "If you were a firefighter, you wouldn't wear a different uniform; you wouldn't wear a low-cut, buttoned-up shirt and have your fingernails painted. I hate fingernail polish in the kitchen. It drives me out of my mind. It's wrong and it chips off and goes into the food; that's just a basic sanitation thing. There are even things about all the jewelry Susan [Feniger][110] wears . . . I just feel like that's a little bit much for the kitchen, too, because food gets all in that shit . . . The reason chef coats have two panels is for protection," she tells me. "So if something spills, then you've got these two layers of heavy cloth on the most important part of your body. Also, then you can switch panels so you have a clean front instead of looking like a dribbled mess. The chef jacket is designed with all kinds of functional

[110] Milliken and Feniger are longtime (30-years-plus) pals and collaborators. They co-own three restaurants and cohosted a television show on the Food Network called *Too Hot Tamales*.

features." For many, Milliken and Feniger included, picking a signature hue for one's chef uniform is about as far as gussying is taken.

There are always exceptions. Surprisingly, Milliken holds one up as an inspiration because, perhaps, of the context in which her mentor broke the rules. "I had worked for a woman in Paris in 1979 for a year," recounts Milliken, "and she had a [Michelin] two-star restaurant—Dominique Nahmias. She would walk into the kitchen in six-inch stiletto heels and a V-neck T-shirt and she was just fabulous . . . She has a restaurant [Casa Olympe] to this day in Paris . . . avant-garde [director] Roman Polanski was eating [there] every day and [author] Jerzy Kosinski . . . Jean Paul Gaultier eats at her restaurant every day now . . . She was a great role model for me, and also it was the first time in my career of cooking where I felt I didn't have to shave my head, wear steel-toed shoes—you know, look like a dyke." When Milliken said this, I have to admit, I smiled with understanding and relief. Something that perplexes me about lady chef culture is the butch aesthetic often associated with it. Why, I have always questioned, on *Top Chef*, for example, do so many of the female contestants have Mohawks and make decidedly masculine sartorial choices? In a way, one of the great things about a uniform is its democratizing effect—it makes everyone look the same. So when a woman decides to put on her stilettos or, alternatively, to draw attention to herself in an equally drastic but opposite manner (i.e., going über-male), I wonder if it isn't motivated by the same thing—to mark oneself as different and to take pride in that difference. In the '70s and '80s, when there were so few prominent women in the industry, Nahmias's racing about her own kitchen in fuck-me shoes was a way of marking her territory (and, to do this in France, where the whites[111]—the training and male tradition they represent—are so revered, is that much more provocative and subversive); it was as though she was belting, "I am woman, hear me roar!" while coyly winking *au même temps*.

---

[111] The ever vigilant and formidable Jane Tunks (the copy editor of this book you're reading) suggested I clarify that those "whites" referenced are sartorial in nature. I'm talking about the uniform, not Caucasians or, as she noted (and cracked me up), a reference to corporate oppression as signified by the phrase "white male."

(Remember, it's Paris; if you're a woman and you get dressed, you're expected to go chic or stay home.) Then for the shorn-headed femmes in steel-toed footwear marching through American kitchens, their self-presentation would say "don't mess with Texas" to potential puerile harassers; it's a form of armor that repels being demeaned or having one's ass pinched.

Today, these seemingly superficial trappings (we're talking about hair and shoes) can have different significance, because, suddenly, male chefs are being held up as sex symbols. The epitome of this *porchetta*-plating pinup is covered in ink and swinging a butchered animal haunch. Where, one asks, does this leave their female counterparts? It's as though the Man Power of the galley has iconographically entered the pop-cultural vernacular (it's worn on a tattooed sleeve). Where do the girls fit in there?

Not one for lazy leave-'em-hanging tricks, I plan to readdress that image problem. It's going on the back burner to simmer for a little while before I stir it up again in a later chapter, because we're here, in the man cave, to talk about what the deal is when you're standing on the line, julienning or deep-frying.

It's not just skin deep, Gina DePalma reminded me. "The thing that used to bother me the most [was that] I always felt like I had to sacrifice my femininity. And I don't just mean my appearance—you have to hide those feminine parts of your nature, of nurturing . . . You have to buy into the whole *pretend to be one of the boys*. I think we're not one of the boys, and it takes a long time to be old enough, to be confident enough to say, 'You know, I'm not one of the boys and that's what I'm bringing to the kitchen, bozo.'" She was also the chef who talked about aesthetic upkeep within a larger framework, that of one's quality of life and how much it suffers in this profession. Enjoying a multidimensional existence is "harder for a woman," she finds, "because if we do want to have kids or have a relationship, it's harder for us to have that balance. You have to have time to not look like a hag and wax your legs and clean laundry, which is all a challenge when you're working twelve, fourteen hours a day. I don't think this is a business where balance is a valued thing. And I don't think we're there yet. I think things are getting a little better incrementally." You could almost describe DePalma's revelation as a Pyrrhic one; getting diagnosed with cancer was what gave her the perspective (and, ironically, the ability) to reprioritize and start making time for other things. It's frightening to think of all the healthy (in body) cooks out there who, because they (luckily) haven't been faced with a potentially fatal diagnosis or other devastating blow, haven't figured this out, and might not until they've missed their chance to change things.

Michelle Bernstein was a late-bloomer vis-à-vis getting out of the kitchen—both logistically and psychologically. "My first few years," she fesses up, "I didn't even let anyone make stock for me . . . I was a crazy bitch . . . I never missed a day of work; I didn't have a relationship. For years it was like that, until I realized I was ready to have a life . . . to have people do things for me. That was the first day off I took after being the chef for three years; I'll never forget that day, because it was probably the first day of my life." She saved herself by unshackling her feet from the stove and, no, she doesn't regret letting some of her destructive monomania go.

There are those who are well aware of what they're giving up—some wouldn't do it differently; others plan to shift gears eventually and find a way to make room for things like marriage, hobbies, or pedicures. Lucas, who unabashedly loves spending the majority of her time in the testosterone den, acknowledged that, because she's "surrounded by guys all the time," she has no time for gal pals, or primping, for that matter (no hair appointments or manicures). She misses a little girl chat or bikini wax now and then, but Lucas isn't complaining. She took a break to work in fashion—modeled for a bit—and, after facing the cattiness she found there, was driven right home to restaurants and the rough-and-tumble life therein. "I just had to have it back; I couldn't really get enough of it."

Take (like Lucas), leave (or ignore, like Tosi and Milliken), or fight (like Aretsky) the banter, taunting, hazing, getting it on, feeling unpretty, shaking in your shoes, because there's still an actual job to be done: feeding the people, getting their food onto the plates. That's what these women do regularly; it's what a workday entails, and what most cooks live for. The daily grind is what you'd call it, and it comprises the bulk of any cook's time. Tina Dang, one of Judy Rodgers's protégées, who recently left Zuni to attend to a slew of projects, including her personal chef business,[112] entered that San Francisco stalwart as a dessert plater on pastry detail, then stepped in for an exiting assistant in that department, moved to "pantry" ("where the famous Caesar salads are made"), and finally made it to grill (not a slot usually filled by girls). She e-mailed me a list of the pros and cons of the line cook gig, and it's a real gem.

Pros

1. Nothing like cooking can give you the rush, exhilaration, and immense pride in the final product—each and every plate. I just love cooking, and a part of me feels like because I can cook on the grill, I have accomplished something no other woman has. Again, maybe it's that masculine aspect to the kitchen and what certain titles can give.

2. Working with such passionate cooks. I have befriended a numerous amount of smart, creative, and passionate cooks with humble attitudes . . . some not so humble. I learned about how salads can vary with sweet [or] bitter leaves; [how to adjust] salt content with acids such as lemon juice; [to have] a consistent product and palate. I learned how to let meat rest; how to grill vegetables; how to grill and butterfly squabs and quails . . . just learning to cook.

3. [Daily] tastings and being a part of a full operation every single night, getting hit with tickets. Sometimes I hated it, but most of the time, especially now, at the end, I wanted more. I love that rush.

4. Honing my energy through hard work and ethics and less talking.

---

[112] An e-mail check-in with Dang found that she'd done some staging in New York City before returning to San Francisco to score the sous chef title at the restaurant Nopalito, a spin-off of Nopa, where everyone I know (in that city) goes for brunch, religiously.

5. BIGGEST PRO: One night on the grill someone told me to peek around the corner. There he was, JACQUES PÉPIN!!! We all waited patiently to see what he would order, and finally the server put in the order and it was a 'Med Rare Burger w/ Cheddar.' At the time, my heart was racing; all arms went up in the air as the cooks yelled with excitement that I WAS COOKING THE BURGER!!!!! I watched him consistently as a small child so I was very eager to cook a burger for him. I also burned another burger because I was so focused on making his perfect. When the time came, Mr. Pépin came into the kitchen. I was inches behind him the whole time, my heart beating as he greeted the other cooks. I was breathless. The server patted him on the back and said, "Mr. Pépin, this is the girl who cooked your burger." He [Pépin] turned toward me and I exclaimed, "I've watched you ever since I was a little girl!" and started to cry. He gave me a gentle hug and said, "It was *ze* best burger in *ze* whole world," and kissed me on the cheek.

Cons

1. Was once told by a male cook "because you are a girl *you* have to work harder than those guys." I actually, at the time, was so shocked by that statement I felt ill; but, well, I guess it was something I could learn from.

2. Long time on your feet.

3. My relationship with my boyfriend suffered from lack of nights with him and early mornings heading into work.

4. I was not able to freely or creatively do more volunteer work or have extra time to myself without always wanting to sleep.

5. You can't always fit in with everyone all the time.

For some, the grueling part never stops. Susan Feniger, who runs four restaurants, discovered that even after introducing her first twenty-eight years ago, she was spending eighteen hours a day in the kitchen, for six months straight, when she opened her latest in 2009. "I'm standing in front of a wood-burning oven fourteen hours a day, and I'm *old*, and I still love it," she says with a grin. "It energizes me."

Dig if you will the picture:[113] You've paid your dues as a cook, are comfortable owning the chef title, have even run a kitchen or two. A modern neighborhood American bistro with seven years and a lot of New York City love behind it has recruited you to take over for a departing exec chef. He's male. His boss, the owner, is male. The GM (general manager), a partner in the place, is also male. And the staff you're managing? Yup, male too. What should you expect? Well, Amanda Freitag can enlighten us on all this, because it's the minefield she walked into when arriving at the Harrison in January 2008. She had already figured out (her last gig helped there) that inheriting someone else's team is a bad idea, but that's what she was doing.

"The Harrison[114] was huge for me, because I'd been cooking Italian for seven years so I was scared out of my mind, you know? And it just all of a sudden sparked all this creativity and, again, I had promised myself I wouldn't go into a kitchen and take over an existing crew. And I did it at the Harrison. And I went in like a warrior. I didn't bring a sous chef with me, I didn't bring a pastry chef, I didn't bring a cook, I didn't bring anyone. I went in by myself, under the impression that this entire kitchen crew is psyched to work with me. [Laughs.] I don't think anybody knows how intense that experience was in the beginning . . . It was all men; there were no women in that kitchen."

At this juncture, I queried whether the dynamic was challenging because the boys were anti-woman, or because they weren't used to being bossed by one. There's a difference. The first is harder to combat; the second just requires adapting. "It was everything. It was both,

---

[113] Prince. Don't pretend you didn't know that. You're singing along now, aren't you? "This is what it sounds like/ When doves cry."

[114] Established in October 2001 a few weeks after September 11, the Harrison lies a few blocks away from Ground Zero.

because it was mainly a Latino kitchen," she replied. "But the sous chef, who I adopted, had worked with Brian Bistrong [her predecessor] and was supposedly excited to work with me, [but] was not really. It was a farce; he was just buying time to go work at Braeburn [where Bistrong had gone]. I thought he was helping me, but he was sabotaging me along the way. I would start talking to the guys about how I wanted things done, and he was eye-rolling behind me. What I was trying to do there in a short amount of time was ridiculous. I knew I was under the microscope. I knew I had to put together an entirely new menu, from soup to nuts, and that we were going to get reviews. It was so intense. From January of 2008 to May, I basically worked seven days a week and, obviously, fired that sous chef." Within five months, Freitag was doing just fine, thanks; she garnered a strong two stars from Frank Bruni at the *New York Times* and brought some needed new energy (and plates) to the eatery.

If you're an executive pastry chef hired to head up that postmeal and bread-related program, you have the added challenge of getting along with the savory side. You have your own team to take care of, but you're expected to answer to the restaurant's reigning executive (as in, of all operations, including yours) chef. You are simultaneously autonomous and dependent. You want to set an example for your crew, show them how it should be done, and make sure your unit runs efficiently and puts out a flawless product; but you and your good intentions can all be thwarted by the people who aren't part of your tiny fiefdom, or undermined by whomever you answer to. That's what happened to an in-command pastry expert at one of New York City's toniest restaurants. Heather Bertinetti had reached the top of the sugar-sprinkled heap by standing up to the men who dominated the kitchens she had worked her way through. She'd made herself numb to the teasing and patronizing, and thought she was giving the women she oversaw sage advice when she told them to do the same. When the taunting reached fever pitch, her employees couldn't tolerate it any longer and advised their boss of what was happening. That's when Bertinetti, who herself had started, finally, to feel the sting, was left with an even worse sensation—culpability. "Now the blinders are off and I really see it for what it was," she admitted. "Like, 'Oh my God, how did I subject other women working for me to this?' They were getting called the C-bomb[115] and all this stuff, and I just kept [saying], 'Oh, you've got to toughen up,' and all these rehearsed answers that I've always been told. Shame on me for saying what they [other chefs] told me to them [her team]. I'm like, 'No. You know what? Yeah, walk out. Give your notice. Tell them to fuck themselves. Who cares? Stand up for yourself. Do it.' " Soon after, she followed her own advice. You can now find her equally exquisite and comforting desserts at Crown on the Upper East Side.[116]

There are chefs who, unlike Lydon or, initially, Bertinetti, did not find the French brigade's efficacy justification enough for the trauma it could inflict on the psyche. Having witnessed tyranny as a cook, Bridget Batson held out hope for alternative ways to govern a kitchen. "I definitely wouldn't run a kitchen like that, but I worked in one and learned a lot about a steady, structured system . . . I learned how to run a kitchen the way I do now, starting with that information, and making it more mine, and a little softer, and more motivational and not fear-driven. That doesn't work for everybody; some people like to be pushed by fear. I know I certainly was a few times. I was scared to death. It's great that it's not the norm anymore." Batson is proud of what goes on in her kitchen at Gitane, but it took her a while to get there. At one point, her city's newspaper—the *San Francisco Chronicle*—profiled Batson in a "behind the scenes" column written by Sophie Brickman, who stepped inside a number of chef's galleys. "Professional kitchens are notoriously fueled by machismo," began the copy; its emphasis

---

[115] The word *cunt* is despicable, true. But part of what gives it the power to slay is that most women are afraid to say it, even in a whisper. I think we have to find a way to own it so that it starts to seem almost silly and meaningless; detonate it, like. It's a Voldemort thing. I'm not planning to call anyone a cunt, let's be clear. I just don't think we need to find other ways to relay it when recounting what some fuckwad of a dickhead said. In related news, my father, upon reading this, is probably never going to look at me again.

[116] When you go, order an *affogato* (ice cream drowned in espresso; think of it as a more sophisticated milk shake) It's her signature. She makes the best ones around.

was on Batson's humility (the opposite of "machismo," as presumed by Brickman) as evidenced by the effort expended on a paella dish. The piece ended thusly: "Before one order was whisked off to the dining room, Batson pulled out her iPhone. In a decidedly un-macho gesture, she took a picture of her dish and texted it to owner Franck LeClerc so he could take part in the team's success."[117] The chef was horrified by this write-up. She doubts that you'd ever see an article like that describing a man anytime soon, and feared that hers would be known as "the gummy bear kitchen." She worried that people would think she was a "pansy" (and, the corollary to that would be, less of a chef). Then, thank goodness, she eventually realized it doesn't matter. But it does show the lasting impact her training had on her.

Ericka Burke's abusive professional upbringing had an even stronger hold; she confessed it prompted her to repeat the violent offense in her own kitchen. Somehow, it had been beaten (I use that word deliberately) into her head that the way to demonstrate power was by invoking fear. "It was, a 'you're going to respect me' kind of thing," she explained, and implied that being a young woman in a kitchen like that might have rendered her more insecure (because, I presume, she felt more vulnerable physically). When she was the one in charge, she found herself following suit in an attempt to command her staff's respect. "If a server screwed something up, like *whoosh*," she said, indicating with a noise that a pan would be thrown. "And then," she went on, "I'd feel bad about it, and I'd go in the walk-in and cry about it." Eventually, she realized this was no way to run the show and that the best way to lead is to do so didactically. "I haven't done anything like that in a long time . . . I see my responsibility as a chef so much differently. I have a responsibility to my crew to teach them skills and teach them the why and how, it's not just, 'We're going to do it this way, because this is *my* way'; I'm going to explain to you why I do this."

---

[117] Sophie Brickman, "Gitane Chef Brings Humility to the Helm," *San Francisco Chronicle*, November 4, 2010.

Michelle Bernstein underwent a parallel transformation as a leader, and her perspective on kitchen violence is provocative and insightful. Her training was among the harsher ones recounted, and she didn't come out of it unscathed; she became a super-yeller. But she was also traumatized by her own shouting. After giving it to one of her employees, she'd retreat to her office, close the door, and cry. "I've learned to yell a lot less and get what I want out of them without screaming at them," she says. But she had "so much guilt about yelling . . . it's hard to live with." That remorse, she believes, has severe repercussions. "I know why a lot of chefs become alcoholics," she told me. Wow. I'd never have made that connection. It's hard to know which drives the other, but it's not such a fatuous correlation. "I wonder why it is you don't see so many women chefs who are addicts or alcoholics," she mused. "At least 70 percent of the chefs I worked for are really down-and-out . . . but I don't know any women with any actual problems; I know a lot of them who party their asses off."[118] If ever there was a sound case to be made for ditching the despotism, it's Bernstein's.

A few years younger than most of these others, Christina Tosi probably takes the most organic managerial approach. She remains open to change and encourages her staff to make contributions; it is essential, she believes, that every member of the team feel as though he or she has a stake in the final product and isn't just a replaceable clone on an assembly line. There are rules and standards and systems, but there's also room for change. "I'm really big on embracing what people bring to the table individually and trying to find a way to put a highlight on that, whether that's a confection or a new way to fold a box or a new way to run service. One of the biggest things in kitchens is, how do you keep good people? There's only so much room for improvement or growth, so how do you keep them interested and how do you keep them

---

[118] I don't know of any studies that have been conducted on chefs and addiction, so I can't corroborate Bernstein's theory or that 70 percent number. I can tell you, though, that she is not the only chef or person to talk about how much chefs drink, or "party their asses off." You can go read Bourdain for captivating accounts of such adventures. If there are any statistics on this subject, I'd love to see them, and if not, it might be worth some data collecting.

feeling challenged and how do you keep them feeling like a part of it belongs to them? Because inevitably, that's how you build something."

Koren Grieveson, the chef (and more recent, an owning partner) at Paul Kahan's Avec in Chicago, underscores the value of team building and of downplaying her own importance as commander in chief. "I'm not the boss; I'm here to work with you and be part of the team. Ultimately, it's my name on the line . . . [but] it breeds a better learning [and] working environment if we're all in it together and I make you as responsible as I am."

Every leader has his or her way of doing things, and Liza Shaw's is well honed and unwavering. She was on staff when San Francisco's A16 opened in 2004. Five years later, a couple of months after receiving the James Beard Rising Star Award for his work there, Nate Appleman, the toque, left for Manhattan. Shaw inherited his hat, and nary a beat was skipped. "The management style has to be firm but also supportive," she instructs. "Support is the most important thing. You take this role where you're molding people into your vision and everybody takes a different way to be molded. And you have to teach them; you have to encourage them; you have to support them; you have to scold them when they do something wrong, but let them know that tomorrow is another day; you have to reward them when they do something right, whether it's with a simple smile, or a congratulations, or a pat on the back, or, you know, a handshake at the end of the shift . . . One thing that is really important to me—that I didn't necessarily get from some of my bosses—is recognition. And it's not like I'm attention-starved. But when a cook does something that's great or when a customer comes to me and is like, 'That octopus terrine was so amazing,' I'll be the first person to pull the cook out who made it and say, 'That was his idea. How cool is that?' I always tell my sous chefs, the day that I got something on the menu for the first time was one of my favorite days ever in the world, and I encourage people to think creatively and to do research and to look at old menus, and come up with things. It's very intimidating for a lot of cooks. But that moment when you become part of the machine and you get that reward and somebody recognizes that what you've done is a significant contribution is pretty great. So I think that recognizing and supporting and nurturing people's talents is a cornerstone of being a chef."

When you are the chef *and* proprietor of a joint, your responsibilities are greater, but you're also allowed to design things to your liking or need. This means that you can change not only the ethos of the kitchen, but also the physical structure of that space. You can truly create a new blueprint.

As mentioned before, Alice Waters removed the French hierarchy altogether when she opened Chez Panisse in 1971. "I don't like a whole group of *commis*[119] to come into the kitchen and chop up my mirepoix for me," she complained. "I think that the chef should be washing lettuce, and examining the quality of the ingredients and making decisions about how best they can be used during the course of the day, and deciding who has the passion to cook what, and that the assignments to certain people to do all of the hard things—all of the things that are unglamorous—just goes against producing the best-quality food." In order to get best-quality results, she makes sure that each person is tasked with a combination of rigorous and less-rigorous labor. She is also known for rotating positions so that employees are exposed to all kinds of kitchen work.

With such functional alternatives to the original (French) template, one wonders—or at least Emily Luchetti does, and I'm so glad for it—why women would condone the latter (or any abusive kitchen for that matter) if she was being ill-used. "Sometimes, over the last few years, people will come to me—not people I work with—and they'll say, 'I'm a woman, I work for this guy, and he's an asshole.' It's like, 'Well, go somewhere else; quit!' This isn't like New York or France thirty years ago when you had to put up with that stuff. There are so many options

---

[119] See footnote 99, page 87, if you decided the *commis* was too lowly a position to remember.

out there. If you're not getting treated well because you're a woman or for whatever reason, leave. There are places you can go . . . It's like being with an abusive boyfriend or something. Why would you stay with them? If you're in a situation where you're still learning but it's not the ideal situation, stick with it for a while. Sitting here and having worked in California all these years, I often find it hard to believe that it still exists, but I know it does . . . But again, get out of those places and go somewhere else, and let them die a slow death because nobody wants to work in them." RIP, Escoffier, after you roll over in your grave, of course.

That's one way to get out. If Luchetti were to tack another word on to that command, you'd have a whole other conversation on your hands. I'm thinking of "get out *more*," as in, you need to. Those on the outside looking in might be compelled to give a female cook that order. If you're someone who thinks women shouldn't be out all night, shimmying, tossing back shots, or, as they say, having a good time, and would rather hold on to your image of their hanging up their aprons, walking out of the "office," and going home to feed their cats, take care of their husbands, or mother their kids, you might not want to read what follows; that illusion's about to be shattered.

"There's plenty of going out," Christina Tosi says in an it's-no-biggie tone. "But I don't even think I look at it like that . . . I think it's a youthfulness. I feel like if you followed any trove of cooks going out after service, if there's a female working in the kitchen, they're probably going to go out for a drink just like everybody else."

You can't argue with that logic. One reason you may not have realized this was going on is that you made a dopey assumption, or preferred to think otherwise. Another is that it has taken some time for the invitations to start trickling in. (Note: I did not say pouring; we're not quite there yet.) Tosi was the first to point this out. "We just started getting invited to things, or we started getting more outgoing about it . . . I don't know, maybe they're [women] not invited? Or maybe nobody's paying attention to them?" She truly believes it's the lack of offers that hold women back from the party scene.

Despite the slow stream of invitations, her faith remains unshaken. But she does offer a few counterarguments to explain why we haven't heard tell of ladies letting loose. "I think [there are] plenty people [women chefs going out], maybe they're less showy about it . . . I don't know what the incidence of, like, men-to-women that just go out in general . . . What do you think a female chef looks like when she gets out of work? It's not as cute as what a man looks like in jeans and a raggedy shirt and a baseball cap, I will tell you that right now."

Ask around, and you'll discover that the late-night romping of sauté sisters is not a new thing. The formal please-attend notices may not have been handed out, the busboys may not have beckoned, but that didn't deter those who baked before Tosi. "No, no no no, no," Heather Carlucci-Rodriguez corrected me right off the bat when I asked if, as it would seem based on what's reported (and blogged about, excessively), the guys were the only ones tearing the roofs off the suckers.[120] I wanted tales from the gritty city, and she complied. "I thought they were amateurs at that level. Back in the day, I thought they were pretty lame. I had a girlfriend . . . and I would have to say, more often that not, when Blue Ribbon was the only place open late for chefs, she and I would close it down, at least, I would say, 200 days of the year."[121] And it doesn't stop at Blue Ribbon. Going out, hard, was a crucial aspect of her young life as a cook and, once in a blue-ribbon moon, her less-young life as a chef. She has raged with the best of them and characterizes most of that "best" as female. It's "totally, totally, totally part of

---

[120] An unfamiliar reference? Ever hear of Parliament? "Give Up the Funk"? (That was the alternative name for this mid-'70s track, originally titled "Tear the Roof Off the Sucker.")

[121] Dear, sweet Blue Ribbon on Sullivan Street, cozy home to hungry marauders craving late-night plates of fatty bone marrow with rich, jammy oxtail marmalade. And, it should be stated, the chef-owner Bromberg brothers (Bruce and Eric) served that dish well before marrow was chic. That's one of the reasons chefs have always dug it there. Now there are more Blue Ribbon spin-offs than I can keep track of, though my preference is for Downing Street's Blue Ribbon Bakery Kitchen, because it's closest to home and has the most outstanding chocolate chip bread pudding (over which hot fudge is poured). Blue Ribbon Sushi, also on Sullivan Street, is another standby of mine.

the culture," she emphasizes. "Hands down. Full-out. And like I said, I really sort of feel like it's amateur hour when it comes to the men, or has been. I mean, there are the heavies, like I don't think anyone can really hold a candle to Mario Batali . . . He's just like a vessel of party like none other, but yeah, I know, going out, eating and drinking, there were many weeks night after night, just like spending what little crappy-ass money you have on that . . . I was not alone. There were lots of them [women], I mean lots, like no joke. I mean everybody does, I don't know anybody who doesn't actually."

I lapped up every minute of this with rapt attention.

"The David Chang[122] thing is a new generation of like whatever . . . "

(There's more!)

"You know, I think that's sort of amateurish as well, and I think there's a better way of doing it . . ."

(Holy fuck, yes, she's going to tell us how it ought to be done. Pay attention, Chang.)

"Whereas, like, I think when we were all going out, you met at a bar, you hung out at that bar till the end of time. It was awesome, and everybody kind of knew each other and it wasn't just the cooks, but it was also like the regular oddball musician or the artist who fell in with it. I mean, to this day, James at Blue Ribbon is my all-time favorite bartender, and we've known each other twenty years. It's awesome, I mean, it's amazing. I can't imagine not having that."

---

[122] I would like to believe that you know who David Chang is, but on the off chance that you don't (shocking, truly), I will tell you that he has become a larger-than-life character on the food scene, not for being on television, but for changing the face of dining in New York City, and beyond. We're talking international impact. He started with Momofuku Noodle Bar, a small space in the East Village dedicated to his passion for ramen; it was a noodle shop like no other. It was where he first threw down the gauntlet and presented what would become his style of cooking, which takes classical training (he worked at some °of New York's best restaurants before slumming it on his own in that scruffy downtown neighborhood), influences and flavor combinations from multiple cuisines, the best ingredients (and every part of those), scientific research, plus envelope-pushing technique, and combines all that, God knows how, to deliver insanely pleasing, amazing grub. His application of fine dining's exacting standards to its casual counterpart was a significant game-changer. He is known, too, for his surliness, his occasionally oppressive perfectionism, his love of the band Pavement and of the 1989 movie *Road House*, and a debauchery of epic proportions. His approach to business development and team building are often admired as well. He now has a cavalry of restaurants under the Momofuku umbrella, including one in Sydney, Australia, and another in Toronto, Canada. Oh, right, I forgot, he cofounded a food magazine called *Lucky Peach* and an iPad app of the same name. He will, I predict, hate that I typed all this about him.

(Note to self: Befriend James next time you're on Sullivan Street; maybe see if Heather's available for a round?)

These days, she's a more "responsible" citizen—older, wiser, and has a wee one at home—but, don't kid yourselves, Carlucci-Rodriguez has still got it.

Beth Aretsky made the rounds, too, and had her own idea about why such shenanigans (hers and those of her fun-times female side-kicks) weren't part of the industry scuttlebutt (as opposed to, say, the exploits of a Bourdain or Batali). "Oh, I would go out. But I think maybe we're just smarter. I think we just leave it at that. We should call a spade a spade. We're just smarter, you know? I mean, really, why do we need to advertise that we have a stripper pole on our bus? Because we *are* the stripper pole."

Amanda Freitag also referenced the Changian stripper pole. It has become something of a touchstone. Forget Excaliber, there's Dave Chang's James Beard Award party bus with its skanktastic focal point. It's kind of the perfect metaphor or mascot—if American chefs had their own guild, their totem would be the pole. Freitag noted that there are lots of galley guys who head straight home after work, but that no one mentions them (everyone would rather talk about the sala-cious stuff, naturally). She went on to say that for women who might want to rent a party bus of their own, (as per usual) a double standard exists. "Somehow, if you're a woman and you're hanging out till 6 a.m., that's dirty and slutty and it's the walk of shame, and there's something wrong with you. But if you're a bunch of guys and you did it, you come in with these war wounds and you talk about it like it's honorable . . . It's that whole thing, you know, guys sleeping with lots of women, they're cool and they're hot, but a girl who does it, she's the slut . . . But it's the industry too . . . it's like, 'Let's see if she can hang, let's see,' and 'Well, if I can hang as long as you, are you going to want to hang out with me again, or is that going to make you feel emasculated?' . . . Because I think they really don't want us hanging around with them." This brings us back to the Lydonistics[123] of it all—act too much like a dude, and it's curtains for you.

Tosi is fortunate enough to be saddled with a male chef-boss who isn't threatened by having the fillies in his mini-empire carouse with him; he encourages them to get out more. You might be surprised to learn that this bro is none other than David Chang. Although they're not all encouraging their female coworkers to gallivant, there are some guys out there who appreciate the presence of a good woman in their (professional) houses. Tosi, who would appear to have a knack for finding the right men to hitch her pastry wagon to, was the only girl at WD-50.[124] Chef Wylie (Dufresne) thinks a small space populated solely by boys with knives is not the best place to be cooking. "I was the only girl working there for a while," Tosi says. "And Wylie would always be like, 'What are we going to do when you leave?' or what have you, and just be like, 'I like having—it could be more than one [woman]—but I like to have at least one, because it keeps all the guys sharper.' " She explained that because they're all working in the same, cramped kitchen, if anyone gets yelled at for screwing up, everyone else is privy to that. Put a girl in the room, and suddenly (if they're straight), the guys become aware of her presence. You could say the Darwinian instinct kicks in. They'll all, she observed, vie for her attention (and, possibly, affection), "even if that person [the woman] is not up for grabs." The sexual tension keeps the guys "much sharper. They trim their beard . . . you know what I mean? Like they set up their station nicely." She sees the competition as a "driving force" that makes them push themselves harder; when they've hit "some sort of plateau" or lose morale, having a lady on the line helps them tap in to "a little of that machismo [that] is left."

Most women are not content to be overwhelmed by that machismo. What they appreciate is a thing called balance, not the same

---

[123] Pertaining to the theories of one Shuna Lydon. See also, Lydonism.

[124] Internationally lauded, WD-50 is that rare restaurant that's executing progressive cuisine (molecular gastronomy would be another term for it, although most chefs who practice that kind of cookery hate that descriptive) on a scary-good level. It is considered one of the pacesetters in this category, and among restaurants at large.

balance of which DePalma spoke—that's different. No less essential to any kitchen slave's well-being is a combination of temperaments. Too many guys or gals holed up in there, and you could find the natives begin to turn on each other (or everyone gets her period at the same time). Karen DeMasco dealt just fine with a line jacked with fellas, but she noticed things flowed more smoothly when a few dames were brought in. "Craft also, at times, would be all men on the line. Then, at times, you had a mix. Here [Locanda Verde], we have a nice mix. I mean, it's not equal but there are definitely women thrown in. It's a different way of just dealing with situations. It's a different feeling on the line; it's not as intimidating . . . Women are more nurturing and I think you need a little bit of that. And they take a little bit more care in certain ways, and I think it helps the whole line to have some of that influence, for sure. It just helps the whole vibe of the kitchen. I remember times at Craft when it would be all men, and it would just be so loud and rough, and just, I don't know, it starts to go down a path; it isn't as nice." A few moments later she wagered, "All women, I'm sure, would have a whole different set of problems." Truer words were never spoken.

CHAPTER 4

An Embarrassment of Bitches

We always have a mixture of men and women, and it just started recently that we started having females who are—fucking female,[125] like none of the women that ever worked for us . . . You know what I mean? . . . In my head, it's probably the most difficult thing that I deal with now, 'cause I don't know how to make sense of it. I can't empathize with it . . . I don't even know how to sniff one of those out, really.

—CHRISTINA TOSI

I already had a bunch of reasons to love Christina Tosi. At the tail end of February 2008, Momofuku Ko, the David Chang team's third and most ambitious restaurant opened, and I was lucky enough to get in on the early action (even now, the infamous online system makes scoring a reservation tantamount to finding a golden ticket in a Wonka bar). It's a twelve-seat counter and the chefs plate the nightly menu in front of you. There's not a lot of fawning or a fleet of servers. The middleman is cut out, so what you pay for is the main draw—the food. Much has been made of the bowlful of shaved foie gras "snow" and, tucked beneath that chilled heap, the jagged, crunchy pieces of pine nut brittle and the softer, sweet globs of Riesling gelée. It's those savory concoctions that monopolize most of a ten-course dinner and the text in any write-up of the place. But in my tummy (and my copy) there's always room for dessert.

What was the last bite I shoved in my mouth that glorious first meal at Ko? Fried apple pie. I was already full, and still, I Hoovered the thing. I had stopped eating McDonald's Happy Meals long ago. I think the last time I'd been on the other side of the golden arches

---

[125] "Fucking female": Translation to come. Have patience and keep on reading. (All will be revealed starting on page 117.)

was in college, on my way from Cannes to Barcelona—it was the only option apparent at a train station and my blood sugar was too low for discrimination. But the one thing I always secretly missed from that clown-fronted capital of the fast-food amusement park we live in was the apple pie. It's really a lame attempt at the Southern fried pie, is what I realized once I'd had the real thing. Whoever this Ko pastry chef was, he or she had brought my beloved dessert-of-shame back to me in concentrated form. It had the familiarity of the cheap-bastard standard, but the flavors were better defined, the pastry an appropriately thick blanket, the fry just right on the crispy and not at all greasy, and the apples had a caramelized intensity. My friend Kyung, who was dining with me, told me she'd never seen me eat as much as I had that night and was particularly impressed with my capacity to finish (and the speed at which I did) the pie. It wasn't just the pie. It was the sour scoop that came with it—like crème fraîche in ice cream form; lighter, somehow, and yet not icy. And then, too, there was the miso ganache. Salted caramel? Please. Next to this almost savory take on butterscotch, with its smooth-creamy, thicker-than-frosting texture, salted caramel might as well be a dipping sauce on the McDonald's menu (if it isn't by now). Heaven. I was in heaven.[126]

That was a Tosi creation.

My next encounter with her was via cookie; her "blueberry & cream" job, to be precise. The Momofuku Milk Bar bakery is a stoner pastry aficionado's wet dream, or if the pot references don't melt your heart, you could think of it as a place where someone with a sophisticated palate and inner child who still longs for Cap'n Crunch would like to be buried. There's a constant jumbling of high—studied culinary technique—and low—the junk food of our nation's youth. The cookies (I endorse them all, really I do—although, I do think the "compost" flavor with its kitchen-sink ingredient list might be a touch overrated) are the softest of soft-bake (glucose helps). Buttery to a perfect fault.

[126] If you wish to pass through the pearly gates, you can re-create this at home. The recipe starts on page 291 of David Chang and Peter Meehan's *Momofuku* cookbook (Clarkson Potter; 2009).

My pick of the litter is the one that sounds the least interesting. You think it's going to be boring—like a scone or a muffin. Wrong. It's the ideal-plus sugar cookie: It has a little salinity going for it and something—ever so faint—sour cream–like that you almost can't put your finger on. Don't forget the star of the dough show—the berries—for therein lies the magic. Each chewy (just a trace of crispness on its outer edges) disk is studded with dried tart orbs that, although not in their plump fresh state, manage not to desiccate completely after baking, but to stay just as they began before entering the oven. What is the secret? Milk powder.

How do I know this? It was revealed to me when we finally met. I'd been asked to be a culinary ambassador for a woman named Josée di Stasio, who hosts a show—*Á la di Stasio*—for French-Canadian television. She was devoting an episode to Manhattan and needed a food enthusiast who spoke (enough) French. I figured no one I knew would ever see the show and signed up. Our first stop, with the camera crew behind us, was to Momofuku Milk Bar, where Tosi was going to do a cooking demo, and I'd asked that the recipe be (what else?) the "blueberry & cream." Tosi, cheerful and on point at whatever that early hour of the day was, gamely showed us how it was done. The blues get tossed in with her trademark "milk crumbs," which are an amalgam of nonfat milk powder, flour, cornstarch, sugar, salt, melted butter (unsalted), and melted white chocolate. These tiny pellets are little bombs—they taste like half-baked (and that's meant literally) cookie-dough goodness (or at least, that's what I think). They also contain the extra fat and moisture (the aforementioned glucose in the batter helps there too) that offsets the total ruination of the dried (so they're already a bit wrinkled) blueberries. How smart is that, I ask you?

As if this lesson wasn't enough of a gift, from that day forward, without fail, every time I saw Tosi, she would hand me my favorite cookie. She never forgets. I think I could take a blueberry bullet for this lady, because such thoughtfulness is exceptional.

But that's not all.

At this moment, it should be noted that I thoroughly enjoy ice cream, maybe too much. I devote a lot of time to it—as an eater and as one who ponders edibles. When I can't sleep, one of my favorite pastimes is to invent new pints.

Ice cream? Sure they've got that at chez Momofuku. At Milk Bar, it's a soft-serve affair. Imagine a gourmet Mister Softee and you're still not close. Maybe if Mister Softee dropped acid you'd be closer. Lots of copycats have jumped on the bandwagon since her swirly-topped cones made their debut,[127] but no one's flavor inventions come close to these. It began with cereal milk, another item born under the sign of the lucky peach.[128] Yes, that's what it tastes like: the sweet, slightly salty liquid that's absorbed the flavors of your cornflakes, Life, Pops, or Cocoa Puffs. Tosi applied not only that base, but also the steeping technique used to make it conducive to the soft-serve enterprise (the milk base retains the essence of what was soaked in it, but remains free of solid particles). And so New Yorkers have been exposed to stuffing and fennel-apple frozen goodness at Thanksgiving or, more directly inspired by the original potable, Lucky Charms and Fruity Pebbles. I quite liked the black sesame and pumpkin cheesecake offerings.

One slumberless night found me coming up with some flavors for the Milk Bar machines. I went so far as to e-mail HQ a list of my ideas.

> **Subject: does tosi take suggestions? for soft-serve flavors?**
> i had insomnia the other night and went off on an ice cream tangent, finally, i fell asleep, but not before these came to mind:
>
> 1. Animal Crackers—you know, the original, generic P.T. Barnum box of animal crackers with that almost lemony flavor. I wonder if the milk would pick that up if you steeped them in it.

---

[127] They first appeared at the Momofuku Noodle Bar.

[128] *Momofuku* (Japanese) translates to "lucky peach," and the brand's logo is a plump, orangish representation of the fruit.

2. a sampling of chocolate chip cookie flavors—just hear me
out. Entenmann's choc chip cookies have a real distinct flavor,
so do Chips Ahoy.
and then you have Pillsbury—the RAW & the cooked. what if
one week, you did an ode to commercial chocolate chip cookies and flavored the base with each of those? just asking.
3. Fig Newtons
4. Ritz Crackers
5. Wheat Thins (maybe the unsalted/low-sodium variety?)
6. Twinkies
7. Pop-Tarts (toasted or untoasted? not sure—you can play
with different flavors . . . blueberry, maple-brown sugar, etc.)
ok
will stop bothering you with my silliness now.
xo

The always-there-when-you-need-her representative, Sue Chan,
forwarded the pastry chef's response:

Already have all of those on our list! We already have an
animal cracker flavor that we ran at ko,
Too.
Thanks,
C

Great minds think alike, I told myself. My flavors were on her list!
And she had actually taken the time to read my nonsense and respond.
Tosi was a class act.

And then she said "*fucking female*."

These new gals on staff, they weren't like their predecessors,
who, as Tosi described, sometimes "talked about something girly" or
might, while changing into their uniforms, pass on a compliment about
an admired sweater or relay a quick anecdote about a boyfriend. "It

was five seconds and it was done, and it was just like, put your head down and go." No. These infiltrators constituted a whole other breed of female. Fucking female.

Believe you me I understand exactly what that means. You don't go to an all-girls school for thirteen years (age five to eighteen) or endure rush—both sides of it—at a notably bratty sorority (in my defense, I was trying to have the ultimate college experience at a university where the Greek system ruled most of campus social life) and not know what "fucking female" looks like. You'll find it at the intersection of passive-aggression, competitive dieting, unnecessary drama, excessive crying, oversharing, intense empathy, low self-esteem, cattiness, pity partying, boyfriend stealing, and mean girls' bullying.

With her two-word phrase, Tosi had just found a way to encapsulate a complicated silent killer of female empowerment. This epidemic is what gives gals a bad rap, and what turns them against each other.

Why am I hanging my sex out to dry? I'm not. If you're going to complain about the frat-boy tendencies of male cooks, then you have to acknowledge the other extreme. Is every man in the kitchen an aggressive, misogynistic douche bag? Of course not. And not every woman is a hypersensitive, irrational, nurturing, emotional mess of a banshee. We're talking about what can happen when you get too many of either together and the hyperbolic behavior of the disadvantageous variety is exhibited.

What Tosi might not realize is that she has a sisterhood of "fucking female" haters behind her. Many talked openly about not appreciating a glut of girls in the galley. Cathy Whims found at her previous restaurant, Genoa, in Portland, Oregon, where she started out as a cook and became a co-chef and owning partner, "that sometimes there were too many women—it got too interpersonal; for example, one couldn't work at night because of her boyfriend or because she had a massage scheduled." She added that lots of women who weren't their household's breadwinners and worked part-time got whiny.

Some of the chefs went further, and admitted that if they had to choose, they'd rather have a majority of men back there with them. La Varenne grad Ana Sortun of Cambridge's Oleana and Sofra is one: "I appreciate balance. I get really freaked out when there are too many women in the kitchen. And I get really freaked out when there are too many men, but to be honest, I'd rather there be too many men than too many women." What has brought her to this conclusion? There are two insidious items on her list. The first is what I call the bond forged in negativity. "Women," she says, "they're dangerous. And the one quality that we all have is commiserating. And it's horrible. It's this 'I hate this person' and so there's this bond that's formed that won't break—it won't break. It's unbelievably powerful." That misery-loves-company pit of darkness into which we climb, together, is a result of the hyper-empathy I mentioned previously.

Sortun's other culprit is also behavioral, but has nothing to do with emotions. She revealed it in an anecdote that some might like to reference when taking on a leadership role. "There was one point [when] I had a lot of women in the kitchen and I sat down and talked to every single one of them, and I was like, 'You know, this is the first time this has ever happened. Let me just tell you what women do and I don't want to see this. We're not going to commiserate and we're not going to walk around heavy boxes.' Because women are strong and they can lift the boxes, but there's something in our nature that, because people have done it for us all our lives—they lift the heavy things for us—I don't know what it is, it's like we don't see them. We just walk over them, around them, push them to the side . . . That is the only difference between working with men and working with women—those two things."

Tosi thinks there's something else as infectious as shared bitterness: girlishness, which is another trait that doesn't translate well to most professional kitchens. "I think being that girly part of a girl, it's contagious even to the most stone-cold female," she says.

Waylynn Lucas has a different way of registering the same complaint about ruffles and bows in the work zone. It's not so much a gripe against the latter as it is a plea for the opposite force to win out. "One thing I honestly hope never ever changes is that manly, crass, kind of fun, perverse, dirty-minded attitude in the kitchen . . . Because that's one of the things, even as a woman, that I love about it . . . I hope that as more women are in the kitchen, we don't find the need to create this sensitive, nurturing, quiet, you-can't-yell-in-the-kitchen, because the kitchen is still the kitchen . . . For the generations and the sake of kitchens and chefs forever, I hope that a little piece of that hardness stays in the kitchen and doesn't go away." The meanness, she could do without; but the thought of a touchy-feely, girlish crew turns her stomach.

One of the most telling theories about gender in the workplace came from Gina DePalma, who also admits to having a preference for dealing with men. It's easier, she has noticed, to take down a man's confidence a notch than to raise a woman's. I think she's right, and this observation speaks to something that is sometimes discussed but always implicit: to establish and keep a name for yourself as a cook, and then a chef, requires confidence. If you're planning to go the distance, as a woman, you must prepare to have your self-assurance undermined at every turn; you must build up a reserve, and if you don't have one, you must never, ever, let anybody see that. It is that confidence that Amanda Freitag references when she talks about what it takes to command more money from an employer, or get a job you want; you need to walk in that room, face the decision-maker head-on, and own it. She has seen it done—by a man—but she has never felt comfortable enough to pull it off. "That's a skill that I want," she said. "You cannot teach that. I swear you cannot teach that."[129]

[129] According to magazine StarChefs.com's most recent (2010) online Chef Salary Report (based on the organization's annual Chef Salary Survey), "A male executive chef makes $16,936 more than his female counterpart on average, and the industry average reaches nearly $15,000. When it comes to sous chefs the gap closes a little—there's only a $2,160 difference between salaries on average. This is cold comfort for women who are in it for the long haul though—they have a bigger pay gap in store as they advance up through the ranks. As for pastry chefs, men are still paid 27 percent more than women." Freitag's comment makes me wonder if women's relative inability to "command more money from an employer" could have anything to do with that salary discrepancy. Our collective

cont'd

Shuna Lydon, as always, has an explanation as to why the "female confidence crisis" (so labeled by yours truly and defined as a shared deficit of confidence among women and the self-consciousness that arises when one perceives that shortcoming in oneself) is more pronounced in this métier. "Within a kitchen that's male and macho and hierarchical and militaristic and patriarchal and definitive, there is no place for a woman, which is why—I think I'm not the only female chef to say—those kitchens which are female predominant are more difficult because it's hard for a woman to find her groove and just be herself . . . Even women talking about women would say, 'She was harder.' "

For some ladies, coping with a back of house teeming with unconfident females is just as complicated as working for a woman chef who, perhaps to overcompensate or as a result of hardwiring, has renounced all feminine behavior and, in a way, behaves like a misogynist herself. "I'm not genderless, I'm a female," asserts pastry chef Katzie Guy-Hamilton, the Willy Wonka challenge winner on the second season of *Top Chef Just Desserts* (her "carrot patch" chocolate-covered carrot cake, shaped like its main orange ingredient and planted in edible dirt, stole the show).[130] "I think that's what my last boss [a woman] didn't like . . . for me to be a woman; to still be a woman and take care of myself." Annihilate commiseration and walking around boxes, yes. Deny every single female attribute you possess, no. Guy-Hamilton lists health, wealth, and happiness among her goals and priorities; in order for her to achieve those in her chosen profession, she has to integrate

lack of confidence might not only be responsible for our lowballing when negotiating how much we ought to be paid, but it might also give employers the impression that they don't need to offer us as much compensation for our work.

[130] Guy-Hamilton, now, at only twenty-six, is the executive pastry chef at the Grand Hyatt Hotel in New York City. She has made two items I went gaga over and subsequently wrote about: one, a beet cake (imagine a carrot cake that's made with beets so it has a subtler, sweeter, earthier profile), and the other, her version of the Provençal (from the Luberon Valley's Lourmarin area, specifically) bread known as *gibassier* (also called a *fougasse*). It consists of an olive oil–based dough and can go in either a sugary or saline direction. This *gibassier*, designed for breakfast, traveled the former route and was orange- and anise-scented, and dusted with sugar. Guy-Hamilton took it over the top with a thick honey and brown-butter spread. Testing the recipe forced me to try baking bread for the very first time. I couldn't have been more pleased with myself when I showed up at my parents' house on Christmas morning with my sackful of *gibassiers* (and my caramel-ish accoutrement). At any point during the day, if someone got ornery or there was a lull in the conversation, I'd just announce, "Hey, I made bread!" and everyone would smile, or at least I would.

what makes her who she is into what she does. To clarify, "take care of myself" does not imply having one's hair done or false lashes affixed before putting on one's whites and picking up one's knives. It entails anything from taking time to get a haircut, read a novel, or shop for clothes, to seeing live bands, going out with nonwork friends, or throwing dinner parties.

Primping, as previously discussed, is never the move; makeup will melt, nail polish chip off into the food, and flowing locks shed onto plates. There's an uglier aspect to all this rationality. Cosmetic enhancements aside, for at least one woman chef, a female applicant's pulchritude can be the reason not to hire her. This biased-against-the-beautiful lady understood she was saying something potentially controversial, and wanted to make sure her truth came out, but didn't want to deal with the backlash. So she asked to remain anonymous. Here goes: She doesn't like having hot chicks (the human kind) in her kitchen. Before you start in with your predictable, go-to, divisive comeback to such a statement and say, "She must feel threatened" or, my favorite, "She's just jealous," you should hear her out. Neither of those conclusions is correct. She avoids the pretty young things because she has found that bringing one into that environment is a distraction that always ends badly. It diverts the male chefs' attention, she claims. Inevitably, the fair lass gets involved with one of the lads, the dalliance goes south, and the damsel gets distressed.

While there are those who have witnessed the unpleasantness that too much female energy can generate, there are women out there who have had positive run-ins with girl-powered institutions. Liz Prueitt had an epiphany in San Francisco in 1987, before she went back east to attend the CIA. She was visiting a boyfriend out west and, having decided to stick around, got a job at chef Catherine Pantsios's restaurant Zola's. Prueitt had never seen a kitchen full of women before, "and it was so inspiring," she recalls. "It was amazing—I was a server, but it was just so inspiring that there were all these women."

Restaurant owner Jessica Boncutter, also in San Francisco, had some really bad experiences in the man cave and, from then on, actively chose female supervisors. She prefers what she dubs the "feminine," a descriptive that implies a set of characteristics that can be exhibited by either gender. "I've always worked for women . . . I didn't seek it out, because, 'Oh, I need to work for a woman.' It just felt better. The restaurants felt better. They felt healthier, they felt better run; they felt more creative, they felt more open . . . I have worked for men, too, but the men I've worked for are very feminine, and very nurturing, and very supportive and lovely people."

Boncutter's list of preferred adjectives—feminine, nurturing, and supportive—could also be categorized as "maternal." And that's one way to guide a team, with a motherly hand. But there are pitfalls here and they're another example of what can go awry when too much of a womanly presence exerts its influence over the stove-heated hot box. That's what alumna of San Francisco's A16 Liza Shaw[131] has found. "I think that some women tend to act like mothers, and people come to them at the end of the shift with their problems. That is not me. If you have a problem that has to do with work, I'm more than happy to talk to you about it. But if you have a problem with your boyfriend, leave that shit at the door; do not bring that inside. I would not call myself maternal in that sense. That's not to say I'm not great friends with everybody in my kitchen outside of work."

If only the emotional dumping and inappropriate sharing were the worst of it. (Those things are annoying enough, and can slow you down, or enervate coworkers, but they're not exactly ship-sinkers). Sadly, as Andrea Reusing has witnessed, for chef-owners, the mama syndrome can have sorry repercussions for more than your staff's psyche. When it extends to studying your spreadsheets, that brand of bossing can jeopardize profitability:

---

[131] By the time this book goes to press, Shaw should be welcoming customers into Merigan Sub Shop, her version of "an old-school Italian sub shop," as she described it via e-mail. When in San Francisco, visit. You'll find her butchering whole animals, pickling and preserving stuff too. Don't forget to order a sandwich.

"I feel like there's a certain style of female entrepreneur, especially in restaurants, who have very codependent relationships . . . it's like a big sloppy mess. And sometimes the women are even having trouble economically—their restaurants aren't making enough money, business is not necessarily going well . . . [There's] this idea that even, as a woman, somehow, you should feel guilty about making a profit . . . [or] that it's not okay to make more money than everyone that you're working next to."

Reusing has brought us back to the theme of compromised self-worth, and, now, she's looking at how that presents money-side. If a restaurant-owning chef doesn't feel that she deserves to make more money than the people she has hired (call them underlings, colleagues, children, siblings, or whatever word the mother of a fucked-up family-galley prefers), then why should those people have any respect for her? Why should they listen to her? Why should they value her opinion or trust the decisions she makes, any of them (from "add more salt" to "I'm moving you to a different station")? And if it looks like she can't afford to pay herself (because if she's living hand-to-mouth, for whatever reason, the obvious conclusion is that she isn't making ends meet), are you going to get the sense her restaurant's successful? Would anyone want to back her in another venture?

If there's anything to be learned from our time here at Camp Sharing-Is-Caring in the Woods, it's that clasping hands as you spill a deep dark secret to the weepy sisters in the circle is not—under any circumstances—acceptable professional behavior. And, most important, when you're on the line or running one, even if you're feeling like a stale bread crumb on the floor that a mouse wouldn't deign to eat, act with confidence. If you can't muster any of that, imagine Julie Andrews as Maria the nun with her guitar case swinging in one hand, hat held on head by the other. She is singing. Can you hear her? It's that "I Have Confidence" song.[132] Now, imagine that everyone else in the kitchen

---

[132] As you well know, it's a song/scene straight out of *The Sound of Music* (the film).

is her. You, meanwhile, should be humming a different tune. I recommend A Tribe Called Quest's "Can I Kick It?" Feel free to find your own anthem.

If you're not a musical type and the estrogen is overwhelming, you might try thinking about ice cream flavors. As I wrote this chapter, my mom e-mailed me to say she'd like to ask Christina Tosi to do a Cracklin' Oat Bran soft serve. Maybe I'll contact the Momofuku hub. At this moment, though, I'm just glad to be back in the land of sugar and cream. Don't think it's all sunshine and Sacher torte[133] over there. Pastry comes with its own piping bag of issues. And in America's restaurants (and culinary schools), it's the first department to which female cooks are often shoved, or presumed to toil. If anyone's entitled to an inferiority complex, it's these bitches, and yet, for all the ethereal soufflés they've baked, they're some of the fiercest chefs I've encountered.

---

[133] A specific kind of Viennese chocolate torte credited to one Franz Sacher.

CHAPTER 5

Gingerbread Girls

I'm a chef before I'm a woman; I'm a chef before I am a pastry chef.

—SHUNA LYDON

I tried to blame it on the snow—or, rather, the pending snow. For what might have been the fifth time in three weeks, the weather people were throwing around the "Storm Warning" alert. The truth is, I love a good NYC winter blitz. Have you ever been outside, on the streets, in the wee hours of the morning (*while the whole wide world is fast asleep*) and stood in the silent presence of a pristine, white-blanketed cityscape? It's even better when giant flakes are falling around you. The next day, of course, the entire thing is covered in dog piss, car exhaust, boot tracks, crunchy salt pellets, and slick ice. So on that evening of January 11, when the meteorologists were sending out the emergency signals, although a small part of me (the part that's prone to falling on ice and breaking things) was slightly put off, mostly, I was unfazed by the inclemency. Why, then, was I dreading my meeting on the Lower East Side? It was with Shuna Lydon. That's why.

The pastry chef, it seemed, had some *ossi di morto*[134] to pick with me. A year earlier (in 2010) an article I'd written had appeared in the tenth-anniversary issue of *Gastronomica: The Journal of Food and Culture*. The rhetorically titled "Why Are There No Great Women Chefs?" addressed something that had been bugging me for a while: the culinary gender gap and what the media (myself included) might be doing to widen it or hinder its narrowing. That rant—the response to it from women chefs, really—inspired this book. A month after that

---

[134] Those are "bones of the dead" and refer to a style of Italian biscuit (a harder, crunchier cookie); since Lydon's a pastry chef, these appeared the most fitting *ossi* here.

essay ran, I started working on another wholly unrelated story for one of my favorite magazines, *7x7*, a San Francisco glossy. I know it seems a little counterintuitive that a (loyal) New Yorker would pen something for another city's rag, but every time I visited the Bay Area, I'd peruse a copy of this publication and delight in its content, especially the food coverage. I subscribed and started to think about how I could contribute to it. Then I noticed a strange thing. A whole bunch of chefs from that city were leaving for mine. There had been a brouhaha made about some kind of rivalry between the two towns, but it seemed more hype than anything else. I wanted to know how these West Coast transplants were faring out East—a progress report of sorts. Was it better, worse, different?

I discovered that the chefs who were relocating—the ones who made the situation seem story-worthy (i.e., they were touted as contenders back home)—all happened to be male. I poked around to see if there were any San Francisco gals fronting (either in name or ownership) new, notable Manhattan projects. There were not. A plugged-in friend told me that she thought an eligible pastry chef named Shuna Lydon was moving across the country to work alongside one of the prominent Bay Area (male) chefs who had unpacked his knives at a West Village boîte near me. But, my pal added, said pastry director had most recently been in London for a spell, which, if you ask me, made her a bit irrelevant when the whole point was to offer a tale of two cities, neither of which Queen Elizabeth II calls home. I also thought that if you do mention a woman who happens to be a pastry chef, whether or not she has been perfecting her crème anglaise across the pond, might she just become a token figure? It felt a little like affirmative action to me, and not in a way that sat well. Bottom line: She wasn't the headliner (as the other subjects were). That was my logic.

The story appeared in the May issue. It was informative and, mostly, tame. No one hated it in either metropolis but I did receive some keen observations in response to it.

Come summer, what should I see in the beginning of the magazine (remember, I subscribe)? A letter to the editor.

Re: "Eastern Standards: SF Chefs Flee to NYC" [May]
Thanks for your thoughtful article. Someone needed to write about the exodus, and I'm glad it was you. But why the complete absence of women and/or pastry chefs? I can't imagine I'm the only female, and pastry chef, who had to move from the Bay Area to find work. I appreciated *7x7* when I lived in SF and have a continued fondness for it even from far away, because I think it's a fresh, upstarty voice the Bay Area needs. But I beg of you, stay off the path so many major media blindly follow—reporting on and from the voice of the majority. My industry is dominated by male savory chefs who overshadow women and take credit for the work of their pastry chefs (who tend to be female). Nate Appleman's[135] pastry chef, Jane Tseng, moved to NYC to continue working with him, and at the time that your writer sent questions to Jonnatan Leiva, I was his pastry chef. Just a sentence or two from either of us could have helped complete the picture.
Shuna Lydon, New York City.[136]

You're not supposed to respond to commenters. That's generally the advice given to journalists who are trying stay out of the fray and act professional. Many of the peanut-gallery members are teched and don't have anything better to do than sit around combing their tabloids of record (whatever those may be) for a typo or (a real coup) a more severe fuckup. But although my initial reaction was 'Why'd she have to pick on me?' some part of me recognized that Lydon had cause to be disappointed. What made me so sensitive about the whole thing was that, in fact, I had thought about including a woman in the story and she was the very one I'd considered. I felt compelled to reach out. (Who's the teched one now?)

[135] Remember him? From A16? Won the Beard Award then left San Francisco for New York? No? Page 104 can fix that.
[136] *7x7*: July 2010, page 24.

So I sent, via Jonnatan Leiva, the chef Lydon was working with a few blocks away—the one I had quoted in my cursed story—an e-mail and asked that he please pass it along to his pastry chef. Yes, I did. He kindly agreed to do just that.

In my first draft of this manuscript you're reading, I included that e-mail I wrote to Shuna in its entirety. My editor, who, most appreciated, is a protective soul, felt that this response of mine had some snark in it and I might want to acknowledge that outright. I'd never meant it to come across snottily, and am now paranoid. Shuna, if you took my note as smugly sarcastic or snide, I apologize. Everyone else, I'm going to spare you (and myself) the possibly snarky (and, coincidentally, irrelevant) or corny (because there were those, too) bits (that's not why we're here) and share the paragraph that counts:

"Please know that I did consider . . . including a woman's perspective, but there were a few reasons I declined . . . There's as much of a potential problem with including (a) a token women (b) a token PASTRY CHEF woman and (c) a token PASTRY CHEF woman who is not the star of the show in a story as there is with not including one."

I waited for a response. Lydon was obviously an intelligent thinker who cared, and I was looking forward to getting, if not an apology, then another point of view. Nothing followed. Ever. (Maybe it was snarky after all?)

Then it's time to write a book about women chefs. If you're me, you've got two choices—you can cut off your nose to spite your face, or you can save your face by deciding not to save face. You know what I mean. What her letter made clear is that Lydon belongs in any conversation about female life in the culinary industry. If you ever read her blog Eggbeater,[137] it will quickly become clearer still that she belongs in any conversation about life in the culinary industry, period.

So, back to that night of portended blizzardry, I was having misgivings. The boots were on, the feet, cold. Lydon, with no mention at

---

[137] That's Eggbeater.typepad.com, yo.

all of the *7x7* happenings, had sent a most enthusiastic reply to my interview request. She congratulated me and followed that with "Zow, this is amazing news. I am so utterly honored to be considered for your interviews & subject. Yes, please, I would love to talk to you." It couldn't have been more encouraging. I knew, however, that she was a sharp one, and I was all kinds of anxious about how she'd process my questions. The day of our summit, I checked in to make sure we were all set and determine the hour of power—7:30 p.m., when she could leave work. "Big massive storm coming in at that time: Put the chains on your shoes," she warned me. Gulp. I told her that if it was looking severe out there, we could always take to Skype (wishful thinking?). Nah, Lydon's hearty. There'd be no cowardly option.

And as the first few flakes whirled through town, I found myself on Orchard Street at Café Katja, that adorable cranny of wurst-spaetzle-and-pretzel sustenance. More than two hours later, when we left Café Katja, the snow was falling like sifting flour and the streets were covered in a plush layer of powder. My favorite. Boy, was I glad I'd met her.

Did we talk about that article? An hour and forty-three minutes into our powwow, boom. There was a lull in the conversation, and I asked Lydon if there was anything she wanted to add, a different topic to cover. "I guess, like, in lieu of the piece you wrote in *7x7* and then the letter I wrote . . ." the match was lit. "That was the thing," she reasoned, "that, like, what was exciting about you asking to interview me for the book is that you considered me a chef, not a pastry chef. Because, in that piece, I think it would have been so much better had you represented any woman, sweet or salty." Here's where, because I seem to have a problem with this, I interrupted and tried to explain myself (it was mostly a rehashing of what I'd e-mailed her initially). When I got to the bit about featuring exec chefs who had either gotten the call to head things up or taken it upon themselves to open their own shop, Lydon cut in with "but a pastry chef *is* an executive chef." Okay, you know how there's a difference between listening and hearing, or knowing and believing? With this small interjection, Lydon made me aware that I'd been on the listening or knowing end of those equations. I understood that a pastry chef was an executive chef in that he or she was in charge of his or her department, but I was so caught up in the titular, that I simultaneously thought of the pastry chef as under the thumb of an über-executive (i.e., savory) chef. In championing the craft itself, Lydon forced me to see that, truly, you're dealing with two separate skill sets—one more general, the other specialized—that require equal amounts of commitment, hard work, and mastery. Somewhere along the way, we in America have either never fully grasped this or forgot that we once had.

I could have also titled this chapter "Nobody Puts Baby in the Basement," since, as Michael Laiskonis, the acclaimed pastry chef, formerly at New York City's peerless Le Bernardin, recently reminded everyone during an interview with the website Eater, that's where the pastry chefs are quarantined. "Sure, I mean you know we're kind of the redheaded stepchildren of the kitchen. We're kind of tucked away in a corner of the basement."[138] It's not really the banishment it sounds like; because of the delicate nature of pastry work, his art needs to be practiced in a cool place, away from the raised temperatures of working ovens and the chaos of the line during service. In Boston, Maura Kilpatrick commented on the basement syndrome. "Here's the thing: Most pastry chefs work alone," she says. "We can't be in the kitchen, with the ovens, and the heat, and the other chefs and cooks. You have to be willing to challenge yourself, criticize yourself, because you don't get the rush of having other people standing next to you on the line."[139]

Pastry has always been segregated, but not because it was valued less. Au contraire. Pastry chefs were (and still are) the profession's specialists. In *Cooking for Kings: The Life of Antonin Carême, the First Celebrity Chef*, Ian Kelly chronicles that early 19th-century French

[138] "From the Eater Lounge: Michael Laiskonis," Eater.com, October 9, 2010.

[139] Louisa Kasdon, "Desserted: Why Don't Pastry Chefs Get More Respect?" *Stuff Boston*, February 23, 2009.

culinary genius's rise to "it" toque[140] and provides a behind-the-scenes peek at how cooking proceedings were carried out, on the highest level, for international royalty. Carême's course parallels the development of restaurant culture in his mother country as well, but, it should be noted, in that epoch, dining at the home or party of a political VIP (like Talleyrand, the Rothschilds, or Napoleon—all of whom Carême prepared vittles for) was the ne plus ultra. What was it that put Carême on the map? Pastry. "The real stars of post-Revolutionary French cooking were not the restaurateurs, they were the pastry confectioners and pâtissiers. And it was as a confectioner that Carême would first come to the notice of the gourmets of Paris."[141] The chef, when he was overseeing all aspects of a meal, always maintained a separate cooled room for confectionary efforts and an additional chamber—his favorite—for pastry. Restaurants are modeled on the same setup. Chefs who had once been employed by aristocrats found themselves jobless after the French Revolution. At the same time, guild laws that had formerly permitted tavern owners to serve food to people outside of their homes were changed so that those who once performed those duties in residences could do so commercially, for the paying public.[142] Those customer-serving establishments and, certainly, professionals like Carême didn't hire womenfolk for cooking of any sort.

At last, today, we're beginning to see the barriers facing female chefs in France come down. Pastry, however, remains the final frontier. You can name a few Michelin-crowned standouts in the saline domain (Anne-Sophie Pic and Hélène Darroze are the most recognized), but are there any in pastry? None that I can think of, and I'm a pastry whore. I can spend days on end wandering the Paris streets and stopping in shops like Pierre Hermé (my favorite), or else Ladurée, Sadaharu Aoki, Jacques Genin, Patisserie des Rêves, or any of the newer additions (I

---

[140] By the way, according to Kelly, Carême invented the toque—he made it himself and donned it in the kitchen.

Ian Kelly, *Cooking for Kings: The Life of Antonin Carême, the First Celebrity Chef* (London: Short Books, 2003), 13.

[141] Ibid., 35.

[142] Ibid., 34.

keep an ever-growing list of must-trys). But I digress. What you need to know: France's pastry world is a men's locker room, and there's not a ladies' equivalent down the hall. This is not to say they don't exist at all, but if they do, they're well hidden.

In America, where we borrowed the Euro foundation for structuring restaurants and adhered it to it as closely as possible, it has taken decades for women to be accepted in the savory spaces; but, somehow or other, pastry slipped through the cracks and became the exception—a field in which women could assert themselves. It has become the feminized discipline in a realm lorded over by men. But why, I wondered.

It's a double-edged sword—women are often pushed toward pastry because it's presumed the "gentler" kitchen; it is said we gravitate toward it because it's the gig that accommodates childbearing and kid rearing.[143] Still, anyone who makes petits fours at a "serious" establishment will tell you that they're the last ones to leave. And if you analyze the nature of the work itself and the haute regard in which it's held abroad, there's a real disconnect.

Claudia Fleming, whose first impressions of pastry were formed here (in her native land), was flummoxed when she arrived in Paris to study that craft only to realize that men had her market cornered there. Suddenly, she found herself an anomaly. "In terms of how it's perceived . . . in Europe . . . I became casual friends with Pierre Hermé[144] . . . His first wife thought it was so extraordinary there was a woman pastry chef, but they thought it was fantastic I was one. So, for

---

[143] According to that StarChefs.com (2010) Chef Salary Report, the average number of hours clocked daily among those surveyed came in at eleven for executive chefs/chefs/CEOs and for both chefs de cuisine and sous chefs, and ten for pastry chefs. The average number of hours spent in the kitchen weekly came in at sixty-one for the first group, sixty for the second, fifty-eight for the third, and fifty-five for pastry chefs. That's not a huge gap, and, although pastry chefs might gain a few extra hours each week, their hours can be the hardest. The pastry chefs I interviewed talked about having to be either the first ones in (at the crack of dawn) and/or the last ones out.

[144] He is, if you ask me, the most formidable pâtissier in France; if we're going on general consensus, then he's one of that country's most revered. You say "macaron," I say, "Hermé." The best creation of his I've ever enjoyed, in case you're curious, was one that Dorie Greenspan advised me to try while in Paris one spring. It's a cherry-pistachio tart with a streusel topping. Greenspan has an adapted version of the recipe on her website, if you're tempted; Doriegreenspan.com.

me, it was confusing because I thought, 'Really? That's where all the women are relegated.' "

The pastry chefs I interviewed seemed, generally, more predisposed to feistiness, due, no doubt, to having to defend the exacting nature of their output to their professional peers (and the misled populace) who believe it the equivalent of a gut course. You can't fake pastry. It's not to say that you can bullshit your way through savory, but there's less dependency on training and precision. Lydon, who started on the "regular" line, finds the work she did there coarse by comparison. It functions differently, she contends, the pastry mind; it's more inclined toward science in its reliance on fixed measurements and temperatures.[145] She expanded on that proposition with the following, one of my most treasured of her aphorisms: "The molecular gastronomists are really savory chefs with a hard-on for pastry." They only wish, those foam sprayers, that they could perform the feats of her people. Also noteworthy, she deemed brain surgeons as medicine's counterpart to cooking's pastry chefs. This analogy does help one fathom both the dexterity dictated by the craft and its male designation in France, where even the lowliest of kitchen slots (allo, *plongeur*[146]) is a challenge for women to score.

Meanwhile, at the CIA, the number of women enrolling in pastry climbs higher each year, while that of men decreases.[147] What's up with the chick magnetism? Lydon posits that women think they're reaching autonomy faster in this sector,[148] but even if that's the case, it is still regarded as the lesser of the divisions of labor here. And one also wants to know which came first, the girls or the pastry? Was pastry denigrated and women pushed to it accordingly? Or were ladies drawn to it and, by choosing it, implicated in its diminishment? Although it might be

---

[145] There is a lot of this in savory, too, don't get me wrong, but there's a greater dependency on formulas and, overall, a narrower margin of error in the bulk of pastry-related procedures.

[146] That would be the dishwasher. (Do you really need to revisit footnote 99, page 87, again?!)

[147] See footnote 49, page 54.

[148] In its accompanying commentary, that same StarChefs.com study mentions that the average time taken to achieve an executive chef position is shorter for pastry than for savory chefs.

impossible to come up with a clear answer or explanation, Lydon has no doubt that the two are directly connected.

If, as she notes, the perception is that "in the world over, women are home cooks and men are professional cooks," then, she deduces, "the same thing has happened with women becoming pastry chefs in America. It's like, it's hard to explain, but in America—and I'm not sure I found this so much in Europe—baking is considered less, so it makes sense to put the 'lesser gender' there. It's pretty harsh, but it's really true."

I asked Claudia Fleming what she thought prompted the shuttling of our ilk to the marble-countered[149] annexes. "My hunch would be, they wanted to get us out of the way," she offered. "And pastry, in this country, isn't that important." Whereas in Europe, she remarked, the final course isn't an option—it is a paid-for, valued component of the meal—in the United States, "it isn't important in the dining culture . . . we don't do prix fixe." She believes that as a result of its being marginalized, "they just put us [women] over there." And it's precisely its underdog status that draws Fleming "there," to the pastry department. "Mom didn't have to make you dessert; she had to make you dinner," she says. "It made you feel special, which is sort of why making dessert is fun."

Katzie Guy-Hamilton reinforces her forte's secondary status. "For every ten restaurants, there's one that has a pastry chef," she counts (and she's in New York City; I'd guess the tally would be even lower in other parts). It's not the most cost-efficient of positions to fill. "If it's not part of the meal, then it's a luxury . . . you know, people have to pinch-hit in pastry," Fleming adds. Even in those recherché establishments that have a dedicated crew, it's not the size of the savory team; it's usually one sole person, depending on the scale and level of business. Gina DePalma rolls it out for you, simple like: "In pastry, you're

---

[149] Marble is the work surface preferred by many pastry chefs because its natural cold temperature prevents butter from melting; this is crucial to dough-making endeavors. If, for example, the layers of butter folded into your croissant dough were to warm and dissolve, you'd be in for a real tragedy.

doubly a second-class citizen, because . . . unless you're lucky enough to work in a restaurant that really values it . . . you deal with lack of space, lack of equipment, lack of just about everything. I love my job, I love my boss, but my needs have not always been met and they haven't ever been front and center . . . You are the last course. In pastry, you have to come to peace with that."

Welcome to the Economics of Pastry, where our visiting professors of *pithiviers* and pennies will be Elizabeth Belkind and Heather Bertinetti. The first, who made a name for herself at Santa Monica's Grace when she launched a weekly "Wednesday Night Doughnut Shoppe" at that restaurant and wowed Angelenos with her menu of made-to-order hole-less wonders,[150] recalls the invisible cap placed on her department's potential earnings. "One of the things I had to contend with was that, in a lot of restaurants, when something goes wrong with a table, they give away desserts, and then, at the end of the month, when you're being questioned about your P&Ls [profits and losses] and your food costs, how do you explain that a huge percentage of it goes out the door for free? There's also a limit to how much you can charge for desserts. People won't pay more than, I would say, ten or twelve dollars for dessert, as opposed to an entree." So if people are paying à la carte (in which case, they're entitled to skip the whole course entirely), they can still only contribute so much to the dessert piggy bank. You're set up, if not to fail, then, at least, to be the weakest financial link. And since cash is king, pastry chefs inevitably get ranked pretty low at court.

"It's true pastry doesn't bring in as much money percentage-wise as savory does," Bertinetti concurs, "but they forget, let's say, petits fours, for instance, and take-home cakes—or things like that. Not only are we the last impression the guests leave with, but we're also what sets the restaurant apart from a two-star or one-star restaurant to [be] a three or four, right? . . . All the extras—all the bread, everything like that—are what's a constant factor throughout the meal that pastry's

[150] Her creations, for them who wish to torture themselves with these kinds of details, included a chocolate hazelnut beignet and a signature "jelly" job filled with strawberry-rhubarb jam.

accountable for, and unfortunately, you don't make money on those things, cause that's the freebie stuff." This I found fascinating. First, I'd never made that correlation between the edible gifts diners receive and the lagniappes being generated from the "basement." Second, and more interesting, I hadn't thought about the star system in such cut, dry, and mercenary terms. I've always wondered why a bare-bones address that serves some of the best food I've eaten and charges squat for it could never be allotted three stars from the *New York Times* critic. My ideal for restaurant reviewing has always been that if a spot delivered on whatever promise it made to diners, and did so in an exemplary manner, it should be heaped with the highest praise—judged on its own terms. I didn't realize that, in a way, you pay for your stars. Obviously, just because you spent all the money on a front of house kitted out for formal service and on someone like Bertinetti and her employees that doesn't guarantee you'll get more twinklers than another restaurant; it only makes you eligible in a way the rest are not. It's a greater risk financially in that it requires a heftier investment, but the potential pay-off (should the critical stars align) is big.

In high-enders like the establishments at which Bertinetti has cooked, her art is undervalued because its ability to put her boss in the black is practically nil. That's what it comes down to—not that the work itself isn't as intricate or challenging. In another profession, like medicine, we accept a specialist's charging more for her time than a GP's for his. Not so in culinary America. "People expect less," says Sherry Yard, and she's all right with that, because, as she sees it, "I'm running my own horse race." The self-ascribed "gingerbread girl" for whom this chapter is titled is Wolfgang Puck's second brain, and a legend in her own right. His may be the bigger name, but she's not invisible. The man, her boss, has more restaurants than I can count. (It's true. I went to the website and was overwhelmed by the lists—yes, there's more than one.) Yard's involved in all of them. She advises those young women enlisting in the gingerbread corps to do as she has and not get thrown off track by those lower standards others might have for the craft. Instead, she looks to those who have surpassed all expectations. En-Ming Hsu is one of them.

A classmate of Yard's at both college and pastry school, in 2001, Hsu won a gold medal at France's Coupe du Monde de la Patisserie or, as we English speakers call it, the World Pastry Cup. Established in 1989, it's a biennial international tournament and it's a big deal. When she scored that victory, Hsu was the first woman to do so. It was also the first time the USA had taken home the prize, and she was her team's captain. I hadn't heard of Hsu until Yard mentioned her. "I guess it's just not being tooted as much," she shrugged. That—the horn-tooting—is what Yard believes can help present and future pastry chefs (and when she talks about it in this context she means the grisettes) garner some recognition and have something they can aspire to, so that they don't look at their streusel-topped lot as a booby[151] prize. She campaigns for herself and those she has worked with, like Claudia Fleming and Elizabeth Falkner. She took over for Nancy Silverton and she trained Katzie Guy-Hamilton. She will tell you all of this. Hers is a close-knit, icing-bound family, and together they compose a formidable legacy of American pastry. The better known they are, the better the girls who decide to follow in their footsteps. Yard suggests that this is the crucial factor when faced with the feminizing of her craft—we can believe and accept that women are being shunted to pastry in culinary schools or galleys, or we can reject that and actively embrace the department.

Anyone who has ever spent more than thirty seconds in her presence or tasted one of her desserts[152] knows that, indeed, Yard does seem to belong in a league of her own. By and large, the public doesn't pick up on the rigor of her discipline, she thinks. Making dessert, most people

---

[151] Oh, *come on!* You must have seen that pun coming.

[152] Even the cookie sampler she sent me packing with was like no other—there were her perfect renditions of a chocolate chipper and that Italian rainbow layered rectangle, plus her signature "rookie," a cross between a brownie and cookie that looks humble but is, on the richness front, awesomely lethal.

figure, is a cakewalk. "People do have the perception that when you're a pastry chef you don't work as hard," says Belkind. "It's intensely physical work. People in L.A. are constantly looking at you physically—and I happen to have a strong upper body, and I don't do anything other than bake. And I say that to people. I say, 'You should try baking' . . . There's definitely the idea that you're just fluffing cream and dipping things in chocolate and it's all sweet and pretty. It's actually, I think, very gutsy, dirty work—like cooking on the line would be."

The biggest offender, when it comes to painting pastry into its shadowy corner, has been the media. It's hard to believe but, according to Heather Carlucci-Rodriguez, before 1999, when William Grimes took over the post of critic at the *New York Times*, restaurant reviewers (or the only ones who matter[153]) seemed to presume that dessert made itself, or, more plausibly, that those who prepared it were extraneous.[154] "Until William Grimes came into play, and that's including Ruth [Reichl], it was really touch and go whether the pastry chef ever got mentioned. He [Grimes] mentioned them by name. Bill Grimes changed my career completely . . . The first year he was in started something that's carried on ever since."

How many food writers or cookbook authors specialize in pastry? I recently asked myself this. All I could come up with was the inimitable Dorie Greenspan. There's David Lebovitz, too, but he's a pastry chef with a knack for prose, so that might be stretching it a bit. If more of us took it upon ourselves to focus on or learn about pastry, we would become more aware of it and those who practice it. And as soon as a few of us began to cover it, that, in turn, would spark repetition of the same—print journalists could explore the up-to-the-minute news broken by bloggers and the latter could pick up and post the stories of the former.

Text-wise, there's a drought. Turn on the TV, and you'll find an equally troubling mis(s)representation. Coincidentally, a few days after

---

[153] Kidding, sort of.

[154] I can't confirm this observation as fact, although, based on my own experience as a regular reader of the *New York Times* restaurant reviews, I find that, in general, pastry chefs are often neglected.

I'd sat down to draft this very paragraph, Alessandra Stanley's article "Viewers Still Drool for Frosting Fantasies"[155] ran in the Television section of the *New York Times* and fortified my lack of faith in the tube. She provided a survey of the programming pantry and, after observing that "There are as many cream-filled series on cable as there are cupcake flavors at Crumbs," listed the crummy offerings. Cupcakes—the trend that won't die and, in its immortality, stands as my constant reminder that mediocrity wins (it's a subpar item even on its best day)—and their progenitor, cake, are the monopolizing megastars. Tune in to the Food Network's how-high-can-you-stack-it *Last Cake Standing* for a glimpse at teetering towers of leavened manhandled shit you most definitely wouldn't want to eat and the drama ("my fondant is melting!") that ensues when people are forced to make bar mitzvah–type eyesores under ridiculous conditions (the "crazy twists and eliminations looming each week," as per the host network's enticing blurb). Or check out *Cupcake Wars*, in which smoked salmon becomes a weapon of mass destruction (note: this ingredient has appeared and been used on the show and, surely, when baked into one of the contestant's morsels, caused an outbreak of diarrhea among the judges). There's *Have Cake, Will Travel*, too, which, as far as I can tell, follows an overly made-up (imagine JonBenét Ramsey "all growns up") cake decorator as she deals with demanding clients in down-to-the-wire circumstances. (Fashion Week! Mardi Gras!) Even nonfood channels are getting in on the easy-bake action. We've got TLC and its *DC Cupcakes* (never seen it, even by accident), as well as Buddy Valastro's *Cake Boss* (seen it, unfortunately) and his two spin-offs, *Kitchen Boss* and *Next Great Baker*. (If we were pitching Hollywood, we'd say Buddy's story looks like this: *The Sopranos* meets *Jersey Shore* meets cake.) In light of the Boss's success, We TV brought Vincent "Vinny" Buzzetta's *Staten Island Cakes* to the party. (Same premise—Italian-American family that bakes together gets on your nerves together.) Then, at 10:30 p.m., just when everyone

---

[155] Alessandra Stanley, "Viewers Still Drool for Frosting Fantasies," the *New York Times*, June 20, 2011.

are for women. And, regardless of his being on television, he represents another aspect of the gender-in-pastry issue. Enter Johnny Iuzzini (a.k.a. Johnny Z), who made a name for himself as Jean-Georges Vongerichten's resident dessert visionary for six years (first at Perry Street and then at landmark Jean Georges), after working for Daniel Boulud, and *maître des macaron* François Payard. A pretty boy with a dark side and a love of high-tech culinary high jinks, Iuzzini is one of pastry's new faces. He's also the head judge on Bravo's *Top Chef Just Desserts*, which, to its credit, is the only show (competition or otherwise) that tries to legitimize pastry as the art it is.

The Z machine and his brethren (it's a boy band) represent the new, the avant-garde; they're positioned, intentionally or not, as the antithesis of the female prototype that came before them (and of the cupcake legion as well). These rebel creators of chocolate soil are in a tiny minority, but they're raking in the validation and hogging the spotlight. It's not just a question of how they look or behave; their approach to pastry is a departure from those who preceded them. While Silverton, Fleming, and Yard established a new genre of dessert—a modern American category that complemented its savory sibling and dealt in pared-down, produce-driven compositions anchored in classical (French) technique—Iuzzini's gang is interested in deconstruction and a manipulation of ingredients informed by the tools and principles of science. A clear divide exists and it's overtly gendered.

Fleming concurred that today's saccharine dishes are "really trending toward the chemistry side," which she, too, identifies as skewing male, and announced that she "can tell men's desserts from women's desserts in a second." Belkind frets that the economic climate might compound the us-versus-them effect in the culinary world at large, and, more pronounced, in pastry. Based on the past economic downturn, she worries about future crises of that nature. She expounded on what had happened to "the fine-dining scene" and "how that affects women particularly, especially if they are in the pastry kitchen." When Wall Street tanked, "the movement everywhere," as she rightly perceived, was "toward food that's accessible and comfortable for everybody." She wonders, anxiously, "if that will be limiting in the long run." She gave me something to think about with that. In one way, you'd think this spike in comfort food might mean more opportunity for women—we are, after all, associated with home-style cuisine. But playing into that cliché isn't going to help us get beyond it. And if the one area in which we're seen as having any clout is pastry, the demise of fine dining deals a huge blow; those are the restaurants in which dessert-making is given a podium. Without that outlet, what opportunities do women have to prove they've got technical chops? Even within that rarefied, ever-shrinking niche, what are their options if, when the final course is on display, the male-dominated, progressive tack is what gets the attention (thanks, media)? On the other end of the spectrum, the casual neighborhood restaurants that are thriving don't have pastry departments (they're smaller in scale and ambition; plus, they don't have the budgets for petits fours). They might have some "homey" confections made by fill-ins from the savory staff. This leaves the majority of pastry chefs with little room to maneuver.

Where, then, can a go-getting gingerbread girl go get? What if she has great expectations for her career (and why shouldn't she)? And what if she has the skill? How can she advance? If restaurants aren't enough, and there aren't enough of them with pastry departments, what's an éclair expert to do? If this were a conversation about "regular" chefs, the answer would be—she should open her own place. But if you're a pastry person and you love the galley lifestyle, that's not the obvious answer. What kind of dining room would yours be? In acts of derring-do, a few have invaded salty territory.

It's a lot easier for a savory chef to launch a cheesecake business than it is for a deacon of *dacquoise* to start peddling pasta—not for lack of skill or height of learning curve (if anything, most chefs would tell you it would be the other way around), but because of general perception. Everyone thinks the blokes who sear venison capable of anything; those who've mastered delicate, lacey Florentine cookies, less adaptable. If you are able to transition from chocolate to forest-based truffles, you'll have a difficult time gaining acceptance or praise from critics or, worse, your own industry. Look at the James Beard Awards program with its strict separation of pastry and savory.[156] Sorcerers of sugar who have tackled salads and roasts don't fit either category, and suffer for it. They're in no-man's-land, and no one is sure what to do with them.

"Why is it savory chefs can do dessert but pastry chefs can't do food?" asks Mindy Segal. In Chicago, she was met with skepticism, confusion, and wariness when, in 2005, she founded Mindy's Hot Chocolate, a restaurant that serves shrimp and grits, and also includes a dessert bar and pastry counter. "When we first opened, no one got it . . . I was the chef . . . all the food was my concept." It was no picnic. She nearly went under once and, because she believed in her concept and the quality she delivered, fought to stay afloat. Like other chef-owners, she has been able to step away from the galley to deal with the bigger picture, and, also like them, it's her vision that's expressed on every plate; hers is the last word on each course. And yet, she remains classified (James Beard style) as a pastry chef (after being nominated five years in a row, she won the award in 2012).

A few others have crossed over: Nancy Silverton, who joined forces with Mario Batali and his business partner Joe Bastianich to open the mini Mozza kingdom that began on Melrose Avenue in Los Angeles and has branched out to Newport Beach and Singapore;[157] Heather Carlucci-Rodriguez, who had my dearly beloved takeout shop Lassi (RIP) before switching back to pastry (to pay the bills until she can afford to launch version 2.0 of that Indian gem); Patti Jackson of

---

[156] In 2011, Christina Tosi—I think you've been introduced—was nominated for the Rising Star Award. I believe she was the first of her kind—not womankind, pastrykind—to be deemed possibly worthy. Stay tuned till footnote 225, page 227.

[157] The heart of the operation lies on Melrose Avenue, where you'll find Osteria Mozza, and next door to that the more casual pizzeria, plus a "2go" bodega that hosts a cooking school event venue.

eighteen-year-old Manhattan gem I Trulli, who, in 2003, stepped up to the plate and took over for her marvel of a boss, chef-owner Pino Luongo, at his much-missed restaurant Le Madri on West Eighteenth Street; and Elizabeth Falkner, whom you might recognize as the polymath (savory and sweet) hopeful who placed as runner-up on *The Next Iron Chef: Super Chefs*. Falkner applied her whimsical, iconoclastic tricks to Caesar salad at Orson, which also housed the production kitchen of her Citizen Cake restaurant-cum-patisserie.[158] Once you get beyond what, in the 21st century, seems like an almost arcane line drawn between the two departments of the galley, you realize how much overlap there is, or can be. "I remember having this dialogue," Falkner says, "with everybody, like, 'Here's the pastry kitchen and here's the savory kitchen. And we're going to define what's savory and what's sweet.' And then at some point I was like, 'No, we're not. We're going to bring it back together. And it's all going to make sense. I like savory desserts and I like some pastry techniques in savory food.'"

Even so, the persistence of labels (and the tidy boxes into which they place people) plagued Falkner and caused her to have a minor identity crisis. In 2005, the same year she put savory ice creams on her menu at Citizen Cake (they would replace sauces; for example, she set a horseradish ice cream atop a steak), she was on the short list for the Beard pastry award and didn't win. The next few years came and went without her being nominated again. She wondered why and, admits,

---

[158] Okay, hold up. I know I'm in the middle of talking about how chefs who have specialized in pastry can apply those skills to savory endeavors, but I have to pause for a moment in honor of the Mocha Mi Su. As I was leaving Orson (on Fourth Street, in San Francisco) after a most fascinating talk with Falkner, she packed up a little treat bag for me. In it was an individually sized version of this, one of the Americana cakes she created for Citizen Cake. If you had read the café's menu, you would have learned that the contents of this revisited tiramisu are as follows: "cocoa chiffon cake with a hint of sambuca, layers of mocha latte mousse, coffee buttercream, and chocolate miroir." (That last term refers to a glaze.) Even though I was having dinner in an hour, as soon as I got back to the artist's studio I called home during my sojourn, I felt it imperative to steal a taste of the boxed mini-cake Falkner had wrapped so carefully for me. You guys? I was floored. As I reported to the chef in an e-mail (sent on February 16, 2011, the day of our interview): "It's like an altered state of being! I just tasted the Mocha Mi Su and am completely stunned by its greatness—like a cloudlike burst of mocha and coffee. It's the happy place." I was moved to tweet about it too: "Have just tasted Citizen Cake's Mocha Mi Su. In a mocha state of bliss." Oh God, I'd kill for another right now. I'm not sure murder would help, though. At the end of 2011, Falkner closed up her Bay Area shops and told me she'd be starting over with a new project . . . a pizzeria in Brooklyn.

became preoccupied with getting that medal. It affected how she saw and projected herself. "Even though I was doing the savory food," she says, "I refused to call myself the chef. I would say 'pastry chef.' And at some point, I thought, 'Well, that's just dumb. I am holding myself back from being the chef that I am.' Does that make any sense? And then I was like, 'Wow, this whole pastry chef thing has turned around and bit me in the ass.' " Once she got her head out of her bitten butt, her mission changed. "I'd like to follow [in] the footsteps of Nancy Silverton and Michel Richard.[159] They're my role models, because they're pastry chefs—amazing pastry chefs—but they're also chefs. I think that it's dangerous to get caught up in that stuff, because, obviously, I think I kind of sabotaged myself."

Not every pastry pro wants to cross genres. Some don't like chocolate in their peanut butter, or peanut butter in their chocolate. Or maybe they're not interested in firing up proteins or having to deal with the main dishes of a meal. For those who wish to adhere strictly to their subset of the craft and to have their own business, a bakery is the obvious choice.

Some, like Belkind, have thrown themselves into that and have no desire to return to restaurants. Then there are those who find the business structure, atmosphere, and duties of each irreconcilably different—that one can't replace the other. The ingredients and product might look familiar, but that's where the comparison ends.

Maura Kilpatrick has found a way to reside in both worlds and, because of that, is able to appreciate their respective pros and cons. She is in a unique position as a pastry chef; at Ana Sortun's flagship Oleana

---

[159] This bow-to-the-master French dude got his start when he apprenticed, at age fourteen, in a pastry restaurant in Champagne, France. Then it was off to Paris to the house Gaston Lenôtre built (see footnote 64, page 61), where, eventually, Richard took charge of that acclaimed pastry shop. Guy's legit. In 1975, he packed his spatulas and headed to the USA, not to New York or California, though. He opened a place of his own in Santa Fe, New Mexico. Here, he served savory and sweet things. He then headed to L.A. and opened a proper patisserie, which he named after himself. From there, a full-on restaurant followed (it was called Citrus; it made quite a splash). Expansion came in the form of Citronelle in Santa Barbara, and then, too, in Baltimore and Philadelphia (there was Bistro M in San Francisco as well). In 1998, the chef bid adieu to California and brought Citronelle to Washington, D.C. That puppy's his flagship. He shuttered the rest, but went on to open Central in D.C. and Vegas.

in Cambridge, Massachusetts, where Kilpatrick is now a partner, she has always been afforded autonomy from the savory program. It's not as though she flouts that and designs desserts that have absolutely zilch to do with Sortun's spice-driven Middle Eastern food. Kilpatrick is known for adopting those themes and expressing them in a pastry-appropriate way. With Sortun, she hasn't glimpsed any of that marginalization that most of her peers do. They are equals; leaders of their coexisting crews. I asked Kilpatrick if this was as rare as it seemed, and she said yes, that it's not normal and she's lucky to be in her position.

The partnership functions so well that in 2008, seven years after Oleana debuted, to showcase Kilpatrick's strengths, they premiered the bakery and café Sofra, which they co-own. Here it's the pastry chef who runs the show, and she looks to her partner, Sortun, to provide inspiration when it's time to do a vegetable tart or cheese-filled turnover. The workload is vastly different. Those who score a job at Sofra subsequent to toiling in restaurants and assume they're in for a break have another thing coming to them. At a bakery, Kilpatrick explains, "you don't think that chocolate chip cookies are as hard as they are—I'm not saying they're hard—but making them the same every single batch, every single day, that's the hard part . . . Because you're producing a lot of products . . . consistency is the biggest challenge."

Like Kilpatrick, Joanne Chang is involved with a bakery and restaurant; she knows all about marketing those entities and giving each a distinct personality. Her bakeshop, Flour, has multiple locations around the Boston area; it's what confirmed her talent as an entrepreneur and culinary maven. With that under her pastry tool–belt, she opened a restaurant, Myers & Chang, with her husband (he's the Myers). Guess who oversees the entire kitchen? The baker. "There is a big difference," she asserts. "If you're an executive chef, you're in charge of an entire menu, which includes pastry and, depending on the restaurant, you're either in charge of the front [of house] or working hand in hand with the front manager . . . When I was the pastry chef, I only had to worry about pastries. I never had to worry about the dishwasher, or the prep cooks, or getting new linens, or anything like that." She went on to talk about why the hybrid group of which she is a part—the pastry chef as restaurant owner—is such a tiny one. "Most pastry chefs don't necessarily want to open restaurants . . . [There are a] few, but it's not because people are telling them not to do it; it's because people [pastry chefs] aren't interested."

Heather Bertinetti falls into that large—according to Chang—cluster of pastry chefs who love practicing their craft in restaurants and have no interest in founding their own, or of planting their palette knife in unclaimed bakery turf. Bertinetti insinuates that bakers are the lightweights of her field because they don't have to put up with the hardships of a brigade. "Bakeries aren't a tough environment. They're not," she asserts. Her anti-bakery stance was comedic, at turns, and also hinted at a strong (if not overtly expressed) undercurrent of what Kilpatrick offhandedly referred to as "snobbery."

Bertinetti's disdain for bakeries reminded me of chefs' misprision of the term *cook*. It's as though restaurant pastry work is revered as professional, technical, and refined while, set on the other end of an imagined axis, the bakery is characterized as the common, untrained, home-style alternative. It's that unspoken, subconscious (or not) polarizing of low and high—handicraft and art. The fact that a James Beard Award goes out expressly to pastry chefs and not to professional bakers buttresses that dichotomy. Her allusion to the galley's male-female dynamic and how it's absent in baguette boutiques calls to mind another previously discussed aspect of that *chef-cook* discourse—its gendered connotations. Based on that prior logic, bakers, Bertinetti's non-"serious" or (as generally pigeonholed) unschooled counterparts undertake the "female" or homey endeavor, while she and her co–pastry chefs, the skilled experts, engage in the "male," professional echelon. Pay no heed, then, to the bakeries—er, patisseries—that offer elaborate, if not plated, delicacies and consistently put some innovative bready stuff out there; the more "legit" thing to do, in the eyes of chefs like Bertinetti, would be to seek employment in a four-star fortress.

When you go back to that original question about what fuels the sociological connection between women and pastry, I think the answer lies here—somewhere amid baking's being perceived as amateurish and pastry's being confused with it. I suspect, in our nation, a conflation[160] of these two microcrafts may have triggered the downgrading of the latter specialty to home-style status. Here, where pastry was never given the same attention or exposure as it was abroad, our idea of dessert was shaped by what we were served at home, by our moms. While savory was more clearly split into two classes—dinner-on-the-table or dinner a la *table d'haute*—pastry was not, so there was no distinction to be made. That's why, I believe, the two entities, bakery output and pastry work, were collapsed into one field dominated by apple pie, carrot cake, and chocolate chip cookies. Do Americans say that they're en route to the patisserie to pick up a tart? No, they use the word *bakery*, whether it's a seven-grain loaf, a pineapple upside-down cake, or an éclair they're after. The pros in either section—baking or pastry—understand the disparity; they're probably more sensitive to it because it's unclear to the rest of the world. To a disinterested or underexposed eater, a bakery is where you go to buy the items you were too busy to make for yourself. It's a retail annex of the domestic kitchen, a place circumscribed as female—a cupcake hut. Maybe this is harebrained and clumsy. I apologize if so. But I think it's a start.

What the bakery offers a pastry chef, though, should not be discounted so quickly. Autonomy, especially for ladies in this profession, and the ability to rig one's own gig is often the best (and only) way to achieve financial triumph and public recognition. The past few years has seen a renaissance in artisanal (a now overused and tired word that implies handcrafted and executed on a small scale) food

---

[160] How this collapse came about, I can only conjecture.

businesses—bakeries being one of the more preponderant of the lot. If that reality offers greater potential to women within the culinary industry, perhaps we're better off taking a page from Yard's cookbooks[161] and assertively claiming the bakeries as our territory and, while we're at it, elevating them to something we can be proud of. Hell, we could introduce our countrymen to the patisserie. There's no limit to how high our cakes can rise (or how long they can stand).

[161] She has two: *The Secrets of Baking* (2003) and *Desserts by the Yard* (2007).

Chefs, Know Your Limits[162]

Question: Do you think a glass ceiling exists in this industry?

"Don't compromise yourself. There will be no ceiling then . . . People look at me and say, 'Wow, you're still working under Wolfgang [Puck].' Oh no. I'm wise. I have a wonderful umbrella. I like my umbrella. It's my family, and it's my choice, and it's what I love to do, and we grow as a family. And soon, I will have one of my own little places and have something I call my pastry clubhouse, because that's what I want to do . . . I think you approach things from a point of: you don't have to; you want to. And everybody does have a choice . . . And when I want to, that's that . . . So there's your ceiling; there ain't none."

—*Sherry Yard*

"There isn't the traditional business model where the top position is the CEO, and if you don't have the CEO [job], you hit a glass ceiling. But here, the glass ceiling would be owner of the restaurant, which I don't want, so it's like you almost have to create your own reality; you have to create your own ceiling in your own world. And yeah, as you move up, the pyramid gets smaller in any business, in any career."

—*Emily Luchetti*

---

[162] This is a riff on "Women, Know Your Limits," the title of a sketch that appeared on the BBC comedy serial *Harry Enfield and Chums*, which aired from 1994 to 1997. Set in the 1930s, this bit was conceived of as a mock public service announcement that instructs women on "proper" comportment (i.e., being docile and unable to develop or utter informed opinions).

"I work in a very specific niche of vegetable or vegetarian cooking. So after working in [New York City] for about thirteen
years, there was just nowhere else for me to cook. I had worked
in most of the vegetarian [restaurants]—you hit a point where
either you stay at the same level or you try something new. I
could have started cooking meat and working in other kitchens, but that would have put me back down on a lower rung,
and I had gone pretty high . . . This is a ceiling you're gonna
hit if you're working in vegetarian restaurants, but it's gender
neutral. Totally different if I was in a fancy French restaurant
world, then I probably would have hit a point where I couldn't
get much past it. All the restaurants I had worked for were
more like mom-and-pop, smaller restaurants; the owners still
worked, they're very involved, and so how far can you go? And
[there are] only so many raises you can get before it becomes
ludicrous. So at that point I really wanted my own restaurant. I
didn't really want to work for other people anymore."

—*Amanda Cohen*

"My whole goal back then was 'I'm going to go out there and I'm
going to make it, and then I'm going to get three stars, and then
I want to get four stars.' To this day, there's only one female
pastry chef [who] ever got four stars in New York City, and that
was Lisa Hershey at Chanterelle,[163] and she's not in the business anymore . . . And I was told a while ago, which affected
everything . . . We were out one night and there were two—
I'm not going to mention who they were . . . but there were

---

[163] On August 11, 2009, the *New York Times'* Frank Bruni, in his restaurant review of the place, gave Eleven
Madison Park four stars, which might mean that Lisa Hershey is no longer the lone lady pastry chef to own this
achievement. Sort of. At the time of Bruni's write-up, Angela Pinkerton was working alongside the restaurant's
executive chef, Daniel Humm, although he was in charge of both the savory and dessert menus. In 2010,
she was promoted, officially, to executive pastry chef and allowed to run the sweet show. I don't know where
Carlucci-Rodriguez would come down on this. Does it count? Can Pinkerton claim the victory?

two gentleman there—owners of four-star restaurants, and we were talking, and they told me straight out, 'Never going to happen. You're a woman and it's just never going to happen.' . . . [One of those gentleman, his restaurant] it's still open; it's successful. He's no longer with us, but, it's open and it's going on and it still goes on. Right there, I had the attitude, because that's just me, I was like, 'Fuck it. Fuck you and your four stars.' And I went on to get three stars three times and then when that was over, I was just like hanging in the air, like, I have to rethink my goal."

—*Heather Carlucci-Rodriguez*

"I miss it [The Harrison, where she was the executive chef] . . . Yeah, it was a ceiling and what happened was Steven [Eckler, managing partner] and Jimmy [Bradley, owner] were doing the new project . . . They had obviously promised Bill [McDaniel, executive chef and partner] from the Red Cat that opportunity; and Bill's a partner with them, he'd been with them for six years, and so that made sense. But what would then happen to me? What would be my opportunity? And, you know, I'm not afraid to say, 'I've done well for your restaurant and good things have come because of all this hard work and this great restaurant, so what happens to me now?' Like, 'We're a team, and go Harrison!' And you know, there was nothing offered."

—*Amanda Freitag*

"I'm certain there is [a glass ceiling]. I don't have personal experience of it, and I think it all comes from if you're working for somebody else as opposed to working for yourself. You kind of get to make the rules as you go, in a way, if you own a business."

—*Elizabeth Belkind*

"It's really the dumbest business you could ever go into. I mean, it's so much work—so little return, so much overhead. What you're selling is perishable, and it perishes before you can get rid of it a lot of the time, so you're essentially throwing cash in the trash can. People have had to branch out . . . When you see chefs opening second and third restaurants it's 'cause they kind of have to . . . [because] even if you're doing well as a small-restaurant owner, you're not making a lot of money. If you have forty seats or less, it's really hard to make money, unless you're doing volume . . . I don't want to work for anyone else, and this is what I love, but I'm at the point where—it's been almost six years—I'm still mopping the floors a lot of nights. If I send someone home, I'm not sitting around with a headset on and clipboard, I'm getting burned and working my ass off and sweating—and this [Dinette] is a great place, and people talk about it a lot. I feel successful, and it's still really hard. So I'm thinking that I have to either open another place, [or] maybe put a little cookbook out—so that's the ceiling, where I'm at right now."

—*Melissa Nyffeler*

"There are plenty of females out there cooking. Is the money going to them?[164] And I don't mean salary. I mean seed money. That brings us to an even bigger question, which is, just in general, about females and start-ups and female business leaders . . . Are people who are investing in restaurants, not chef-owned restaurants perhaps, but other restaurants, do they have the confidence to put a female in that position? For me, it all goes back to the money."

—*Gina DePalma*

---

[164] For answers to DePalma's question and others related to opening your own joint, turn the page. To exit this program, close the book.

CHAPTER 6

Owning It

The following set of guidelines contains advice, admonishments, and alternatives for setting up your own shop (you know, a restaurant) from those who've done it.

1. YOU HAVE NO IDEA WHAT YOU'RE GETTING INTO, AND YOU MIGHT BE BETTER OFF THAT WAY.

"The more you think you know, the less you know," says Mindy Segal. However, the more you know, the less inclined you might feel to undertake the endeavor. Consistently, the women who threw themselves into the task with short-depth tunnel vision had the "easiest" (so relative, that is) time of it. When Renee Erickson, who has endured four launches, looks back on that innocent period when everything was a first, it's with quasi-fondness. "I, for sure, feel lucky that I had the opportunity and took it . . . to buy a restaurant when [you're] twenty-five—I don't know if it was the smartest," she muses. "I'm glad I did, but my life kind of came to a screeching halt for five years."

Mary Sue Milliken recalls the madness that she and Susan Feniger faced when they took on their first major establishment.[165] "When we opened City Restaurant, it was a 125-seat restaurant, and neither of us had ever opened a full-service restaurant in our lives. We'd never worked for anyone through an opening. You know, restaurants weren't opening every five minutes like they are now. That opening almost killed me. [Laughs.] We did not know what we were doing. We had like three days in the kitchen and we opened . . . Susan, at one point, almost fainted on the line. We didn't go home for a week . . . It was

---

[165] To get you sorted on the Feniger-Milliken time line, I should tell you that before City Restaurant, their initial foray was the eensy City Café, where, because there was no stove in the kitchen—only a hot plate—they cooked on two hibachi grills in the parking lot out back.

really excruciatingly difficult—worth every minute, but nobody would do that now. There's a whole bank of knowledge around how to open a restaurant, what to do, there are books about it . . . But something about the naïveté is really also very energizing. If I hadn't been twenty-three when we opened City Café and twenty-six when we opened City Restaurant, I might have been more cautious . . . I wouldn't have had as much passion . . . So I think those things served us well."

Although Milliken believes launching a restaurant would be a lot easier today, Melissa Perello, who planted forty-seven-seat Frances in San Francisco's Castro neighborhood at the tail end of 2009, might disagree. "It was probably one of the most gratifying experiences of my life but also probably one of the most torturous, especially the first six to eight months. Opening and operating is just so, um, so exhausting. It just sucks every last bit of energy out of you. When we opened Frances, I had no idea what to anticipate—what to expect—and I never expected it to be quite as busy as it ended up being . . . There was just so much that came into play—making sure we had everything we needed, from equipment in the kitchen to plates and glassware and heaters in the dining rooms . . . things like how we were going to take reservations."

2. MAKE IT PERSONAL.

Yes, listen to what "they" say, but trust your gut. When Feniger and Milliken opened the first of what would be, thirty years later, a fleet of L.A. eateries (plus a Vegas satellite), there was no formal strategizing, concept honing, or heeding of dining trends; there was only what they craved. In her description of how it all began, Feniger mentions the kind of details that make your mouth water and your tummy wish the pair's original, ramshackle City Café still existed.

"There was no vision, it was, 'I wanna do food that I love to eat,' which was really country French food. With all my training, the food I was most drawn to were things like *brandade* of salmon, confit of duck, cassoulet, pot-au-feu, those sorts of things—not the beurre blanc, not the foie gras. Mary Sue and I being from the Midwest, we were cheap, so when people were doing veal chops and rack of lamb, we were doing things like getting whole baby lambs, cleaning them completely and using every single part of 'em . . . We never did a veal chop, but we took veal breast and stuffed it with a duxelles of veal and braised it. That sort of thing . . .

"We started doing country French food, and then I took my first trip to India. I came back and we put on [the menu] this incredible vegetable plate, back in '81, that had a dal, a *biryani*, a curry, and then all sorts of sweet and sour vegetables, or *raita* [or a] chutney—back then, that's when vegetarian plates were steamed vegetables, if you could even find that. So then, Mary Sue took her first trip to Thailand, and when she came back we put Chinese sausage salad on the menu and Thai red curry . . . We weren't thinking about . . . 'Is it okay to have [cassoulet] side by side with red curry duck?' We just didn't think about that . . . We weren't doing fusion; we just had things we loved to eat on the menu.

"And then, when we decided to open up the big restaurant and make it City Restaurant, we had to figure out what to do with the little one, City Café . . . We thought, 'Well, we're either going to do a noodle shop or we're going to do a taco stand. And it was Mary Sue and myself and one kid in the kitchen at that point, 'cause it was so small—you know, the bathroom for the customers was in the kitchen. So we took our first trip to his [the kid in the kitchen's] house; we stayed with his family in Mexico City. We explored the city with his mom, going to markets, eating *huaraches* and gorditas. We'd bring back all these ingredients to the house, and she would walk us through all of it, and we would cook all day with her . . . And then we drove around in a Volkswagen Bug and traveled all over Mexico . . . and when we came back . . . we had our notebook filled with all the little stuff."

And so Border Grill, of which there are now three (along with a to-go kiosk and truck), came into the world. Leap ahead to 2009, and Feniger decides to get something else started—a canteen called Street. When I asked her if she were starting on this restaurateuring journey now, would she do it the same or would she be more measured or structured in her approach, this is what she told me: "I think we would do it the same. Street's a perfect example. Kajsa, who's my partner—Kajsa Alger, executive chef—and I basically just said, 'Okay, what do we love to eat? Let's think, you know, about ethnically influenced food. What are some of the street food dishes?' I thought about my travels to India, to Turkey, to Israel, her travels, and we just started playing around with the food and started doing dishes and going out to Koreatown and to Little Saigon and tasting dishes . . . That's what we did. It wasn't any more thought through than that."

When chef Suzanne Goin and Caroline Styne drafted the story of their first restaurant, Lucques (est. 1998) in Los Angeles, "I really wanted to create a place I wanted to go to," the former reminisces. "I wanted to be able to cook my food, have an environment that felt warm and comfortable but also felt chic and special. Lucques is a very personal place—reflective of what we want and how we want to feel when we go out . . . When we opened, we had to tell managers to be welcoming . . . it was that era of snotty anorexic hostesses . . . I just wanted to cook what I wanted to cook, without being boxed in by it needing to be Italian or French." By adhering to their personal tastes and preferences, they broke the mold and put L.A. dining on friendlier, more inviting footing. Their stories (all three of them, and a quick-service café too[166]), once composed, have proceeded to direct culinary traffic in Southern California.

Their second scheme, A.O.C., was, to Goin and Styne, a logical outgrowth of a specific audience that had emerged at Lucques. "The bar developed its own culture and clientele—the crowd was more relaxed and casual. People would have cocktails and snack from the menu. At some point, they stopped wanting to sit in the dining room and preferred the bar. So A.O.C. came out of that," Goin explains. When they

---

[166] There's The Larder at Tavern, an annex of the latter restaurant in Brentwood, and The Larder at Maple Drive, a freestanding outpost in Beverly Hills; good to know, should you find yourself feeling peckish while driving through town.

introduced it, the hybrid wine-food bar was an unknown entity in that city. This, too, was a novelty derived from the chef's predilection. "Having a wine bar morphed with a food bar—as a chef, I love traditional wine bars, but I wanted more—that's where the idea came from . . . It's a full-service restaurant with the heart and soul of a wine bar . . . We were worried people wouldn't get it. Then, it wasn't a known thing; now, it's normal," she says. Echoing Feniger and Milliken, Goin went on a trip to Spain to shape her menu. She could explore the flavors she had just sampled and combine them with others that appealed to her, such as those of Portugal and North Africa. There was no market research conducted, no consciousness of a "platform" being built. One investor asked them about their demographic and, as Goin amusingly recalls, "we were totally clueless about it . . . we were like kids breaking out. That's how we like to do things. It's more from the gut or the heart than from research and demographics."

3. BE AWARE THAT ALL RESPONSIBILITY FALLS ON YOU (NO PRESSURE).

Opening a restaurant "really preys on your fears and weaknesses," cautions Johanna Ware, who, when we talked, was about to quit her day job as the sous chef of Cathy Whims's Nostrana to make her own proprietary mark with Smallwares in Portland, Oregon. "No matter what I'm doing in the business, I'm always the one who wakes up at 4 a.m. thinking about it . . . Once you take on a managerial role, it's never-ending."

One of the things that a new owner often grapples with—in addition to insomnia—is dealing with the front of the house. Some hired executive chefs have an active role in guiding that section, but many don't. It's a whole new bag of tricks. If the two halves of your whole aren't in sync, that will be reflected in the dining experience. If your food is scrumptious, but the service is crap, people won't come back. Budgeting might also prove difficult. There's a wider field of vision, and unlike your days supervising the back of the house in someone else's joint, when the keys are yours, so are the ledgers, all of them.

Amanda Cohen is a self-taught budget master. She acquired the skill OTJ,[167] taking it upon herself to do so as the curious head chef of a restaurant that never made money. First off, the place was overstaffed, so Cohen sat down with her employers, the owners, and figured out who could go. Then she took to balancing the books herself. "I really started to look through the numbers," she says, "and I started doing payroll, which most chefs hand off to their managers, and I started looking at the budgets and how it was all working." After that, at future jobs, she did the same. When potential investors in a new venue she was involved in asked her to draft a budget, she did it and, in the process, learned how to use Excel.

That new venture didn't pan out, but the task the investors assigned her—it was, in its way, her lucky break. It taught her the following, which any aspiring chef-owner (or owner, period) in this industry needs to know. Ready? "You should never open a restaurant." Got it? In case you didn't: "There is no way restaurants can make money; I mean, this is crazy. More people thinking of opening a restaurant should just sit down with a spreadsheet and look at it. When you do, you'll be like, 'Okay, but my staffing costs, my food costs, and insurance and rent,' and all this comes into play. 'There is no way.' " Still, Cohen realized that, with her newly found superpowers (budget-busting and mastery of the computerized systems for that procedure), she just might beat the odds. And so she has at her modest vegetable mecca, Dirt Candy on East Ninth Street in Manhattan, which opened four years ago. If equations bore you, skip the next paragraph.

"In a vegetarian restaurant, typically you get thirty to forty people a night and you're doing really well," Cohen explains. "So I was like, 'Okay, I need to make a restaurant where that's the highest number of seats I can do.' So then we started looking for really small places. This place [Dirt Candy] seats between eighteen and twenty-one in one seating, and I thought, 'Okay, if I do two full turns, then that's forty people

[167] See footnote 80, page 71, and let's not speak of this again.

and that's a really successful restaurant, and that's what I have to look at.' There wasn't this huge optimism on my part. I was more like, 'Let's take the worst-case scenario and go from there,' which allowed us to be really successful. Luckily, we do three full turns a night now."

4. YOU NEED MONEY.

Keeping track of the cash and knowing how to allot it is crucial, which, of course, presupposes that you've got it in the first place. If you don't have enough of your own (first-time proprietors are usually lacking here), you'll have to secure some, which is not easy for most chefs and, many would argue, even harder for the females of the group.

Unable to rely solely on her assets when she created Chapel Hill's Lantern, Andrea Reusing had to explore external fonts of tender. Here are her thoughts on the process:

"It's so hard to get financial backing to open a restaurant, period. Some banks even require you to show you have a separate stream of income that would pay the rent . . . like, just assume you're not ever going to make any money . . . You have to be a lawyer that has a full-time job to open this restaurant because you have to show you're going to be able to pay the thirty grand a year. I had one amazing meeting with a banker once who—when I told him I was thinking about opening a second restaurant, and buying space for it—asked me how I could open another restaurant when I had two kids. That's how he opened the meeting. I'm in a small community and have a very busy restaurant. I'm known to be somebody who's had a restaurant for ten years, so you'd think if anyone [were] going to get money for another restaurant, it would have been me. But I could tell from our conversation that I probably wasn't getting any money from that guy. That was a chilling moment for me. You can go through your life for a pretty long time without experiencing that kind of sexism, but when it happens, it's surprising."

When she opened Lantern, her first and (still) only restaurant, she'd bypassed the banks and went into business with her younger brother. It was a setup she describes as "nice, for a while, until it was not." She explains: "My father had this kind of vested interest in us being partners; he thought it'd be a lot easier for me . . . [He] naturally wanted me to have a partner and my brother to have a partner and for us to be able to support each other in doing this thing that we like to do together, and that made a lot of sense [to him]. I don't think it really made sense for either one of us in a lot of ways, because we're siblings, and so there was a lot of tension there. [My brother] left the restaurant a couple of years ago, but we're good friends now. When we first opened, people often assumed that he was the chef; people assumed that he was in charge; people would direct things to him, from purveyors to customers to certain male staff—even though it was made pretty clear that I was the chef."

A. ASKING FOR IT

i. Begging at the Bank

When she was building Mindy's Hot Chocolate, Mindy Segal skipped the bank because she'd "never opened a business before and had no track record." If she wants to expand, though, she might consider consulting a loan officer. (I'd recommend she bring a bag or two of her cocoa, with a package of homemade marshmallows on the side.) Banks appear less reluctant to dispense dough to second-time owners, especially those who show they run a viable operation. Whether you're a man or woman doesn't seem to matter much in this case. In San Francisco, when Nancy Oakes embarked on Prospect, her follow-up to Boulevard, "We got a loan down there [Prospect], but it was based on the achievements of all of us here [Boulevard] and our seventeen-year track record." When she says "we," Oakes is referring to Pam Mazzola and Kathy King. The three opened Prospect as partners and, to that end, they borrowed three million dollars from the Small Business Association and raised nearly the same amount from investors. Securing the SBA financing, which is done through a bank, was the easy part because, Oakes notes, "the office was all women, and they were foodies." Winning investors was tougher. "I never want to do it again," Oakes said, followed by "ugh." She was spared that task at Boulevard, because Pat Kuleto[168] took care of the fund wrangling. "I have to say," she reflects now, wiser for having gone through the process herself, "that I appreciated Pat's ability to raise the amount of money that he has over the years to open all the restaurants that he has . . . He did it with 100 percent investor money in all of them. He never went to a bank. So I really appreciated his chutzpah." Ah, the chutzpah. Would that it were bottled.

ii. Courting Investors

Amanda Cohen gave up on getting bank money for Dirt Candy before trying because she didn't know where to begin. She turned to private investors, which wasn't easy either. Her gender was a deal-breaker exacerbated by her vegetal mission. "There's a double-edged sword here. I am a vegetarian vegetable cook, which was not the most popular thing at the time." What was popular back then in the aughts? "Really, like, macho cooking." She elaborates, "You look at it, it's about barbecue and pork belly and all this, like 'Let's butcher!' It doesn't seem very female-friendly, although [there are] great female barbecue cooks; it's just not what springs to mind."

Cohen figures could-be shareholders see it like this: "A man's going to run this kitchen better; a man's going to be able to organize it better; he's going to have a better sense of the financials. [He's] going to be able to multitask better than a woman, who he thinks is going to cry." Despite providing seed money, Dirt Candy's backers didn't give her any reason to doubt her conjecture. "Even my investors were like, 'Well, you know, if we didn't know you, we probably wouldn't have invested in a woman.' And some of those [investors] are my family . . . Men in kitchens seem more reliable. You see women at home in the kitchen and you see the people who are in charge in [restaurant] kitchens are white men."

---

[168] Oakes's business partner at Boulevard.

One way to get around this roadblock would be to follow Phoenix chef Charleen Badman's lead. When campaigning for cash to get her joint FnB[169] off the ground, she wasn't discriminated against because of her sex, but that's because, she suspects, she hit up her own kind. It makes feel-good sense, the idea that women would support each other in entrepreneurial endeavors. But regardless of who your target investors are, you've still got to step up and put your hand out.

Cohen contends that one of the reasons men continue to monopolize the position of kitchen leader and why people are, if not more reluctant to give women the funding they seek, then at least more responsive to men in search of the same support, is that the boys are better at asking for it. It all goes back to confidence. "You're just not taught to have the balls to go out and be like, 'Give me money. I can do this.' And I do think women, in general, are shyer, and I think we don't take as many chances. It's hard to ask people to take a chance on you. And I think men are more willing to screw up. 'Yeah, okay, I'm going to lose your money; I don't care.'"

Alex Raij, the chef and co-owner of Spanish-inflected treasures Txikito, El Quinto Pino, and La Vara in New York City, believes this reluctance to request capital holds back chefs of all stripes, pink or blue. "That's what's really hard for people to wrap their head around— be they women or men—especially cooks," she says. "I think all cooks, including men and women, are looking for approval, and food is currency and love and everything you get back. I think it's really hard for people like us to ask for money. We also feel like we aren't doing things that are important enough to be valued by other people. But once you learn to ask for money once, you can ask for money [again]."

Goin agrees that practice helps, although petitioning for greenbacks isn't her forte. "I am horrible at it. That was part of the problem; we were so scared to ask people. It was people who asked me." She and

[169] A year after our interview, I learned, with FnB going strong, she and her business partner, Pavle Milic, were about to launch a triple-threat concept. Housed in one space, there's a gourmet neighborhood grocery, the Bodega; AZ Wine Merchants (I think you know what's sold there); and a wine bar at which to sip the stuff.

Styne had a particularly tough time with their first place, Lucques. After raising the initial $450,000 from family and friends, they received a line of credit for the rest. For Goin, the impasse was her own timidity. When she was able to muster the courage, she was usually pleasantly surprised by the results. "I'd get my confidence up and ask somebody . . . One man I grew up with, who lived four houses down . . . he invested and brought in three lawyers from his firm. Twenty-five percent—approximately—of that money was raised by him." When she recounts this, you can still hear the genuine, surprised delight in her voice. With momentum behind them and the coinciding flush economy, their second project, A.O.C. (est. 2002), was a breeze by comparison—people had Lucques as a familiar, booming reference point. By 2007, when they were cooking up Brentwood's Tavern, they actually "ended up turning people away," Goin says. This time the bankrollers were lining up at the door. "We were better at selling when it came to Tavern," observes Goin. "For example, we did an event at a filmmaker's house and served our food, brought our designer. We raised over one million [dollars] in shares in that one night."

A final note: When you meet with potential backers willing to give you a listen, make sure you're ready, that you've done your homework. Amanda Freitag received her crash course during a meeting with a possible supporter. "I talked to some crazy high-end hedge fund guy immediately after I left the Harrison, and I wasn't ready for it. He was like, 'What's your brand? Where's your business plan?' You know, all of those things somebody like that needs before they give you a whole bunch of money, obviously . . . unless they know you." Even when they're acquainted with you, they might want to know what you've got cooking.

iii. Family Funding

No one knows you as well as your kin. That's probably why we're always cautioned against signing on to business ventures with our relations.

There is plenty of advice out there advising you not to do it. After struggling to run a restaurant with her brother, Andrea Reusing could easily dissuade you from attempting the same. Then again, there are chefs like Mindy Segal. She says she "wouldn't be in business today if it weren't for [her] parents," who helped her raise the money—a lot of her investors are family members—and have guided her throughout the entire development process.

Some mamas and papas invest their dollars in an offspring's cause; others invest their dollars and dictate how the cash should be spent. "Who better to manage your finances than your mom?" asks Jessica Boncutter. I can think of a whole lot of alternatives, but for Boncutter, it's a perfect fit. "My mom is a businesswoman," she explains, "and is an excellent partner. We get along great; she's shrewd; she's great with money . . . and she is the last person who would ever steal from me . . . I was a little nervous in the beginning, like, 'Oh my God, I'm going to partner up with my mom. Am I crazy?' She's taught me so much about the business side of it. I'm really, really fortunate to have a role model like her."

B. SPONSORING YOURSELF

Marcie Turney and her longtime girlfriend Valerie Safran have quietly built a mini kingdom on South Thirteenth Street in Philly. They're responsible for seven businesses (there's a home furnishing shop, three restaurants, a gourmet grocery, and a jewelry boutique housing their line of artisanal chocolate) and more than one hundred employees. Aside from taking out an SBA loan and borrowing $50,000 from their enterprising landlord, Tony Goldman, a locally known neighborhood developer, for their first eatery, Lolita (a small Mexican BYO), they've bootstrapped their other ventures. They've also managed to repay Goldman in full, as well as their SBA debt. "We've done this our own way," Turney tells me, laying out their modus operandi for me. "We don't come from money . . . we've just worked our asses off. . . . Val is great on budgeting. . . . We have no investors and not a cent of debt . . . We make some money, save it, and then invest it in the next project. With guys, it's about being hot right now and getting everything you can while you're hot. But we ask ourselves the question, 'Where will we be in a few years?' "

5. CO-OWNERSHIP CAN BE A BEAUTIFUL THING.

A. DO IT WITH ANOTHER CHEF

As you've already no doubt deduced, Angelenos Susan Feniger and Mary Sue Milliken are model citizens of joint restaurant custody. You could say they wrote the book on efficient chef-owner alliances, except that someone else beat them to the punch. Former Disney CEO Michael Eisner recently published a tome called *Working Together: Why Great Partnerships Succeed*, for which Feniger and Milliken's union provides one of his ten case studies.[170] These ladies are evidence that two chefs (and friends) can work together brilliantly. What resonates in Eisner's portrait is the ease with which the duo gets along; Susan is all drive and fiery, often unharnessed energy, while Mary Sue craves structure and reigns as the prevailing cooler head. They are equally matched in their levels of industriousness. They also have an ability to work individually on separate projects without encroaching on what they've built together; consider Milliken's role raising her three kids or Feniger's launch of her groundbreaking restaurant Street.[171]

---

[170] Michael D. Eisner, *Working Together: Why Great Partnerships Succeed* (New York: Harper Collins, 2010), 198–219. At the end of 2011, Eisner went on to sell his concept for a TV comedy project based on Feniger and Milliken's preliminary exploits to ABC.

[171] Everything needs to stop for a second so that I can tell you about the *kaya* toast. Many of you might already know what I'm speaking of because you watched the second season of *Top Chef Masters*, and you saw Susan Feniger make the dish for a whole slew of people and then get sent home because the judges, while finding it undeniably delicious, felt it was somehow not sophisticated enough to be called Master-worthy. This is bollocks. I demand a recount. I interviewed Feniger at Street, home of this *kaya* toast, and the chef kept asking me if I wanted anything to eat. Now, I know what you're thinking. *What kind of idiot passes up such offers?* This idiot. I learned that it's impossible to do your job (if your job entails taking notes, asking questions, listening to responses, following up with more queries, and steering the conversation) while distracted by a plate of food (the better that food, the greater the distraction). I'd order a coffee and forget about it until, at the end of the interview, I'd spy it next to me, full to the brim and lukewarm, at best. Also, though, my ethics policies (and those of many of the publications for which I've written or currently write) dictate that I do not accept comped (that's pro-talk for "free") meals. Feniger insisted I try just one thing and that it be the *kaya* toast. I capitulated,

Up north from the land of Feniger and Milliken, San Francisco chef-owner Nancy Oakes implements a related brand of job sharing with a different ownership structure. Yes, she's the one who opened Boulevard in 1993 with restaurateur Pat Kuleto and, seventeen years later, added Prospect to her holdings—this time, with two partners who were part of the original Boulevard team, GM (General Manager) Kathy King and chef Pam Mazzola. Mazzola, the employee, and Oakes, the boss, split the responsibilities for overseeing Boulevard down the middle so that they could each have a life. It's an appealing and functional template, especially for anyone who wants to build a career as a chef and be a present parent. Coincidentally, like the Feniger-Milliken collaboration, Mazzola and Oakes's arrangement consists of one chef who has children (the former has three) and one who doesn't. They met at L'Avenue, Oakes's initial restaurant, a significantly smaller fifty-seater.[172] Mazzola's first child was nine months old when Oakes asked her to come on board at fledgling Boulevard. Mazzola ran the restaurant on Oakes's evenings off, and they toiled together a few nights a week. "So we've worked together for twenty-three years," Mazzola adds it up and goes on to describe their alliance:

"I really have to thank Nancy for enabling me to be one of the really few women to stay in the business and raise a family . . . It's also allowed her to maintain a relationship and not work quite so hard. But it's not always easy. Sometimes it's hard always getting someone else's opinion. Sometimes *you* just want to make the decision. Partnerships

but under the impression that I could take the vittles to go. That way, I could focus on her and our chat, and then, on the way to my next meeting (which, coincidentally, was with Mary Sue Milliken over at her and Feniger's Border Grill on South Figueroa), gleefully inhale my snack. The *kaya* toast waits for no woman; it does not travel. As our interview was winding down, a dish was placed before me. There was on that plate a perfectly fried egg, sunny-side up, about to burst. (For the record, being able to make hundreds of these, to order, which is what Feniger had to do on that fateful *Top Chef Masters* challenge, and to get each egg just so, which she did, is not for amateurs. It's a test of precision and consistency.) Dark, syrupy soy sauce had been drizzled over it. There was also a piece of toast slathered with a thick coconut jam. If I lived in Singapore, this would be my daily afternoon snack; that's where this edible *kaya* was born. But I don't, and I realized, as soon as I'd taken a bite of this sugary, salty, gooey, fatty, crunchy miracle, that my time with it was limited. I was already running late, and, no, I couldn't take it with me. I managed to get three bites in. That is all. Parting was such sweet sorrow. I still pine for that unfinished masterpiece and expect to get closure on my next visit to Los Angeles, when I will surely go to Street and eat one of these puppies in its entirety. The end.

[172] To give you a sense of proportion, Boulevard's dining room seats at least 130.

frequently work because somebody's in the front of the house and somebody's in the back of the house, but we not only share the same role, we also have a lot of the same sensibilities about food. On the other hand, that's what's made us successful . . . We listen to and respect the other person, and realize that sometimes you just need to go with the other's instinct. It's really a matter of trust; I know Nancy always has the best interest for me and the restaurant in mind, often taking unselfish positions to do so."

I asked Mazzola whether the transition she has made with their new venture, Prospect—acting as an operating partner instead of an employee—has altered their relationship. She acknowledged that it has, though there doesn't seem to be a downside. "It's a little bit different. She hasn't had a vocal partner while she's had Boulevard. If you look at what a partner is or you evaluate ownership, it's different. Being an owner is different than being a co-chef." All in all, Mazzola's heartily in favor of the team-up: "I think having a partner is a great thing," she says.

B. DO IT WITH A MANAGERIAL COUNTERPART

Traci Des Jardins also gained her independence with the help of Pat Kuleto, who became the kick-starter for her Jardinière, which recently turned twenty-five. Des Jardins, while enjoying her role at the time as top culinary dog at Rubicon,[173] wanted her own place, but was clueless as to how to make it happen. That was when, like magic, Kuleto showed up to guide her. He'd drafted the business plan, gathered the investors, et voilà. Des Jardins would be a coholder, and stand as the Talent portion of the enterprise. She could play to her strengths and

---

[173] Whoa, how many careers did this iconic place catapult? Countless. In 1994, New York heavy Drew Nieporent (he's the same restaurateur who opened Nobu, in Manhattan's Tribeca a few months later) and a Master Sommelier by the name of Larry Stone opened Rubicon. The following year, its chef, Traci Des Jardins, picked up the James Beard Rising Star medal. While wowing diners with her food, she also managed to hire those who would also make names for themselves—Elizabeth Falkner, whom you've already met, is an excellent example; Chris Cosentino, the country's overlord of offal is another (his eatery Incanto, also in San Francisco, comes highly recommended, by yours truly; and if you think you might like charcuterie even a little, and you don't try the cured delectables from his *salumeria* Boccalone, you're mad). Rubicon is *no más*. It closed its doors in 2008. Tyler Florence took over the lease. Shame, as the Aussies say.

spare herself a lot of the labor pains that come when, overnight, you are obliged to master budgeting and fund-raising on top of everything else you are already being overwhelmed by. The plan gave Des Jardins time to gradually hone those beyond-the-kitchen skills, which she did. Once she was comfortable running the business side of Jardinière, she was able to build her next venture, a Mexican cocina named Mijita, from the ground up.

C. DO IT WITH A SPOUSE[174]

Restaurants are a risky proposition to begin with; gambling with one's home life and family structure on top of that is—many might say—greatly upping the ante. For some, opening restaurants together has strengthened the nuptial bond and uncertain professional enterprise; for others, it has led to strife, even divorce.

"To me, everything I've done that's been successful has been a collaboration." That would be L.A.'s Nancy Silverton. In 2006, she signed on to helm Mozza with the legendary restaurateur-chef (respectively) team of Joe Bastianich and Mario Batali.[175] Prior to that auspicious arrangement, in 1989, she founded and operated the restaurant Campanile with her (at the time) husband, chef Mark Peel, and also built La Brea Bakery.[176] Theirs was a business adventure that ended in the dissolution of both their marital and professional associations, though this hasn't necessarily soured her on future restaurant partnerships, even of the spousal variety. In fact, "I think it could be an ideal situation, because it's a way of sharing a life with somebody," she observes.

---

[174] The term *spouse* applies for same-sex couples that consider themselves hitched, even if they're not legally allowed to tie the knot. And the same holds true for significant others who take their relationship seriously—it's not for me to say who counts and who doesn't.

[175] Silverton wouldn't let me leave the Mozza premises without singing the blues. Okay, not that, but she urged me to take something for the road and presented me with the spongiest, moistest, most wondrously doughy and crisp-topped focaccia you've never had—there was one studded with sage and caramelized onions, one with roasted red peppers and chiles, and another, simple as could be, with olive and rosemary. When I die, the afterlife issue is unclear, but I hope, wherever I'm left, they're serving some of this.

[176] Silverton and her partners unloaded La Brea Bakery (it comprises a retail and industrial baking entity) for multimillions in 2001; when she and Peel divorced, Silverton sold her interest in Campanile.

When Atlanta's Anne Quatrano and Clifford Harrison gave birth to their first spot, the acclaimed Bacchanalia, they "worked really intimately together," Quatrano recounts. This was not a scenario unfamiliar to either of the two; they met at culinary school in San Francisco and remained attached—in the galley and beyond—from there on out. They were hired as a chef team, a package deal. When they unleashed Bacchanalia on the world, Quatrano says, "for the first seven or eight years at the restaurant, it was the two of us in the kitchen, perhaps with one or two others." But once they conceived their second property, Floataway Café, she took up professional residence over there and he stayed anchored to the first spot. Six eateries later, their responsibilities are greater and have developed in different directions. "He's more involved with the growing of food now, tasting the wine . . . He does the beverage programs and oversees all the protein, which means foraging for meats and seafood," she explains. "Now we have a system—we try to stay in separate places most of the time." While they've got that nailed down, Quatrano admits, "I don't think we're great at separating the restaurants from the rest of our lives . . . I try harder at it but I don't try hard enough, which means that a good amount of time at home is spent talking about [work] . . . Sometimes, we'll get home and he'll start talking about work and I'll say, 'Please, can we not talk about that now?' and then he'll say, 'Okay, I'll e-mail you.'"

Michelle Bernstein admits that teaming up with her husband, David Martinez, has "made my marriage, but it's also the thing that could make me lose it." She stresses the importance of respecting the marital relationship, of "remembering we're together not because of work . . . making sure we have date nights." Keeping their on-the-job rapport removed from their at-home dynamic is something she is mindful of at all times. "I'm aware of the need for daily balance, which is not easy . . . I love working with David and I can't imagine it [any other way]." At her Miami restaurants Michy's, Sra. Martinez, and Crumb on Parchment, Bernstein's the authority on food matters, while copilot

Martinez, an industry pro, has a strong hand in staffing and commands the wine and beverage agendas. She knows it's not exactly common to "find a man who would back me in my career and would stand behind me to make me greater . . . for the first few years, I know people called him David Bernstein instead of David Martinez . . . That is a test of ego."

Naomi Pomeroy tried the "& husband" experiment, followed by the "& boyfriend" experiment, and can say with authority that she's best when she leaves the "plus one" out of the professional equation. At Beast, the Portland, Oregon, eatery from which she has arisen from the ashes of failed culinary ventures and romantic relationships, she finally understands what it's like to be in charge, and her career has soared. She describes that evolution with brave openness:

"I am going to be straight-up honest: The way I've come to everything I've gotten in this business has been that I've had these boyfriends who really wanted to exploit my cooking talents. They saw my skill and my ability and realized that there was something in it for them . . . I'm not being a hater in saying that—they also had something that I needed . . . With my husband, he is really good at promoting stuff and he's supergood at creating, you know, curating experiences for people, and that's his real strength. But he needed a product that he could sell, and that was my product.[177]

"And then, the next thing that happened was that, after that all imploded,[178] I needed a man to sort of, like, pick me up for a second . . . I just needed some comfort and there was somebody there . . . He [her new beau] saw that I was totally busted and he knew that I didn't have any work in front of me, and he got the deal on this space [that would become Beast] . . . And so, he designed the interior and said, 'Do you want to be the chef there? Because you don't have a job right now.' And I said, 'Sure.' " Taken on its own, that act—his suggesting she run the

---

[177] In case you forgot (it was noted back in chapter 2), Pomeroy and her now ex-husband started with a catering company (followed by an underground supper club), and then launched three eateries. It didn't end well—the personal or professional endeavors. Pomeroy told me she was left to inform all twenty-two of the couple's investors that their money had been lost. And, yes, there was the divorce, too, with a child to account for.

[178] Re: implosion, see previous footnote.

restaurant—is responsible for relaunching Pomeroy's career and teaching her that she could operate independently of a romantic interest. It became clear to her that her designing boyfriend wasn't interested in contributing to the place once he had spiffed it up. She was doing all the work and, even though she might have felt frustrated for the lack of support, she was coping just fine without a wingman. Once she ascertained how much she could accomplish by herself, she decided to take ownership—of her life and her restaurant. She "started making a lot of executive decisions without asking" and, finally, after changing the locks, told him she was buying him out. "That's how that went . . . It was time."

Because of her blistering trial by fire—the roller coaster of professional success and failure plus domestic upheaval and heartbreak—Pomeroy discerned what she wanted to do and, more important, got it done. "I've earned my own respect now, you know, and the respect of others, which isn't nearly as important to me as it used to be. Ultimately, I've realized it's really a solo journey . . . it has everything to do with trusting yourself." If anything, going it alone granted her more recognition and esteem than functioning in tandem with a lesser half ever had.

6. EMPIRE-BUILDING

"The only thing that changes once you own multiple restaurants, you're not part of the kitchen anymore, it's more about the paperwork and getting the business side done," says Avec's Koren Grieveson. That's not an insignificant shift.

A. ALL THOSE IN FAVOR OF THE MOTION . . .

If, like Denver chef Jennifer Jasinski, the proprietor of three culinary pit stops, your primary motivation is to support your crew, then you find that the only way to give them promotions is to have another kitchen. "Basically, I think of myself as creating jobs for the people around me." When she builds a new venue, it's "for them; I want to move people up, but when they're ready." Their readiness dictates hers.

David "The Momofuku Messiah" Chang's perspective on setting up multiple camps resonated with Amanda Cohen. "People, like David Chang, are able to open lots of different restaurants and do a great job. In an interview, he said [her words], 'You know, to make a financially successful operation, I had to open more restaurants.' I liked the way he looked at that. He was like, 'I want to give health care to my employees, but I couldn't do that just at Noodle Bar; I had to be able to open other restaurants so I could have enough people on staff to make it worth all our whiles to get things like health care.'"

The initial impetus to go forth and multiply for Feniger and Milliken was not power-hungry ambition. They simply had a deficit of room combined with a surfeit of ideas. Each time they started bursting out of a space's seams, they'd look for a larger one and convert the original into whatever excited them at that moment. The "bug to open more [restaurants] hit in 1997 and '98," Milliken says. That's when the pair's television show, *Too Hot Tamales*, took off and gave them a wider fan base. As business continues to grow, their goals have also evolved, always directed by the chefs' sincere, deep-rooted commitment to educating everyone in their sphere of influence—staff, customers, readership, and television audience.

"Why more restaurants?" Milliken was repeating my question, since we'd managed to meander off our interview topic. "There is a two-part answer, which is that we love working with other people and we also love working with each other, collaborating. You can get kind of stagnant if you're not growing, which means you're not offering new experiences to people anymore; and people crave new experiences . . . We want to keep our employees engaged and excited about what they're doing even seven, eight, nine, ten, twelve years later—we have a lot of people who have been working for us for decades. And then, Susan is a very driven person who is interested in growth, while I am more interested in financial stability, something I didn't grow up with.

The other impetus is bringing our food to and sharing our ideas with more and more people . . . The more restaurants you have, the more you can do that."

Des Jardins, who, in addition to Jardinière and Mijita, has ties to two other spots,[179] is on the same wavelength as Milliken. Her recent eagerness to increase her holdings was catalyzed by a desire to advance deserving personnel into the empowered positions they've earned. "For me, it's happened a little bit by chance so far, but going forward, there is more intention that I have, and that has to do with the people [who] I work with and providing them with guidance and opportunity and help . . . The reason, going forward, for opening more restaurants is really going to be based on people who I want to help to get their own dream."

While Des Jardins is all about giving folks a leg up in the industry, she can't say the same for everyone else—or, more precise, she can't say that hands are being extended to the girls. "I don't think women are approached with as many opportunities. I don't know why, but I think that's true. I think if you could find the male equivalent of me and ask them how many times they're asked to take on new projects, you'd find that the percentage is much higher. I don't know that for sure, but I have a pretty strong feeling."

Feniger, who otherwise doesn't dwell on her gender in terms of being a chef-restaurateur, has picked up on this vibe too. She suspects that the kind of expansive commercial growth that she and Milliken are now after might prove harder to come by for women. "Even with Border Grill—which has been around for twenty-five years, and is built on a strong concept and is running great profit—we've never had real interest from a big investor group who wants to grow the company, which is surprising. On the other hand, I have to say, we haven't gone after

[179] A relevant and fascinating aside, Des Jardins is a chef-partner (she differentiates this from chef-owner—the Mijita Cocina Mexicana situation—and chef-co-owner—the Jardinière setup) at Public House, a tavern in San Francisco, and Manzanita, a French-Cali–style restaurant at the Ritz-Carlton in Lake Tahoe. Hers is an empire based on a less traditional model. As she explained, there's no single company behind her projects—a different team runs each one.

it. And maybe guys like Wolf [Wolfgang Puck] have. If I was an investor looking to put money into a restaurant company, I'd be looking at Border Grill, because when you put it out there side by side, its efficiencies, how it's stood the test of time . . . you would think one of those big companies would try and snatch it up. That hasn't happened."

The good news is that because of the Des Jardinses and Fenigers in our midst, there's hope for a new and bigger crop of culinary empresses.

B. ALL THOSE AGAINST . . .

There's an expectation that chefs, especially those who have attained a certain level of recognition or respect, should front a fleet of places. Carrie Nahabedian, the Beard-winning[180] chef of Chicago's Naha, told me that she definitely feels "pressure to open more restaurants." It comes from within the industry and beyond. There are her peers' accomplishments—for example, she mentions "seeing Sarah Stegner, who has two restaurants," or Tom Colicchio, whom she remembers from his earlier days at Gramercy Tavern, where he was a partner before launching his own restaurant group and getting aboard the *Top Chef* train. "They're all businessmen now," Nahabedian says in reference to her peers. Her customers like to add their two cents on the branching-out issue as well. She recalls an unnerving exchange where "I was told by one heavyweight patron, 'You need to be more of a whore. You're leaving too much money on the table. You need to open more restaurants.' And when I said, 'That's not my style,' he said, 'You need to make it your style.'"

7. YOU DON'T HAVE TO BE AN OWNER TO CLAIM A PIECE OF THE ACTION.

Those chefs who are risk averse and don't think their place is to operate a business, but who wish to have an active role in shaping the restaurant

---

[180] That's my shorthand for James Beard Award (she won hers for Best Chef: Great Lakes region in 2008). Since it ties in to the familial business model, it's worth mentioning that she opened Naha in 2000 with her cousin Michael Nahabedian (his brother Tom designed the space and her sisters are also part of the team).

and a stake in the profits, have managed to find the happy "Goldilocks" medium that suits. Alex Guarnaschelli is content to be an executive chef, straight-up; she's currently doing that job at two restaurants while also giving on-air love to the Food Network. I asked her whether she had any interest in taking on a project herself. Nope. "Nah, I'm too lazy," she confesses. "Bobby Flay has been very encouraging in that regard . . . I have a three-year-old. I don't think there's any excuse for not opening a restaurant, but I think I'd rather spend those extra four hours a day with her. There's the privilege of time that not owning my own restaurant affords me . . . I think I'll be a late bloomer in that department." Sounds like it's there when she's ready, which is a privilege of support (Flay's and that generated by media efforts—she has an audience full of hopeful reservation-makers).

If, ten years ago, you'd asked Missy Robbins what she intended to do with her career, she would have told you she was going to have a small dining room of her own. Plans change. She's the executive chef at New York's two A Voce restaurants. These are large operations, both of them (the smaller of the two seats one hundred in its dining room), and she commands what comes out of their kitchens. I asked her if she continued to aim for that initial goal of running a smaller place. "I think there's a part of me that will have an opportunity to open places with these guys[181] as a chef-partner down the road, if I stick it out. And I think that there's a lot of benefit to that and a lot less risk. I don't have control over every aspect of this restaurant, and I never will; it's just not the way that this company works. So, yeah, there is still a part of me that wants a fifty-seat charming little place and to do my own thing and have total control over it. But I also know that if you open a fifty-seat restaurant, you go back to the other side of being a chef. I'm in my forties—do I really want to work the line every day? I don't. I like what I get to do now, being in a different place all the time. I never get bored."

[181] That would be restaurateur Marlon Abela and his management team at his London-based company MARC (Marlon Abela Restaurant Corporation).

Bridget Batson, who imagined she would go solo at some point, has done an about-face, with September 11 as her turning point. When she saw how hard it was to keep something afloat and how many factors were beyond a restaurateur's control, she realized she'd rather stay under someone else's umbrella. She's happy to be an employee as long as there's room for growth and new opportunities. So far, there has been. At the end of 2011 (after our interview), Franck LeClerc, owner of Gitane, the roost Batson rules in San Francisco, introduced Claudine, next door, and asked the chef to take charge there, too. Her husband, Robert Patrick Kelly, who's also a chef (at Angèle in Napa), does want his name on the door somewhere. Batson says she's keen on taking part, but doesn't want, physically, to be in there with him. It's not that she would like to take a backseat; she would rather be in a different car, work-wise, and she'd like to be driving that car (as long as it's someone else's property, you understand . . . sorry, just finishing out the metaphor).

Melissa Perello couldn't have asked for a warmer reception for her "baby," Frances, than having the place receive a Beard nomination for Best New Restaurant in 2010. Proud as she is of having embarked upon business ownership, she recognizes that being a hired hand has its perks. "There are a lot of advantages to working for other people. There's something nice about getting a paycheck every two weeks."

8. DON'T GET TOO COMFY.

The hardest thing to do, says Jasinski, "is to keep a restaurant at the top of its game year after year, staying on trend, reinventing what we do, making sure service gets better." Watch it on that trendy factor, though, because there's a fine line between keeping current and staying true to your own vision and the identity you've created for your establishment. "I fight the trendiness of it," acknowledges Jasinski. "I don't want to make something because I saw someone else making it . . . I want to make it because it's delicious and I have well-thought-out reasons for making it."

9. REMEMBER TO HAVE A LIFE.

Restaurant ownership, like parenthood, is an all-the-time responsibility. As long as the place is open, it's not something you can step away from. If you're doing double duty as sole proprietor and chef, everything—from the gas being turned off down to a wine spill that lands on a diner's lap—is, ultimately, all on you. Your employees are dependent on you, diners too. And there's that whole bill-paying albatross. It's easy to lose perspective and burn out. Those of sounder mind (and sometimes it takes hitting rock bottom, or feeling the effects of aging to get there) have sought ways to stave off the madness. "One of the reasons that I committed to having my restaurant close one day a week," Perello confides, "is that the doors are shut and I don't have to worry about what's going on there at least for twenty-four hours."

"I think if I was going to give advice to chefs who are frustrated with how to balance," Milliken offers, "and as unnatural as it might feel, you have to create a structure that allows your personal life to flourish. And you have to stick to it . . . You have to be as rigid and structured about it as the way you run the kitchen. You wouldn't allow for somebody not to show up for a shift, so don't allow yourself not to show up for a shift at home with your kids or with your husband."

If only from a purely biological standpoint, having a baby often forces women to actively seek more balance between the personal and professional. No one's saying motherhood is the cure-all for overworked, obsessive, monomaniacal chefs, but from the chefs I've spoken with, I've gleaned that being your own boss makes it easier to pull it all off, especially when you've launched the restaurant before the kid.

It's a relative term, *easier*.

The Motherload

Being a single mom and deciding to be a chef was a weird decision, and I remember the exact moment I decided it . . . I looked at taking a desk job that would enable me to work from eight o'clock in the morning, when my daughter was in school, till three o'clock in the afternoon, so I could then pick her up and be home with her every night. I'd also have weekends off. But what I decided was that the kind of girl that I wanted to raise was the kind of girl who would say to herself, "What do I want for myself? What's going to make me happiest?" It's like putting on your oxygen mask before putting on your child's oxygen mask. You can't really take care of other people unless you're taking care of your own needs, and if I wasn't going to be happy—which there's no way I would have been happy pushing a pencil and answering the phone—I had to step outside of all of the social norms of what's right.

—NAOMI POMEROY

A few minutes prior, at the coffee shop across from her mother's establishment Beast, August, Pomeroy's angelic-looking daughter, has left us to chat and gone over to the restaurant to wait for her mom. She has done so reluctantly but obediently, and I understand where that acceptance comes from when Pomeroy talks about what she perceives as her unorthodox way of raising her towheaded ten-year-old. The chef becomes noticeably upset as she describes how the other moms at August's private school, many of whom don't work, make her defensive of her choices. "I constantly feel like people might think that I've skewed my priorities incorrectly toward my own self," she says, but she goes on to confidently stand up for her choices. "What I've done is taught her that you can be happy; you can do a good job of taking care of somebody else just by—almost just by—doing a good job of taking care of your own self." Perhaps more significant than this perspective is the fact that she discusses it with her daughter—that there is an ongoing, open dialogue. "When [August] says that she's lonely and she says that she misses me, I say: 'I know that you've made a lot of sacrifices, too, in order for me to do what I want to do, and that I hope that you know that when you're older and I can make sacrifices for you, I will. And, you know, I have.' And we just talk a lot about that kind of stuff. We talk about quality of time versus quantity of time spent together."

As Pomeroy tells me this, there's an unhinging under way. I'm being blitzed, you could say, by a revelation, and it's overwhelming enough—the effect of her words and what they're drumming up—that, as I'm registering that her eyes are tearing, I realize mine are brimming over as well. Not cool. I don't cry in public[182] and I'm certainly not keen on losing my shit whilst on the job.

I'm not sure that Pomeroy saw how close I came to crying on that Sunday morning, and if she did, I hope she knows it's because I am in awe of her. She reminds me of a group of women whom I held in the same regard when I was in high school—my classmates' mothers. We'll get to them in a few. My immediate response to Pomeroy was to share Nancy Silverton's words on the subject.

Silverton, in an interview we had done in Los Angeles, also talked about raising her kids in her professional orbit——at Campanile, the restaurant she owned with her ex-husband, Mark Peel, and upstairs, where the family lived. "There are certain things I think I regret about it," Silverton admitted, also conceding that "maybe it wouldn't have been any different otherwise." She had presumed that "when people had more regular hours, their lives were more regular," but, having spoken to many of those people, she learned that regular life eluded them too. Irregularity, for her, looked like this: "When my kids were young and I did traveling for work, I always brought them and somebody to

---

[182] Except, sometimes, at movies, or plays, or in front of certain works of visual art . . . There may have been a wedding or two as well.

help take care of them with me. Everything that I earned went to [pay for] their child care. So it wasn't that I abandoned them. What my kids got was being around two parents who loved what they did. They always could feel the excitement and the pleasure that we got in our workplace. I remember my daughter, when she was graduating from high school, being very nervous about not finding what she was passionate about."[183]

I remember being nervous about that too. I always needed something to be passionate about, or else I'd feel lost and as though I was failing. That's not a complaint being filed, by the way. I'm not a mom yet, but I believe Silverton's is some of the best parenting advice anyone could give. It's one that my parents passed along to me, although in a less obvious way—it wasn't the example they set themselves; it was the one they exposed me to, inadvertently, perhaps. Thank goodness they did. And thanks all the more that Pomeroy reminded me of it as my cup of coffee sat untouched and forgotten.

When I was just a little girl, I asked my mother, "What will I be?"[184] . . . No, actually, I didn't. I told her. Many times. I was going to be a singer on the Broadway stage (Evita, watch out; Éponine, I am you); an actress; a singer-songwriter; a novelist; a lawyer; a journalist. Point is, I was going to have a career. This was as obvious to me as breathing or drinking milk (I drank a *lot* of milk) and inhaling chocolate chip cookies (in the school cafeteria, I was the one who bypassed whatever the lunch entrees were and headed straight for dessert.) Having a career was what Brearley girls did, you see. Or, at least, that's the ideal my alma mater promoted. We were supposed to be great thinkers, or leaders, or Nobel Prize winners, or humanitarians, or something.

---

[183] Vanessa, Silverton's daughter, has, in case you're wondering, found that thing. As per her mom, "She now is a segment producer for *The Rachel Maddow Show*; and she's very outspoken and she's very politically driven, so it's a perfect fit."

[184] "Que Sera, Sera." It's a song. Starts like this: "When I was just a little girl, I asked my mother, what will I be. Will I be pretty? Will I be rich? Here's what she said to me." And what do you think she said? "*Que sera, sera,* whatever will be, will be [because that's what the phrase means]." It was written by songwriters Jay Livingston and Ray Evans in 1956 and made its debut in Hitchcock's *The Man Who Knew Too Much*, when Doris Day sang it. Won an Oscar too, that ditty.

Underlying all of this, I suspect, was some of that old-fashioned educated-lady business that was presumed de rigueur for young women of a certain social echelon (in the same way that you might find pedigreed Radcliffe girls of the 1950s applying their expensive degrees to doing their husbands' laundry) combined with a slightly more progressive agenda. There was a sense that we would be difference-makers, but not necessarily contributors to our household budgets—and certainly not the sole breadwinners thereof.

My mother works. She has sold antiques at a well-known French dealer's New York outpost since I was three. She loves it. But she has never treated it like a career; she has treated it more like a hobby. (No offense, Mom—I know you're quite good at what you do.) Mom isn't someone who could have stayed at home all day. She likes being busy, and she loves the art, history, and people who surround her at that gallery. However, when offered more responsibility, she wasn't interested. And though she may have toyed with the idea of becoming an independent agent, she never seriously considered it. My younger brother and I always found this frustrating. We'd ask each other why Mom didn't want her own business; didn't want to be boss.

If I only had my mom as an example and accepted the somewhat mixed message Brearley delivered, to what would I have aspired? I'm not sure. What I figured out, almost twenty years later, as Pomeroy talked about her relationship with August, was that the main reason I think having a career never seemed like it was an optional goal or a recreational confidence-booster came from my friends' mothers. By the time I graduated from that institution, among my chums, only two (maybe three) of us could claim parents who remained married to each other. Of the rest, most of the girls were raised single-handedly by working mothers. And when I say working mothers, I mean forces to be reckoned with. The one who had the greatest impact on me was my friend Felicia's mom, who was the president of Planned Parenthood. She had this crazy high-powered job that was all about fighting for women's rights and health, yet her parenting style was close to that of my folks'.

They underscored old-fashioned values like hard work and good manners; they stressed the importance of ethics, education, cultural awareness, tolerance, and human rights; they encouraged us to talk to them about anything and to speak our minds (respectfully); and they always showed up to school plays (unless advised not to). Then there's another pal whose mother is an acclaimed novelist and screenwriter. For many years, I wanted to do what her mom did, and the fact that she could write those books, and lead that life, while raising a daughter was, well, awesome. Other do-it-all moms were educational administrators, or nurses, or entrepreneurs. Each of them raised—and maybe I'm biased, because, to me, they're all my extended family—extraordinary women. They didn't have a choice when it came to working. And yet most chose professions, like Nancy Silverton, that they were passionate about, and they passed this on to their daughters and to me. It is one thing to be told that you can do whatever you put your mind to; it is another to see it firsthand.

As I shared with Pomeroy that morning in Portland, she is doing for August what my friends' mothers did for me. These role models resurfaced a few days later in San Francisco when I met with Traci Des Jardins. She has a son, Eli, from a previous relationship and has chosen the role of part-time parent while her ex-partner acts as his primary caregiver. "I really didn't feel like I could do him justice having him half the time when I knew he was going to be spending a lot of that time with a nanny. So now he's with me about a third of the time. But I think I'm a more committed parent now, as a part-time parent, because he's all mine when I have him. My ex is great—we have a great understanding and she does a lot of the heavy lifting. Without that support, I'm not sure how good of a parent I could be." What Eli gets from Des Jardins, among other things, is what Silverton's children and Pomeroy's daughter receive from their working chef-restaurateur mothers. "Eli sees my struggles. He knows that I would like to be with him and that I'm torn. He sees me in that crazy dance that's our lives. He gets it . . . You give your kids this model for passion for something."

"You can't have it all," Des Jardins says with certainty. "I didn't give birth to Eli—was not his birth mother. Shortly after he was born, I thought about having a baby—I always thought I would—and I came close. But I realized I had to make a choice. I wasn't really going to be able to be the kind of parent I wanted to be. And, I am to Eli, but I knew that I couldn't do that as a single parent. So I decided not to do it. I chose not to have another child."

After I spoke to Pomeroy, and before I sat down with Des Jardins, I found myself trying to think of one woman among my friends who has done what Pomeroy has—or what my former classmates' moms did. At my age (mid-thirties), my friends' moms were already writing their novels or spearheading campaigns to distribute condoms in public high schools, and their daughters were in middle school. I'm sad to say, on some level, that until I had that conversation with Pomeroy, I hadn't come across anyone, personally, who was holding down the fort that way. At thirty-seven, she is raising a ten-year-old and running a restaurant. It's not that I wish divorce on any of my espoused girlfriends who have kids, I'm just wondering how everyone has escaped that—either they're married mums and not performing astounding professional feats, or, like me, they're single and focused on their careers. I looked at Pomeroy and wondered, "Could I do what you are right now?" The answer is probably no.

I've always wanted to be a mother—I think I took that for granted too. I assumed I'd do things like get married and give birth later in life, but I had no idea how it was all going to come together; I definitely hadn't entertained the notion that it might not. Recently, however, an old comrade of mine (he knows who he is) pointed out in the kindest of ways, via Instant Messenger, that many of his fortyish female friends have expressed regret at not having frozen their eggs. What he said was well intentioned, but it still made me want to throw up. It's true; the cursed clock is ticking. These are conversations guys don't need to have with themselves or their buddies. No matter how much society morphs and its established roles shift, the biological and physical realities of motherhood remain. We have to decide, either way—to give birth or not, to be mothers or not—and be okay with those choices. It's not something you can come back to later on; it'll be too late. "[Men] don't have to give anything up because society doesn't expect the same things of them, and that's a huge part of the issue," Des Jardins asserts on the subject. "I have to be analytical about how I am as a mom. If I were a guy, it wouldn't come across my spectrum. And that's where we hit that stumbling block in our careers, because we are the keeper of home, and the keeper of relationship, and the keeper of children, by virtue of our sex. That's the stumbling block in the restaurant business for women . . . That's why women drop out. We realize at some point in time that maybe you can't have it all."

The restaurant industry is bleaker than most on this issue. The job is not only harder on the body and demands being on your feet for hours on end, but also adheres to an inflexible routine (dictated by the hours of dinner—or lunch—service). Maternity leave is, unless you own your venue, a foreign concept in most professional kitchens. Once you leave, it's not likely someone's holding your slot open for you.[185] "And how do we make this industry supportive so that if a woman takes a break to have children, you can get back into it later?" Amanda Cohen wondered before observing: "There are very few working chefs with children who are women." Many of the chefs I interviewed, not just Des Jardins or Cohen, believe that motherhood is the deal-breaker that drives women from the galley.

---

[185] Once again, three big whooping cheers for Jane Tunks (the only copy editor you need to know), who gave me a proverbial tap on the shoulder with a note about the FMLA (Family Medical Leave Act), a federal law that obligates a business to keep someone's position open. Legally, you can take up to twelve weeks (unpaid) leave (parental leave included) and employers are required to hold your slot, *if* (and here's the crux, folks) they have more than fifty employees. How many restaurants employ fifty or more people? Or, rather, how many don't? That caveat alone exempts a slew of employers from this act (signed into existence by William Jefferson Clinton, 42nd president of these here United States of America, in 1993) and renders their employees ineligible for its protection. A few states have amended the law to lower the "fifty" cap.

For a practical understanding of how FMLA applies, I asked Anita Lo, chef and proprietor of Annisa in New York City, her thoughts: "One of our servers had a baby and we kept her position open. But we have much less than fifty employees. If she were a kitchen employee, it would be impossible to hold her position, as we have only four cooks and couldn't cover her shifts without cloning someone. (And training someone for that period of time would hurt the business.) I don't know what, exactly, the law says, and we support maternity leave in theory, but in practice for a tiny restaurant like ours, it's sometimes not possible."

Alice Waters agrees: "I think that's the greatest impediment to women's careers in the kitchen . . . Unless you have a completely understanding husband who's willing to participate and you share the raising of the child, and the work that you're doing. I'm just beginning to understand the kinds of things that we can do to facilitate that. A whole lot more has to be learned . . . You have to leave room for picking up children, for kids being sick—things that aren't issues for men. So men are thought of as more reliable. We have to figure out how to make room for children." It's interesting, this idea that working fathers are thought to be more reliable than their female counterparts because they're not tested in the same way women are, and are expected to do less where the home and family are concerned. The exception to this, of course, is, as Waters dubs it, the "completely understanding husband," or as he's referred to in pop cultural jargon, the "househusband." Waters had one, which was one of at least two factors that enabled her to be the culinary heavyweight and activist she has been and a committed parent at the same time. He, thankfully, "was willing to take care of her [their daughter] and feed her at home," as he had a flexible work schedule.

Luchetti, who doesn't have children, notes: "This is a business that works seven days a week, weekends and nights. And if you have children, you have to be able to fit that in somehow, or else you never see your kids . . . A lot of women give up their careers because they can't do it all. Maybe they get out for five or six years and then, when the kids are older, they get back in. But it's really hard to balance it. And it's not the kind of business where, if you can't come in one day 'cause your kid is sick, the papers just pile up on your desk and you can get to it later on. That's just the unfortunate part of the physicality of the business; you can't be in two places at one time." One of the draws of working at a restaurant is that every evening is a new performance, a chance to start fresh. The downside to this, especially for parents, is that it doesn't allow you to work from home or get creative about catching up.

Mary Sue Milliken found an understanding business partner and co-chef in Susan Feniger, but doesn't believe she could have held up her end of that bargain and raised her three kids if her husband, architect Josh Schweitzer, hadn't opted to retire early. Milliken recalled the couple's earlier days, when they had two young'uns and she was pregnant with their third. During that time, she would leave Los Angeles for one week out of every month to shoot *Too Hot Tamales* in New York. Back on the West Coast, she and her husband "would talk on the phone every night at around five—we had a nanny, you know; she was full time—and [try to] come up with a better excuse why one of us couldn't come home by six to relieve the nanny. It got to a point where he was so frustrated, he just closed his office and said he was going to take a one-year sabbatical. He's never gone back. So he's Mr. Mom . . . He is just fantastic. I often feel a little bit guilty because I got to keep my career and he didn't. But he has started painting; he's had two or three gallery shows. Our marriage has improved enormously, without having two people with high-powered careers who are constantly in the press and getting all kinds of recognition. You know, he bakes bread; he makes salami and sausages; we have a huge garden he tends. He plays tennis five times a week . . . It has worked really well for us . . . His move to do that and having Susan [as a business partner]—both of those have allowed me to juggle both things." Milliken and Schweitzer are unusually lucky; not just because they found each other and have such a strong marriage, but because they are fortunate enough to be able to structure their life this way. They don't both *need* to work to support their family.

Milliken's arrangement raised three questions: (1) Why aren't there more Joshes, and if there are, why can't I find them? (2) Is guilt an unavoidable consequence of being a working (and career-driven) mother? (3) What does *family* mean today? (Is it more like a village? If so, Hillary Rodham Clinton, please report to the front desk for footnote duty.) There's no need to discuss (1) further. I've put out the call. You

Josh types know where to find me. But (2) is an unavoidable by-product of the motherhood-chef pairing.

What Andrea Reusing conveys so clearly is that the guilt goes in two directions—you either worry that you're neglecting your children or, alternatively, that you're abandoning your restaurant:

"I think that if a customer in a dining room is told that a male chef is not there because they're at their other restaurant, [he] gets a pass, or gets applauded; it's not acceptable for a woman chef to not be there because she's simply putting her kids to bed. And so there's that inherent feeling that it's somehow okay for a chef not to be there for a professional reason, but not a personal reason." Reusing added that this dilemma isn't limited to the restaurant world; it extends to any demanding profession, whether you're a mother who's working on an oil rig or Wall Street.

What distinguishes the life of a chef from that of another career mom is the galley gal's hours. As Reusing points out: "The most important time of the day for a kid is bedtime in a lot of ways, in terms of an emotional closeness and a vulnerable and bonding moment. And the most important time of day at a restaurant is, obviously, dinner. It's the same time." She realized how much the tuck-in counts after missing many of her first child's. Reusing went back to work when her daughter was three months old. Then there was a period, around a year later, when for at least six months, Reusing was only able to put her little one to bed once a week—the night the chef wasn't working. Seven years later, the repercussions linger. "I think it still has an effect on our relationship in some ways, 'cause it took away this very special bonding time between us. She developed a strong preference for her father during that time, which was painful to me."

What she missed with her daughter, Reusing tried to regain with her son. She didn't go back to work as quickly after he was born. Devoting more hours to him meant taking them away from her restaurant, and that caused a different set of misgivings—she knew it "might not be good for my career; it might not be good for my business." But, in her mind, she didn't have a choice. When people ask the million-dollar how-do-you-do-it-all question she can only offer one she knows they'd rather not hear: "I do both of them really shittily . . . Everyone wants more from you and you can never give them what they want." Her trick to not disappointing everyone is to manage expectations—make sure they're not too high—and "to find the pleasure in the stuff you're doing at work and the time that you have at home too."

Reusing confessed that even not checking her e-mail for two hours while hanging out with her kids turns out to be a challenge, something Suzanne Goin, a parent of three munchkins, can relate to as a multi-restaurant owner. Goin keeps rearranging her daily routine to land on the perfect formula for packing each day with a few quality children's hours and, also necessary, enough time to handle her three eateries. "I haven't figured it out yet," she says. "Sadly, I'm not joking. I think it's inherently really, really hard. It's definitely the biggest challenge of being a chef and restaurant owner . . . I'm in the eye of the storm of figuring it out." Goin's husband, David Lentz, is also a chef-proprietor of three spots (The Hungry Cat, with locations in Hollywood, Santa Barbara, and Santa Monica), so it's not as though one can compensate for the other's hours.[186] "Mate-wise, it's easy," she acknowledges. "We're on the same schedule—we're used to hanging out late at night. The children thing is really tough . . . I feel it and they feel it. They just really want me now, and I can't . . . There are literally moments [when] I say, 'I have to go to work,' and they say, 'Why do you have to go to work?' And I wonder, 'Yeah, why?' "

There's another layer of guilt, and it dovetails, ever so nicely, into that third question on the agenda—what kind of family are these chefs

---

[186] This might be the right moment to give a shout-out to the silent (paid) helpers who allow so many of the female chef-owners out there, especially those without househusbands, to carry on in the kitchen postpartum. Elisabeth Prueitt, whose spouse, Chad Robertson, is her co-owner and co-chef at their Tartine franchises, reminded me of this: "There are some women who opt to have a serious full-time nanny, just like any other profession . . . A lot of people in our business, they're married to people in the business, so forget it." The takeaway: To be successful at a certain level, you should expect to outsource the child care.

creating? The Cleaver regime under which the Beav grew up is extinct. Divorce, remarriage (and the stepsiblings it brings), same-sex parents, dual-income households, latchkey childhoods—these are all ordinary sights here in today's USA. For those born in an earlier time—who had what we still define as a traditional home life—it's not always easy to accept the current reality. Is the old way better? Silverton, for one, is left pondering what she did and didn't give her children. "The way I grew up, for the most part, doesn't exist anymore. My kids never had the experience of having a nightly family dinner at home, ever. And that was such a part of my life growing up. My father came home between six and six thirty; we all sat at the dinner table—we all had our own seats—for a minimum of an hour. My youngest is seventeen, and when we do have dinner together, which is not often, I think he's done within seven minutes. I didn't take it for granted in those days. I loved it. I was home, having dinner with my family, and that's when I learned about politics; that's when I learned about what it was like to be a trial lawyer; that's how I learned what it was like to write soap operas.[187] I learned so much and I gained so much. I loved having friends over and they loved having dinner at our table."

Are these kids-of-chefs really losing something that Silverton and her peers cherished, or might they be partaking in another version of it? You could say that the proverbial (and literal) table has expanded. Many of these minors become part of their overseers' restaurants—they are adopted by the staff, hang out in the kitchen, and are privy to that same cocoon of grown-up attention and knowledge. Those in Silverton's shoes don't necessarily *tell* their wards of what they do; they show them.

And, yes, this is where that Village thinking comes in. Although it's far from provincial, what emerges is an invested ensemble that, blood ties or marriage certificates notwithstanding, performs the child-rearing functions of a clan. Pomeroy's represents the epitome of this

---

[187] Her dad was a lawyer and her mom, a soap writer.

CSP.[188] Her sous chef Mika Paredes lives with her and August, and then, always present, there's the Texan nanny and the latter's sister. "It's just this real small family," the chef muses.

After that interview with Pomeroy, we stopped by her restaurant, and there was August, helping the staff out with the evening's *mise en place*. She was happy as a clam, confident and busily chatting away about what she thought should be done with the ingredients in front of her. It looked to me like a life I might have fantasized about as a child.

Waters told me how fortunate she was to be able to take her daughter, Fanny, to "the office" (that would be Chez Panisse), though she also sees how those circumstances were special.

"I, of course, had the luxury of bringing my kid to work, which I did. I'm really lucky, because this is a place of eating, and I could feed her here. And I had a lot of friends who could take care of her here, while I was working. But I realize that I have a really privileged position." How, I asked her, do you extend those kinds of opportunities to others? "Well," she responded, "in the summer, we give priority [for time off] to people who have kids—though it's our busiest time and we want everybody to be there—because we understand that summer is vacation time for children, and we'll just have to figure it out." She also outlined a rotation system developed so that no one has to face five night shifts a week—it's two lunch and three dinner services instead. Waters spoke idealistically about seeing more day care centers in big companies, and how that initiative could be applied to her industry in the future. "I think that's a great thing," she said in a tone that was simultaneously dreamy and assertive. It is a great thing, but it doesn't come cheap; for a small business (like a restaurant), it's not typically a financially sustainable option.

If, however, you're a chef-owner and mistress of your dining domain, you can, as Pomeroy and Waters do, institute take-your-child-

---

[188] Community Supported Parenting.

to-work-day regularly. Do note, as Goin mentions, this is a policy better implemented when the kinder are well past infancy. "My problem is, I have three kids within eighteen months. I have four-year-old twins and a two-and-a-half-year-old, so they can't hang out at the restaurant." Bringing them into her galley world is, she says, "something I look forward to when they're older, when they can come after school and help prep in the kitchen." Sounds like the best after-school activity ever, if you ask me. It was, in fact, one of mine, except I engaged in it at home.

I know what Silverton's childhood looked like; I got double lucky on the maternal front. On the one hand, I had all of those honorary mothers to inspire me. On the other, I had my mom, who was there every morning to give me breakfast (I still miss "Cream of Wheat weather," for the record, NRD[189]) and home every night to tuck me in, or even, on my favorite evenings, to cook family dinners. She designed her hours around my brother's and my schedules. The best was Thursdays. On those days she came home an hour or two early, at 4 p.m. And that's when we (mostly she, with a little help from me) would bake. Would it be Dolly's Crisp Toffee Bars or Ralph's Cookies (both in Maida Heatter's *Book of Great Chocolate Desserts*)? Would there be rice pudding? If I hadn't had those other maternal presences around, I might not be writing this book, that's true. But you might say the same for those Thursday afternoons. They're, in part, responsible for my love of and interest in food, without which, I never would have begun reporting on that topic, or contemplating what it's like to be a chef. It's never one person, really, who sets it all in motion. It takes a coven.

---

[189] Nancy Robbins Druckman.

CHAPTER 8

Media Rare

I'm thinking in particular of a question that always bothers me when I read stories about chefs winning awards, chefs opening spectacular new restaurants, chefs starring in yet another new TV series—congratulations, but why are all of you male? Where are the women?[190]

—LAURA SHAPIRO, AUTHOR AND ACADEMIC (AS IN <u>NOT</u> A CHEF)

I could have picked a plum quote from among the many women I interviewed who spat out on the subject of the media and its involvement in the culinary industry. But then, I thought, if everyone's speaking from experience, I should maybe let the experts—as in, the content providers themselves—have a moment. Who best to represent the media than one of its congregants? Laura Shapiro is many things: a food critic, a culinary historian, a journalist, and an author. Her topics of interest include women chefs, gender studies, and, which you've already deduced, food. She is responsible for the tomes *Julia Child: A Life*, *Perfection Salad: Women and Cooking at the Turn of the Century*, and *Something from the Oven: Reinventing Dinner in 1950s America*. She also penned an online story for *Gourmet* magazine, "Where Are the Women?" which is where the above lines first appeared. I came across Shapiro's article while working on that *Gastronomica* story I told you about (see page 125), "Why Are There No Great Women Chefs?" wherein I challenged the media's relationship with chefettes and, in so doing, appropriated this very same citation.

In the context of that *Gastronomica* piece, Shapiro's borrowed words, along with my own ramblings, were directed at the media, which means they were pointed in my direction as much as Shapiro's or

[190] Laura Shapiro, "Where Are the Women?" Gourmet.com, June 12, 2008.

anyone else who considers herself part of that sprawling conglomeration of depicters. What that essay didn't do was look at the situation from the point of view of those depicted. And that's what brings us, now, to the land of "Media Rare." We're here to check out the type of coverage these ladies receive, the impact it has on them, and how they figure one should go about getting it.

So lest you were concerned, yes, I'm perfectly aware that I'm part of the media and as such, presume that any stones cast in this chapter are headed as much in my direction as in any other food writer's, journalist's, editor's, publisher's, or producer's. Obviously, it's a little *difficile* for me to remain unbiased, but, if anything, speaking to all of these chefs has made me less inclined to defend my profession and more ambivalent than ever about what it is I do and how I do it.

As can also be said of those who track the food world, increased interest from the mainstream has provided chefs with more business opportunities and turned them into public heroes. At the same time, the portrayal of this bunch is, by and large, inaccurate and limited, and those raised on pedestals tend to look and behave a certain way—like white alpha males. But it's also true that some of the same media outlets responsible for the skewed presentation of women in the culinary business can be given credit for putting more of them on the radar.

I'm going to jump right in to television, because that's where you find the frenemy-ship at its most tenuous. If you're turning on the telly in search of vittles, the obvious destination would be the Food Network. Alex Guarnaschelli, a regular on channel 50[191] (she is a judge on *Chopped* and the host of a couple of cooking shows), kindly distilled something I've been known to rail against—at length—into three sentences, and without the harsh ruling. "I think men on television are more referred to as authorities, and women are more authorities for the home cook. For a large part of it, there's truth to that. Whether it's damaging or not is another story." The distinction,

---

[191] That's the Food Network's station, where I'm from.

and I believe Guarnaschelli was saying as much, is that men are typically portrayed as the professional experts (you know, Chefs, capital C) and women as the home-cooking experts. Her stint as a decider on *Chopped* is one example of a lady chef's representing the toque-topped set, true; but those half-hour tutorials known as *Alex's Day Off* and *The Cooking Loft* that put her on the set of a residential kitchen in nonworking costume (the ubiquitous V-neck included, to flash a hint of cleavage) are par for the course.

Those shows, the instructional ones geared to helping the residential stove-tenders, air during the daytime (when the stay-at-home parents are presumed watching). When it gets dark, it's a whole other story, packed with adventure, travel, competition, and challenge. How many habaneros can one man eat? Which pit stop serves a cheesesteak with chicken-fried chicken? Who's the next Iron Chef (Guarnaschelli competed for that gig too)? These programs are usually hosted by men and tend to feature that sex more than the fairer one. Collectively, some of these duke-it-out serials have introduced quite a few other-than-white-male chefs to the American public, although those included culinary minorities are often pigeonholed in some way. Watch *The Next Food Network Star* and observe how many of the women on it are interested in cooking for their families, peddling healthier cuisine, or bringing the traditions of their "ethnic" mothers and grandmothers into everyone's life. Then see what the fellas are up to, especially the white ones (sometimes, the non-Caucasian males can veer into that "flavors of my people" column too). I may be exaggerating a bit (you've got to laugh at it), not as much as I wish, though.

"As much as I hate these reality cooking shows . . . it's one of the few places where you see women chefs," Amanda Cohen chimes in. "It's really different, and you see minorities . . . you see women, and you see people from all different kinds of backgrounds cooking." She's proof—a self-titled "vegetable cook," the chef-owner competed on *Iron Chef*. That's one point for food television, right? Maybe. Cohen told me she knew she wouldn't win, and that she was encouraged to have fun and "turn it on" while she had her golden on-camera moment. As part of their preparation for the challenge, she and her team smile-trained (go back and watch the tape—the girl grinned big the whole way through). "We didn't lose huge . . . but I think [my] being a woman hurt us." She was pleasantly surprised to find that the harshest judge, resident curmudgeon Jeffrey Steingarten (should you need an ID on this guy, he's *Vogue* magazine's food columnist and author of *The Man Who Ate Everything*), liked her food a lot. The two other judges—both women, as it happens—were more taken with Iron Chef Morimoto. Cohen assumes their preference was informed by the victor's being "a TV personality, famous person" and her being a girl who "looked very young." And she's not sorry she got up there and lost. "We held our own and so it was worth it."

That's the deal *Iron* side. Bravo, home of the *Real Housewives*, sets a better example (not for housewives, mind you). With its program *Top Chef*, Cohen notes that the network has introduced the audience to women chefs who have their own restaurants, but also to someone like Jen Carroll, who, up until August 2011, was the executive chef at Eric Ripert's restaurant 10 Arts in Philadelphia. Seeing a female chef who has excelled in the world of French-style fine dining was almost more important for Cohen, who, if you'll recall, harbors some regrets that she didn't have access to those types of kitchens, than watching others like herself, who own small, less formal eateries. "It's also great to aspire to be someone's right-hand person, and she's one of the few people, and few women, who has this amazing job, and people don't talk about that enough."[192]

Cohen's right, *Top Chef* has put a few new faces on the toque. It's not to say you won't see some predictable casting, but it's more a character type that's being filled each season than an overtly gendered tack. Is there always one caterer? Yes. Is *she* a woman? Probably. Does she

---

[192] Cohen and I talked about it—climbing the rungs of the kitchen ladder beside a culinary giant—on pages 73–75.

pack her knives and go early? Definitely, except in one triumphant defying instance, that of *The Chew's* Carla Hall. She was, naturally, billed as the underdog, and her classic training as a chef was often downplayed, but she prevailed and finished as a runner-up.

I asked Hall to talk about her relationship with that show. She was on the fifth season, set in Washington, D.C., and then returned in the *All-Stars* round where she was voted fan favorite. (Confession: I was rooting for her to take it, and that was before we spoke.) Despite appreciating the attention she received from the show, she admitted it wasn't easy to handle all of the enticing prospects that came her way. "I think, honestly, it has been amazing. The one thing that I don't think people realize—they will ask me, 'Oh, hasn't it brought all these opportunities?' But you have to pay for those opportunities." It was an intense case of growing pains. There was a flood of demand for her talent (as a personality and as a chef), and as the owner of a small catering company, she didn't have the infrastructure or financial base necessary to deliver the supply. "It almost killed me . . . All of a sudden we were growing really, really fast, so I needed to have a bigger kitchen, I needed to have more people . . . and I really needed an influx of capital, but there weren't a lot of people. It was really hard . . . and I made really fast decisions that I probably wouldn't have made [otherwise]." Between putting in appearances, driving her company, and getting married, she had barely a moment to catch her breath. "For two years, I was running around and stressing . . . and never felt like *Top Chef* ever ended. I mean, here I was having Quickfires [challenges] on a day-to-day basis when you are having an event, you're doing the food, you're running to do something else, you're coming back, you're delivering it, you're running through the streets, you're overscheduled, and just overcommitted. It was really crazy." That was one outcome she hadn't expected; the other was fame. "I didn't realize how popular the show was. I didn't know. I watched it, but I wasn't talking to a bunch of people who watched it. So after the show, when

I went out and people were like, 'Oh, Carla!' I'm like, 'Huh? Do I know you? I don't remember you. Did we go to school together?' "

Post–*All-Stars*, she has made out pretty well; she was able to quit catering, start a cookie company, and score a deal as a cohost on a new daytime food-centric talk show, *The Chew*.

I also had the pleasure of conversing with Stephanie Izard, who was the winner of the fourth season of *Top Chef* and since then, opened Girl & the Goat in Chicago, which was nominated for a Best New Restaurant award by the Beard elite, been chosen as one of *Food & Wine's* Best New Chefs, published a cookbook, and has a second eatery on the way. Would this have happened without that on-air victory? We'll never know. But her televised achievement is directly responsible for most of the opportunities that have followed. For Izard, though, that shining moment remains slightly tarnished by an ever-present reminder. "My press [PR] person keeps telling me it's a good thing no other woman has won, because then I'm the only one. I want to be seen as one of the better chefs who won, not as the woman who won."

Her remark reminded me of a conversation I had with Allison Vines-Rushing. She became a chef de cuisine under Alain Ducasse at twenty-eight and, soon after, in 2004, received the James Beard Foundation's Rising Star Chef Award. This, of course, was a rarity—her being a woman and all. Thrust into the spotlight as a young, easy-on-the-eyes Southern wunderkind, Vines-Rushing has henceforth found herself the go-to gal whenever a lady chef is needed for a reality show. As frustrating as that is, it's not nearly as detrimental as the fact that her husband, with whom she works, is never hit up for these gigs. She delivered quite the earful:

"I'm constantly, constantly bombarded with TV opportunities. It's mainly those, but I've really had to be like, 'No, no, no, no, no.' Here and there, that's been hard . . . [It's] because I'm a woman, and they tell me that straight-up . . . It's not because, 'You're a very talented chef that we're interested in,' or 'We think it's amazing that you worked for Alain Ducasse.' It's none of that; it's 'Well, we need women for this' . . . They say it all the time."

The onslaught of requests has been disruptive to life at home with her spouse and co-chef at MiLa in New Orleans, Slade Rushing. "Magazines have been really respectful and interested in us and our food and what we do. TV is not interested in that at all. They're interested in me, as a woman, my face, and, potentially, really harming my career—maybe making it better or being some superstar on TV, maybe; maybe doing the total opposite . . . My husband gets a little offended, because he's not really approached and he feels like, 'I work beside you every day and I work just as hard and they're not interested in me' . . . And it's just because he doesn't have boobs; that's the only thing it is. It's not me being a more talented human being."

Even if these casting agents were more excited about her talent than her gender, the ideas they're pitching are untenable to someone like Vines-Rushing, who takes her craft seriously. It sounds funny, the way she tells it, but then you remember this is a real scenario and the laughter ends. "I got a call—this was last week, I think—and it was the second show pitched to me that has the same concept to it. It's like *MacGyver*-type shit. They're like, 'Well, so, you have this challenge where all of your ingredients are frozen in a block of ice and so you have to get the ingredients out of the ice with a chisel,' and I'm thinking, 'Wow, that sounds like fun.' Like, why would I do that? . . . I'm no *MacGyver*."

What chef is MacGyver? As Vines-Rushing said, her job is to lead a team and, also, to be supported by that team. She isn't working alone like some rogue magician to get all those plates onto a table. Aside from the offensiveness of the solicitations that come her way, there's a certain lack of *reality* being considered. Which restaurant do you go to where the cooks are in the kitchen chiseling your trapped T-bone out of an ice block? These shows are designed to put people in extreme positions and see who can survive (and hope that the ones who can't go out with a recordable nervous breakdown).

One of the few projects pitched to both Vines-Rushing and her husband was one of the most unreal I've heard of and obviously contrived for maximum drama. It was, as far as she is concerned, the final nail in television's coffin. "We were actually approached about a show—they were like, 'We really want both of you on the show to compete against each other.'" They were, of course, unwilling to participate. There you have it, folks: the vérité of reality television where helpmates who work in the same field, as equals, are asked to demonstrate their professional legitimacy by going neck and neck in front of a national audience. Nice.

For people like Vines-Rushing, celebrity is a difficult thing to grapple with; becoming famous is not what they set out to do. They're chefs who were recognized for their work and, because America is currently mesmerized by the wide world of food and needs its public heroes and villains to worship, subsequently became big-time purveyors of entertainment too. They are not to be mistaken for wannabes who start with the desire for fame and see cooking as their way in.

A number of women I spoke to seemed to carry a chip on their shoulders when they got talking about the Johnny-come-lately "chefs" who, without much experience in or dedication to the culinary profession, have jumped at the chance to get known quickly as food celebrities. Heather Bertinetti is outspokenly perturbed by the ease with which the charmers championed by content producers sail into success when there are so many hardworking people who hope to make their reputations the old-fashioned way, by doing hard time in kitchens. "When it comes to this industry, the people who are portrayed in the media—let's take Paula Deen or Food Network people like Bobby Flay and whatnot—the way they're perceived on TV is, we're all supposed to look up to them and be like, 'Oh my God! They must be so knowledgeable and they're so good at what they do and cooking.' I'm not discrediting them at all. They've accomplished plenty of things, but it's different than, let's say, the underdog who could come from a small town and is cooking his way through Per Se and Jean Georges and those places, and paid their dues on a different path than these people who got one restaurant, did very well, and then got on TV." Bertinetti would feel less antagonistic toward the celebrity contingency if she believed that the programmers and charisma scouts cared about presenting audiences with the kinds of chefs who haven't taken shortcuts, and whose rising in the ranks is merit-driven. "At what point," she asks, "is the media actually going to recognize people who work really hard, who have achieved things, and do a serious show about cooking so people out there can actually understand that it's hard work?"

Christina Tosi isn't clueless about the ways of the media or the classism; she understands, though, that if you're ambitious about your career today, self-promotion could be a requirement. You may not have trained or wish to be an entertainer, but if that allows you to do more with your talent—to cook the food you want, the way you want, or get whatever your message is across—then show's on. "You can't half-ass it . . . I think people get media attention for a lot of different reasons. But a lot of the people who are at the top of their game are at the top of their game because they want to be the best, and they're not afraid to do their best to get there, whether it means [seeking] media attention or not."

If you talk to those who preceded Tosi and Bertinetti, and made their marks before this golden age of food-as-entertainment was in full swing, you find a less self-conscious attitude toward the hype machine. "I think media's been very important, but we never did what we did to get media. There's a big difference in that we did TV because we love teaching, and it fell into our lap," says Susan Feniger, who, with her partner Mary Sue Milliken, had one of the first shows on the Food Network with *Too Hot Tamales*. All told, between that program and their second, *Tamales World Tour*, from 1995 to 1999, they wrapped more than 400 episodes and, in 1996, started one of my favorite radio shows, *Good Food*, on KCRW in Santa Monica. "The media is a fantastic way to boost your restaurant," adds Feniger. "If you ask me, if you had a choice of being just a TV personality or just a restaurateur, which would you do? Not even any question for me. I would be a restaurateur. That's where my passion is . . . I believe, if you're going to be a chef, you should be focused and let that drive you. The rest—the cookbooks, TV—is gravy." She and Milliken embraced each of those projects because they wanted to have those experiences and saw them as extensions of what they were doing in their restaurants.

Traci Des Jardins has come around to seeing Feniger's side of things, but only after taking a lengthy and deliberate hiatus from the scrutinizing lens. Eventually, she deduced that boycotting the entire spectacle—declining any and all invitations to get involved—is no way to run an operation. "I'm the reluctant person in front of the camera," she shared. "I had an early taste of it in my Rubicon[193] days—that was like sixteen years ago—and I did not enjoy being recognized." She was on a few national television shows on CNN and NBC and "suddenly became recognizable." When her photo was on the front page of the *San Francisco Chronicle*, locals started chatting her up, much to her consternation. "You're in Peet's Coffee in your sweats and you're not quite awake, and then someone comes up and says, 'Hey, are you Traci Des Jardins?' and it was horrifying. I didn't want any part of it." And so she didn't partake, not for ten years. "I really didn't pursue that kind of media exposure that puts your face on something," she relayed. Once she perceived how much that exposure does for revenue, she realized that her having "crawled in a hole" was "a real detriment" to her businesses. "Being out in the media is part of what I have to do. And it's part of my job." That's how she looks at it. "I could [choose to] not do it," she expounds on her enlightened viewpoint, "but I feel like I've got everybody who's running my restaurants, and the chefs who are cooking, and they're all doing their part. Now, this is my part." This part, she

---

[193] See footnote 173, page 168.

says, is that of "figurehead," and it necessitates her being "the spokesperson out there promoting the restaurants." Putting that aspect of her job in this context, she discovered, "made it easier for me and easier to accept my relationship to media." For the record, Des Jardins's change of heart has made an impact—she was a finalist on the third season of *Top Chef Masters*, and not only made herself known (again) across the country, but she also won $30,000 for her charity, La Cocina.

Celebrity, or simply being known, has its privileges. It's also, many will tell you, a necessary evil if you're someone who dreams big. If your goal is to run a small establishment in a town where everyone knows your name, more power to you. If you're in a major metropolis and/or you want to establish a colony of stations, pandering is unavoidable. On a related note, I asked Chicago's Mindy Segal how important media is to her career. "Hard to say. I tend to shy away from media. Not that I'm shy, because I'm certainly not"—she is not, I can attest. "I have a core value that media is earned, not given . . . In a spiritual world, if you're good and you cook well, you'll get attention for your work. I like the work to speak for that . . . Buying press [by hiring a publicist] doesn't make sense to me, though my feelings on that are changing . . . since I'm doing an expansion in my business, and will have to do national press."

In order to attain that national press she's looking for, when we spoke, Segal was beginning to shop around for a public relations company that could handle her account. Although you might assume the only way to pay for coverage is to buy an ad, there's another option: You can pay a liaison (a.k.a. a publicist) to share your achievements with magazine editors and television producers. Some of these attention-getting pros will even help you market and brand yourself—hook you up with product endorsement deals, get you screen-tested for a reality show, and help you with cookbook deals. Most of the time, though, these conduits send out e-mails to people like me, suggesting stories about a (billable) talent's tips for throwing a fun tailgating party, or a new trend (gooseberries, they're everywhere; lamb fat? it's the new pork fat) that their clients happen to be on the forefront of (woohoo, chef Kendrick is serving all of his courses in drinking vessels! Wilhelm only cooks animals he killed himself—please try his ant tapenade). It's not to say they're all bombarding their media contacts with balderdash. There are some highly skilled and most likable publicists out there. Hire a good one, and you'll probably get a lot more traction. Hire a great one, and you might find yourself up for an award, or being courted by investors. Chefs who have reached that celebrepreneur (celebrity-entrepreneur) status find they can't do without a marketing and publicity program, which can be outsourced or developed in-house.

Whether or not wooing the populous floats your boat, if you're an ambitious chef, you have to figure out how you're going to draw a client base. You could decide to go "guerilla" style and run an anti-media operation wherein you keep your planning under wraps and open stealthily, for the neighborhood and some carefully selected early adopters[194] who will get the groundswell started for you, albeit slowly. Either way, though, a strategy must be sorted. We live in a world where, like it or not, story-hungry bloggers are always on the prowl, and the public can't wait for another restaurant to open. (If it's wondrous, they'll want to visit; if it's a disaster, they'll love reading about the abysmal failure.)

Melissa Perello, whose Beard-nominated Frances was listed among both *Esquire* and *Bon Appétit* magazines' Best New Restaurant selections in 2010, endorses spending money on a PR company. "I think it's important. Sometimes, honestly, it's painful. Maybe you put on this facade, this persona; it's not really me, but you kind of have to sell yourself in order to get exposure so that more people know about your restaurant and more people will come to your restaurant . . . There's a handful of chefs who are always in front of a camera, and they're getting all the recognition and all the business. And they're not necessarily better chefs, [and] their restaurants aren't any better." Perello isn't after

---

[194] This works exceptionally well if you're in an on-the-rise neighborhood that's on the cusp of cool and just beginning to be co-opted by hipsters. It also helps if you have a few regulars (or backers) with ties to the music, fashion, art, or film industries. In short, if you can get the beautiful people and/or hunters of cool to dine at your new spot without seeming as though you're trying *and* you let them find it first (so they feel like they discovered it), the media will follow and crowds descend.

celebrity, but she wants to ensure her eatery remains on the radar and is recognized for the quality of food and service it delivers. Committing to that agenda requires more effort than she anticipated. "I work with a PR company . . . In general, they're just really good at managing me and pushing me, because I have a really busy job . . . It doesn't leave me a whole lot of spare time to answer e-mails in regard to, 'What are your top five favorite things in San Francisco?' or 'Can you take this media person on a tour of San Francisco?' or 'We need seven recipe ideas that have to do with Meyer lemons,' and it's sometimes just, like, literally overwhelming. I have a call with them [her PR company] every week for an hour, and they give me a project list of all the stuff I have to do . . . They ride me for it until I respond. It really is hard and it's a lot of work sometimes."

Seattle's Renee Erickson doesn't have a publicist. For one thing, she can't afford one, but she also has other reasons for going without. "I don't know that it's going to get me to a place where I'm striving to be. I want to try to be closer to my work, not farther away, by going on tour to talk about my restaurant . . . We do a fair amount of nonprofit stuff and that's kind of where I do PR for the restaurant, by doing events for organizations that I'm happy to work with . . . at least once a month, if not more. So then, you're trying to be part of a community and support things that matter to you but also try to make sure that Boat Street [her restaurant] gets attention enough so that the people remember to come here . . . The whole system of trying to get in print, or whatever, either I just don't understand it or I'm not trying to very hard." Erickson's brand identity—the fact that I used that phrase will probably make her cringe—is shaped by a connection to her purveyors and the city she cooks for. So her not giving a hoot about national props and her inclination to stay close to home actually suits her platform. It has worked for her too.[195] "We get

---

[195] Our reporter in the copyediting field Jane Tunks chimed in with an astute remark when she asked if Erickson's being in Seattle, a smaller market, might also allow her to get away with going publicist-free. It could, yes, and because Seattle's food scene appears to be a notably community-driven one, her strategy seems particularly well attuned to that market's tastes. But, to play devil's advocate, a number of Erickson's peers in that city have hired publicists and seen positive results for having done so.

lots of great local press and are included in lots of things," she says, and in June 2011, the *New York Times*' Frank Bruni gave some love to the bivalves and "palpable conviviality" at Erickson's "embellished oyster bar," Walrus and the Carpenter, in his recap of a tasting tour through Seattle for that newspaper.[196] She spreads her message through the channels that feel right to her and, because of that, is, in fact, on point with everything her personally directed businesses stand for. That symbiotic relationship between nonprofit organizations and restaurants is one that might make naysayers a bit more receptive to dabbling in PR.

Here's Tosi with another unexpected reason why chefs should care about publicizing their achievements: "I want to learn from people I admire, from the best. How did I know I wanted to go work at WD-50? Because of the media . . . I knew that I wanted to work for them because [of] everything I've heard and learned and read." Like any diligent, committed culinary student, Tosi did her research and discovered that WD-50 restaurant was considered (by the media, at least) the best in what interested her (progressive cuisine), so she went after a job there (and if you've been paying attention, you already know she got it). In addition to gathering diners, chefs in search of potential, young talent should consider press a way to attract eager beavers who are serious about their careers.

Tosi leads with how media can influence a young cook's trajectory, and then—thanks for reminding me of this, Christina—she follows up with how that prestigious chef can, in turn, withhold from or grant you publicity (once you're on his payroll). Just how generous with the dispersal of credit is the proclaimed genius you've chosen to tie yourself to? "It depends on who you're a pastry chef for," she says—remember, she abides by the Tao of Dough. "If you're a pastry chef for David Bouley, you're not gonna get any press. No disrespect to him, but it all belongs to him and he's never even going to mention to your name in an interview, even if you're the one who's slaving away." Looks good

---

[196] Frank Bruni, "Seattle, a Tasting Menu," the *New York Times*, June 12, 2011.

on the résumé, so there's something, but the traditional Frenchie *système* isn't one that appreciates the praise-singing of underlings.

If you're a Tosi-in-the-making and you're doing the research she did, odds are, your goal is to land in a New York restaurant. It's where you'll find the highest concentration of serious contenders and the chefs who garner the lion's share of attention and awards. It's where trends are outed and shaped; where one officially "makes it." Wanna know why? Well, it's the city where all the national magazines (including the food-related ones) are based, not to mention the Food Network's headquarters. If the nabobs at those institutions call soda-making the next big thing, you're going to see that craft crop up everywhere before you can say "egg cream." It can take the form of an old-fashioned drugstore-fountain revival or a barrage of bottled artisanal syrup, first on gourmet grocery shelves and then those of Whole Foods. If the same pundits say the guy who opened the restaurant on the premises of a defunct funeral home in Spanish Harlem is the maverick who will lead cuisine into the future, soon enough, they'll know about him in Des Moines and Detroit. It's partially because New York City welcomes novelty that discoveries are often made there, but there's a practical tie-in as well. These found phenomena are conveniently located within the newsmakers' vicinities. The closer something is to home (or work), the more likely you are to notice it, and then, since the inclination is to write what you know, it's easy enough to spin a story from there.

Change is afoot. Localization has spread like wildfire. And editors or writers in need of content can scan what's brewing elsewhere with a quick visit to their Internet-rigged devices. One of the strongest forces behind this is social media. Eyes may be on New York, but people everywhere are just as enthusiastic about the places in their own backyards. They have opinions, and there are many outlets for them to express those. Crowdsourced dining has arrived. In a world where people have stopped trusting journalists and professional critics, why not take the temperature of your peer group or, better yet, some random composition of neighbors and tourists? There are those public opinion sites like Yelp, Chowhound, Urbanspoon, or MenuPages, to name a few. You can use these portals to gauge the sentiments of others, or vent about last night's dinner. If you'd rather share your discoveries in a more immediate and "personal" manner, you can tweet a little tweet about the "amazeballs fried green tomatoes" served down the street, or protest a touted table's gluey gumbo on Facebook. Who actually reads those personal news blasts? Unclear. I don't think we should be determining whether or not to eat somewhere for dinner based on some tangential "friend's" update (unless, of course, that friend has a trusted, proven palate). I do, however, appreciate a favorite local canteen's tweeting of a winning daily special, or if a restaurant changes its menu diurnally, posting that on its Facebook page or blog.

What about the editorial blogs?[197] Sure, many are merely deardiary wastes of e-space, but there are those that provide service-oriented (we in the biz say "servicey") content and are, at times, the first places we look when deciding where to go for dinner or when we want the lowdown on that asshole of a chef whose hubris has led him to open a pop-up where he—and he alone—cooks with a blindfold on.[198]

All of these posters—individual tweety birds and blog-backed scoopers—seek bragging rights. They want to be first with story. If it's a property's opening night, they descend like vultures on a carcass. Prior to that, they're tracking construction progress. They're beyond a restaurateur's or chef's control. All of this, if you think about it, is unsolicited press, which is to say, it's press. The attention places extra pressure

[197] Editorial blogs are those that provide their readership with editorial (usually service-driven) content that has been created and/or selected (er, edited) with that audience in mind. Examples of food- or restaurant-related editorial blogs are Eater and Grubstreet. They are not to be confused with personal (or what, in jest, I refer to as dear-diarrhea) blogs.

[198] I was exaggerating there. There's no chef I can think of, asshole or no, who has attempted to open such an operation (so there's no blindfolding going down). But there are such entities as Ludo Lefebvre's LudoBites, which began in Los Angeles in 2007 (this according to the official Ludolefebvre.com website) as a location-changing pop-up and now exists as "a 'touring' restaurant." Read on and you get: "Like a club band we have been touring locally since 2007 and 'playing' different parts of Los Angeles, West Hollywood, Culver City, Downtown, Sherman Oaks, with more to come." More came, and it did so nationally. In 2010 Lefebvre and his business partner and wife, Krissy, took a televised road trip to "play" in big and small towns across America. *Ludo Bites America* premiered on the Sundance Channel in July 2011.

on restaurateurs and chefs to perform, and perfectly, right out of the gate. It also generates buzz and, if your reviews are favorable, drives traffic (to your restaurant).

Yonder in Denver, Jennifer Jasinski made me aware of how fine the line between professional and amateur critics can be. "Every city is different and the caliber of their food critics varies," she started. "I don't always agree with all the people who get to name themselves food critics . . . It's just someone's opinion, like blogging or Yelping. Someone gets to put in their opinion about something you've put your heart into and you love . . . It's such an emotional thing—eating, food, dining—and there are so many moving parts, and so many operational things that go wrong . . . If you're having a fight with your boyfriend, you're not having a good experience; that's what you'll remember or associate with the restaurant. As a chef, that's completely out of my hands. Good food critics know that. They come back multiple times, on different days and at different hours. They shop you to see consistency." Sadly, though, we live in a world where all opinions count, trained or untrained—albeit maybe not equally. The opinion of a critic at a local paper (or a national-local paper like the *New York Times*) carries more weight (and can do more damage) than one angry Yelper's, but a group of inexperienced or closed-minded tasters who are all too familiar with the contents of Happy Meals and, because of that, prefer them to untried lamb burgers, can make an impact as a whole (there's strength in numbers). "Some of the things people write are so damaging—I don't know if they intend it or not," complains Atlanta's Anne Quatrano.

On the flip side, some of the things people write are awfully advantageous. Unless you've built a destination dining room tourists flock to in droves, it's the local love that keeps restaurants in business. In addition to receiving favorable reviews from regional publications,[199]

[199] I wasn't aware of how vital mentions in local media (as opposed to the highly coveted national shout-outs) are to sustaining business until Suzanne Goin told me that the best press she and partner Caroline Styne ever received, in terms of filling the house, came when *Los Angeles* magazine ranked the city's restaurants from one to fifty and Lucques was numero uno. Reservations poured in. More than the Beard Award or the review in the *Los Angeles Times*, that ranking, which appeared just as the economy was about to tank, kept them alive.

social networking can be a powerful tool for retaining and developing business. It's a cheap way to create a virtual community and stay in touch with your patrons once they've come through your doors and Yelped their initial happy thoughts. It is also, as Quatrano reminded me, yet another task for the already overworked chef-owner.

Whether it's a Chowhounder's bashing the burger at an old standby, an Urbanspoon[200] member's lavishing praise on a two-day-old restaurant, a chef's tweeting about a new tattoo, or a blog editor's spilling the beans on a just-signed lease for a new joint specializing in barbecue chicken wings, what all of this editorial democratization and localization points to is a widespread development of from-scratch projects fueled by a surge of community building (virtual or on the ground) across the country. Nancy Oakes observed that the folks behind these spots tend to apply a grassroots method to growing a groundswell of interest and that their premises have a certain shoestring appeal; they don't spend much on decor, but they "believe in [their] product" and "do something really good." A perfect example of that where she is, in San Francisco, is Mission Chinese Food.[201] You might lump New York City's Momofuku Noodle Bar[202] in the same category of enterprise.

Although the Mission Chinese and Momofuku revolutions have been fronted by male chefs, Oates sees their brand of business

---

[200] Both Chowhound and Urbanspoon are examples of popular crowdsourced or aggregate review repositories online. Chowhounders (those who post on the "Chowhound" message board co-opted by the food website Chow) are known (and sometimes, even, appreciated) for taking their "jobs" as amateur critics quite seriously, by the way.

[201] Mission Chinese Food would be the establishment that shares kitchen space with and borrows the dining room of Lung Shan restaurant (a quiet, permanent fixture in the Mission District). What began, in fall 2008, as a truck serving innovative, hybrid, scrumptious cuisine like the PB&J (flatbread folded around pork belly and jicama) morphed into dinners served on the premises of the formerly mentioned Chinese restaurant twice a week. At these events, cofounders (and spouses) chef Anthony Myint and manager Karen Leibowitz invited different chefs to pick a theme and cook accordingly, then donated a percentage of the evening's earnings to local nonprofit organizations. Eventually, the duo went for something a little more consistent and turned their part-time restaurant into full-time Mission Chinese Food (sautéing six days a week), where they've installed Danny Bowien as chef. Myint and Leibowitz published a cookbook, *Mission Street Food* (2011), to document the experience and, in February 2012, announced a New York City franchise was on the way.

[202] Momofuku Noodle Bar was developed in what was, at the time, not much more than a low-rent district, and done so economically, cheap-and-chic style. There, David Chang (sorry, I'm sure you're sick of him; he's sick of himself) quietly started to play with ramen, and well, look where he is now—opening Momofuku spin-offs in Australia and Canada, that's where.

development as a female-friendly outlet. "I think that's another opportunity for women . . . [There are] a lot of fun things, and it's all made possible by Twitter . . . and bloggers letting people know about stuff that's great . . . [and] not depending on traditional media for reviews . . . If what you have is real, and by real I mean that you are doing something that's really delicious and it's priced fairly and your spirit is behind it then . . . I think the bloggers, for the most part, are on your side." Getting the resident bloggers rooting for you, that's how you lure the bigger fish.

Since the mainstream media glommed on to the charms of regional discovery, spots like Reusing's Lantern can garner national coverage. She observes: "Media food coverage has changed a lot in the last ten years . . . it has really opened up, because I think there's a sense that readers and consumers of information about food are very much interested in what's out there, outside of urban markets, in regional cooking, in smaller towns, in places where agriculture is more at the center than foodie-ism . . . Now they're dying for the story of the small-town chef with only a twenty-seat restaurant." This, one would presume, would be exactly the type of shift that would be favorable to female chef-owners, since theirs are often those smaller venues. And yet, ratio-wise, coverage of the regional finds favors those helmed by men. Is that because small-town populations remain relatively conservative and don't roll out red carpets for, or produce as many, independent-minded entrepreneurial girls? Do the mold-breakers leave to go to the big city? That seems like a pretty lame explanation.

Reusing has a theory, and, as uncomfortable as I am with it, since, on some level, it implicates me, I have to agree with her: The food media's female population is biased toward guy chefs. To that, let's add my own observation, the food media's male population is too. Possibly out of defensiveness, I challenged Reusing with another contributing factor to our (female content-creators') collective tendency to ignore our own kind: a fear of singling out or giving some kind of preferential treatment. Call it the backlash of feminism, or just a certain hyper-sensitivity to being handled with care because you have jugs.

Reusing's take on that premise of mine wasn't quite so over-analytical. "Well," she said, speaking about the ladies of the media, "it kind of feminizes them in some way, like they want to be like the cool kid, and the cool kid is often not the woman." Why be pigeonholed as the girl who writes about lady chefs (so not ideal for one's social life) when you could, instead, be touted as that fun chick who runs around town with boys—you know, the ones whose sweet(flat)bread[203] every-one's lining up to sample late night because she, coincidentally, wrote about it. Waylynn Lucas knows what I'm talking about; it's a regular thing, according to her. "I think a lot of these powerful women in the food industry, whether editors or journalists or bloggers . . . It's almost like they're chef groupies. They're not going to get anything from me, but to be in with the hot chef or the sexy dude guy chef or whatever, they get more out of that, so they're going to put more of their focus and attention into that."

Fine, point conceded. Still, us girls, we're not acting alone. Boys lavish a lot of ink on mister chefs too. Once any food writer ("groupie" that you are) chooses the cool (male) kid de jour and exposes him to the public, there's some enjoyable wave-riding ahead of you, with a ripple effect that provides others with seemingly endless material to publish. You've created the culinary monster, and, thanks to you, everyone else wants to write him up and be apprised of his every move. Sadly, instead of moving on to a new scoop-worthy hero, most members of the press would rather restate the obvious. How many stories can you read about a single chef? A lot, it turns out. Since most of these objects of endless fixation tend to be penis carriers, their monopolization of the media doesn't do anything to put more ladies on the map. Christina Tosi has witnessed this monomania and its effects firsthand, because her boss, David Chang (yes, again), has been pegged as one such wonder boy.

---

[203] I just made that up, you like? It's a flatbread with sweetbreads on it—get it?

The reason—or one of them; there are so many—Tosi enjoys working for Chang, is that, she says, the Head Peach doesn't claim responsibility for every Momofuku-related invention. "He's not afraid to be like, 'Hey guys, what are you all squawking about? I don't do it all by myself. I have a chef de cuisine at each of the restaurants. These are their names. If you like this, that's what this person over here made.' And most of the time, the media is just like, 'Oh, David Chang and his famous Beef-7-Ways,'[204] or 'Oh, David Chang and his famous Compost Cookie,'[205] and it's like, 'Okay, do you really—purposely?' You could give them all the information in a fact-checking thing and it will just bounce or sometimes not." That's pathetic. Dude is actively correcting his followers to promote the unknown creator of the deliciousness served at one of his eateries and the groupies would rather write about him.

Carlucci-Rodriguez has some advice for us on this point: "If you're a food writer, stop kissing everyone's ass who's young and a male and really start looking at what's going on, because you're missing a lot of people." (You know, I was just thinking my next book should be about the cute guy who parks his newfangled Thai-Moroccan food truck down the block—it's a flatbed, and he turned the back into a makeshift garden where he grows all his herbs and vegetables.)

Veggie-peddling Amanda Cohen, who believes that the future success of female chefs hinges on the press changing its boy-crazy agenda, comments that it "has to start supporting women more. I really feel like on blogs, in magazines, women chefs are not supported. You don't hear about them. They don't talk about them; there's a lot more talk about male chefs, which, I think, is because that's who we know about. The press has to step outside of their comfort zone and start to look for women chefs . . . And it has to become a focus. It has to become actually important to the people writing about chefs. Or there just will

---

[204] The work of Tien Ho, the former executive chef at Chang's Má Pêche in Manhattan's Chambers Hotel, this updated traditional Vietnamese feast comprises seven courses, each showcasing a different part of the cow.

[205] Tosi's, obvi. You can find it at a Momofuku Milk Bar near you or order them online from Momofukustore.com and they'll show up at your doorstep.

not be a change . . . It all comes from there; investors read these blogs, investors see the women chefs, they see the male chefs, they think, 'Oh, this would be a good guy to hang out with,' or 'a good girl,' or whatever it is, so you really need that outside support from the press."

You might be nodding in accord with Carlucci-Rodriguez and Cohen—hard to disagree, really—but as soon as you start looking for the missing, you run into the awkwardness of the "single out." Reusing saw what, in my convoluted way, I was getting at when I tried to explain it. After she suggested that female members of the food press might be prone to go where the boys are in an act of cool-by-association, she added: "You know, that said, I think there's kind of an affirmative action feeling about a lot of press women get . . . I can't remember who wrote this piece a long time ago . . . [that] was kind of like, when you see one woman world leader in a picture, it's more jarring than if there were none, because it serves as a reminder that it is a male universe. And it's the same thing with the *Food & Wine* [Best New Chef award], like, if it were all men, it would almost be less disturbing, but it's like that one token woman always. [Laughs.]"

Yes, every year, *Food & Wine* magazine crowns ten honorees (individuals or duos) as the country's Best New Chefs, which only goes to show how hard it can be to make a clear demarcation between media attention and award-receiving (they're intertwined and Gordian-knotted). Even when one understands how both systems operate, working them to your advantage isn't necessarily a possibility. If you or what you're selling isn't relevant, it's as though you're learning the rules to a game you haven't been invited to play. "They're writing songs of love, but not for me,"[206] is that how the standard goes? It's the one I'm hearing in my head. Does it mean women like Cohen should change their styles? Is there hope of achieving legitimacy from the time-honored institutions? Or else, are there new ones that will, by appreciating those chefs' contributions, put them on equal footing with their peers

---

[206] That's how it goes. It's a Gershwin tune (music by George, lyrics by his brother Ira): "But Not for Me."

who have been recognized by the old guard? The constantly changing media landscape has given lesser known regions and unconventional restaurants a visibility they haven't previously enjoyed. What of awards programs? We're going to check in on them next.

CHAPTER 9

Proving Your Medal

It doesn't have to be equal opportunity, but it's a huge problem. And I will go back to this over and over again. Food & Wine's *[Best New Chefs] . . . You know, there's maybe one woman on that cover, maybe two every year. And I'm not saying it has to be ten women on that cover, but boy would it be exciting for a young female chef to see . . . I think it's really depressing every year. And I'm established. I'm a lucky one. But that cover, it's always like, really?*

—AMANDA COHEN

Food & Wine magazine established its Best New Chefs program in 1988. Each year, ten recipients get the call and are then celebrated on the magazine's July cover (and within that issue's pages). That first year, there was one woman included. From then on, there were just one or two with two exceptions—there were three in 1996 and zero in 2003.[207] This is what Cohen cites as a source of depression.

I've been a freelance journalist for seven years, but I once worked at *Food & Wine*.[208] For the record, I loved life on staff at that magazine and am incredibly proud to have been part of its team. Still, to say I don't have the same response as Cohen to those annual July covers with their cluster of nine guys and one girl would be a lie. It was one of the initial bees in my bonnet that, ultimately, led to this project.

If there weren't a lot of female executive chefs, then, although that annual magazine cover might smart a bit, I would also have to acknowledge that the women weren't out there to be found. But when

---

[207] The official count is as follows: 1988: 1; 1989: 2; 1990: 2; 1991: 1; 1992 (hiatus); 1993: 1; 1994: 2; 1995: 2; 1996: 3; 1997: 2; 1998: 2; 1999: 1; 2000: 3; 2001: 2; 2002: 2; 2003: 0; 2004: 1; 2005: 1; 2006: 1; 2007: 1; 2008: 2; 2009: 1; 2010: 1; 2011: 1.

[208] I covered home (kitchens, cooking appliances big and small, tableware, restaurant and residential interior design) and entertaining, a.k.a. "style."

I began tackling this book, I figured I would interview forty women (all executive chefs or chef-owners, plus maybe a chef de cuisine who was running a kitchen for someone with multiple businesses). As I went on, I kept discovering others—one chef would recommend another, or I'd hear about someone, somehow. Before I knew it, I was up to seventy, and I could have kept going. There are tons more lady exec chefs than I realized (still a whole lot fewer than the male version, true). Maybe the editors of *Food & Wine* are already aware of this and still aren't finding enough women who are up to Best New Chef par. Maybe, though, none of us has figured out how many of them exist. I was mainly focused on the country's major metropolises, so I'm not as familiar with who else is out there. If you want to rail against me for not getting to smaller towns, go ahead, I can take it; that's a fair beef. If I had more resources—time and funding—I'd love to scour the less-slogged portions of this country to discover additional chefs, male or female.

Although the Best New Chef honor has been known to predict future glory, Denver's Jennifer Jasinski doesn't believe it's the be-all and end-all. "It's one magazine's perspective—and as the people who work there have told me, they're only looking at hot, trendy stuff.[209] I've found lots of good people there, and then people who have fallen off the face of the earth." Other chefs are indifferent to blue ribbon prizes across the board. "It's not a goal of mine to win awards at all," Renee Erickson says. "I'm sure hundreds of other restaurants like mine get overlooked, because [there are] a lot of apples to oranges as far as comparisons . . . There's a typecast of what people consider great or of high quality, and if you fall into that, great, and if you don't, too bad.

---

[209] Here's what *Food & Wine* is seeking, in its own words, as of September 19, 2011: "We are looking for chefs who are going to rock our world. Each year the magazine names 10 extraordinarily talented men and women as the Best New Chefs in America. The hunt for the 2012 winners has begun, and we would love you to nominate chefs you feel deserve consideration. The style of restaurant isn't important: It could be an elegant dining room or a shiny taco truck. What does matter is that these chefs in the kitchen are the superstars of the future: creative, thoughtful and passionate cooks with a personal culinary style that always results in unique and delicious food. Here are the specific criteria: The nominee must create menus and oversee the day-to-day operation of the kitchen. He or she must have held the top chef position at one or more restaurants for no more than a total of five years. The restaurant does not need to be new, and the chef's age is not a consideration." According to Nancy Nichols, who posted that quote the very same day on SideDish, Dallas-based *D Magazine*'s food blog, that "call from *Food & Wine* magazine went out to editors all over the country."

[Laughs.] . . . The system that exists sort of leaves out a whole category of restaurants, whether there is a male or female running it."

Melissa "Mel" Nyffeler shared the sentiments of her fellow Seattle chef-owner Erickson about those who, as they do, own small local restaurants that don't aspire to four-star-level bedazzlement or the awards that those honored venues were built (and invested in) to win. When you spend that kind of money on a business, it's with the expectation that it'll yield a hefty profit, and how else can it do that without an endless stream of paying customers who are charged accordingly? These palaces are designed as destination spots. Press nabs (often traveling) diners and awards (or nominations), which will snag more eaters. In her own way, Nyffeler, whose fuss-free, ingredient-loving Dinette falls into the "neighborhood" genre, feels the pressure to be more competitive, but chooses to ignore it:

"I think that PR has a lot to do with people getting recognition. Talented chefs who get nominations often have PR people working for them, sending press kits or whatever to whoever's doing the voting or nominating. There are just so many talented people who are lost and just sort of buried in the restaurant world, who never get any recognition. I also don't feel like I'm a cutting-edge cook—I'm not inventing anything new here. I'm a good, creative cook, but I'm not out there trying to win the James Beard Award because of some new techniques that I'm using. I like being a humble cook, but it's not about being humble; it's about survival, basically. If you want to survive, you have to talk about yourself and tell people how great you are, in this business . . . Self-promotion is a way to increase your chances of winning more awards."

A flowchart emerges as you realize how the influence moves up the food-media chain until it reaches the institutional acme, Casa Beard (the James Beard Foundation—or JBF—has its HQ in New York's Greenwich Village; it is called the Beard House). Local buzz manufactured by PR initiatives, the critics who received the press releases or did some unaided scouting, nosey bloggers who harass the poor construction crew as it erects a new site to find out when it will open, and chefs who enjoy tweetfests or otherwise engage in attention-getting stunts (some culinary, some not) pique the curiosity of national food or ahead-of-the-curve style websites. That's followed by print publications like *Food & Wine, Bon Appétit, Saveur, Every Day with Rachael Ray,* or *The Food Network Magazine,* and then, beyond that, to travel and lifestyle magazines like *Travel & Leisure* or *Vogue.* With the right kind of exposure, chefs can sell themselves to book publishers and pen culinary tomes, and they can get the most important thing of all: backing. They can open bigger, more expensive restaurants—just the thing appreciated by the Beards. The better known you are, and the more money you have behind you, the more likely it is you'll be nominated for, and even win, the award. *Food & Wine*'s Best New Chefs is the first major step in that direction; once you're slapped on that cover with the other nine Bests, you're expected to arrive at the magazine's Food & Wine Classic in Aspen (it's like Sundance, for food people, without the self-righteousness or the indie cred), where, after you do some demos for the crowd, you can mingle with some serious players (read sponsors), and you're also treated to frequent editorial check-ins and write-ups. So the Besties (why not call them that; it's catchy, no?) can really get you started. They are, however, but a stepping-stone to the Beards, which helps to explain why the concerns raised by talk of the BNCs (perhaps you prefer an acronym) apply to and are heightened by the Beardness (couldn't resist, sorry).[210]

If you're looking for gravitas, you've come to the right event. Often referred to as the "Oscars of the food world," the James Beard Awards are undoubtedly the most prestigious and renowned medals given to chefs and restaurants in this country. Our honorary MC for

---

[210] There is another organization that hands out awards—StarChefs.com, the online magazine with the annual Chef Salary Report you learned about in footnote 129, page 119. Theirs are the Rising Star Awards, and of course it's an honor to receive one, but they dole out many more per annum (they do a series of medallions for each region) than the James Beard lot, and they don't have the same status attached to them outside the industry. Non-food-biz people have heard of the Beards; they're not familiar with this other bunch.

this on-page decoration program, Cohen, had a lot to say on the subject (shocker), and I've distilled her diatribe to three main cavils that deserve extended conversation.

1. **The Girl Powerlessness:** "I'd love to see somebody who's a woman who gets those awards. You want to have something to live up to . . . I aspire to be this New York chef, competing with all these men, getting this award, and it doesn't really happen that often."

2. **The Critical Conditions:** "The criteria [are] actually insane. To be nominated to be a Rising Star—whatever that younger award is called—you have to be under thirty[211] . . . There's no way I could be there [at that level] in my career. Now, there are some people within that starred system who could, for sure, but if you're working at smaller restaurants . . . It's not just about being a woman in that case; it's just outside of the system. And then to be the best chef in New York City, which is supercompetitive . . . look how established you have to be. You have to be a Tom Colicchio or a Daniel Boulud, or [a] Jean-Georges [Vongerichten]. So then you have this whole middle range of great, talented cooks who are too old and not established enough."

3. **The Bottom Line:** "It also seems financially unfair. If I open a second restaurant and make it superfancy and . . . get a real review—which Dirt Candy's not had yet anywhere—and we make that supersuccessful, then yes, maybe, possibly, we'll be considered."

Let's start at the top: Women chefs aren't the favorites at the annual awards ceremony. True dat. There's one heat in which their odds are significantly improved: pastry. Since 1991, when the first ribbon-strung, gold JB pendants were handed out, of the twenty-one years' worth of Outstanding Pastry Chef recipients, twelve have been women. That's more than 50 percent, giddyup! Funny how everyone

---

[211] It's actually thirty and under.

thinks ladies dominate that sweet field, though (*dominate* would have them bringing home a few more than that, right?).[212] Meanwhile, this award the institution is giving out isn't doing much to strengthen pastry's image; if anything, the Beard's sweet "honor" reinforces the already infuriating fallacy that this branch of the culinary profession is the weaker link. While there's a Best Chef Award bestowed upon eleven chefs (one for each of ten national regions plus another for New York City), as well as a singular Outstanding Chef Award, there is only this one Outstanding medal handed out to a pastry chef. That's it. (If you're counting, that's twelve for savory; one for pastry.) So people of the crumb[213] can consider themselves fucked on that score.

Patti Jackson, who's biculinary (does pastry, her initial specialty, and savory[214]—yes, I came up with that one myself too), agrees that this lone girl-friendlier prize is a ruse. "That's the Erica Kane award too," she said, referring to the role made famous by soap actress Susan Lucci (*All My Children*), who was up for a Daytime Emmy fifteen times before anyone was willing to let her have it. "They'll just nominate the same five people every year, and then the five people they nominate continue to be nominated until they win."

Another voice from the pastry squad, twenty-something Heather Bertinetti, is already disenchanted with the antics. "The Beard Awards [are] a joke, I'm sorry," was her succinct assessment. Although she can—at such a young age—claim that, under her dough-eyed watch, her affiliated restaurants have garnered nine *New York Times* stars, four Michelin stars, and a Best New Restaurant Beard Award, she has yet to receive a nomination from the JBF in her area of expertise. She blames this on her refusal to campaign. "It's because I don't play the

---

[212] Do note, however, in recent years, you'd be lucky to find one male nominee in the annual crop. And, in 2012, all six nominees for the Outstanding Pastry Chef Award were chippies.

[213] Before Jane Tunks (copy editor par excellence) tells me my "people of the crumb" thing is obtuse, I'll make a preemptive strike with this clarification. It's a reference to Pulitzer Prize–winner Geraldine Brooks's 2008 work of historical fiction, *The People of the Book*, which I never read, but have heard wonderful things about. It won the Australian Book Industry Award for Book of the Year and Literary Fiction Book of the Year.

[214] See page 144.

political game and run with that same circle of friends, and I don't socialize and blog, and I'm not all over Eater. And I don't go to my PR company all the time, with like, 'Hey, I think I want to go to Spain and write about it,' and all this stupid stuff. You know what I mean? I just, I don't care."

The cliquey activities that Bertinetti avoids, I suspect, contribute to the Erica Kane syndrome. The short list for title of Best Chef: New York City edition always seems peopled with the same rotating roster of predictable toques.[215] There are five nominees and each one usually spends four years on that list before getting the victory. Seniority rules. Once a member of the group wins, he, or once in a while she, is kicked out, but because these awards can help make such dreams come true, that same victor will probably go on to open a new restaurant and then, possibly, get a Beard nod for that. Or if he (and this is very much a he thing) starts opening multiple joints, he (Mario Batali and Daniel Boulud can flash you their golds) may then get thrown in the small pool for an Outstanding Restaurateur emblem. All the while, these dudes are growing in fame, popularity, and resources.

No matter where you're cooking in these here United States of America, if you've got a bosom—nature's display shelf for a medallion—enjoying a brush with Beardness is only slightly less challenging than pushing your camel through the eye of a needle or, if that's a bit hyperbolic, we might say than finding that same needle in a haystack. When Ann Cashion got her ticket (Best Chef: Mid-Atlantic) in 2004, she was the second of her kind in her region to have one. Nearly a decade later, this remains true. You'd expect her to be trotted out for photo ops, right? Not according to her: "What I find really interesting is that—because

---

[215] Here are the nominees for Best Chef: NYC from 2008 to 2012. The * indicates the victor.

2008: Michael Anthony (Gramercy Tavern), Terrance Brennan (Picholine), David Chang (Momofuku Ssäm Bar),* Wylie Dufresne (WD-50), Gabriel Kreuther (The Modern)

2009: Michael Anthony, Terrance Brennan, Wylie Dufresne, Gabrielle Hamilton (Prune), Gabriel Kreuther*

2010: Michael Anthony, Wylie Dufresne, Gabrielle Hamilton, Daniel Humm (Eleven Madison Park),* Michael White (Marea)

2011: Michael Anthony, April Bloomfield (The Spotted Pig), Wylie Dufresne, Gabrielle Hamilton,* Michael White

2012: Michael Anthony,* April Bloomfield, Wylie Dufresne, Mark Ladner (Del Posto), Michael White

I don't have that swagger and because that isn't my focus and I don't have a PR person—I've actually found that people have no idea that I won the Beard Award. None whatsoever. It's really interesting . . . It's definitely hard to get taken seriously at *that* level."

Mary Sue Milliken thinks it's hard to get taken seriously at that level if you're not aspiring near the Eastern Seaboard. When I ask if she feels the media overlooks West Coast restaurants and chefs, Milliken's first thought is not of the press, but of good old James. "Absolutely, without a doubt. Before it became the Beard Awards, it was the Who's Who [of Food and Beverage in America] and Susan [Feniger] and I got that honor in 1985.[216] Craig Claiborne gave us the award onstage. Then it transitioned into the Beard Awards, and ever since,[217] we've never even been nominated." I'm amazed that with the number of businesses Milliken and Feniger have successfully launched and sustained, they've never been nominated for that restaurateur award. What's their fatal flaw? Milliken thinks it's their California location, that "if you don't make a huge effort to be part of the East Coast food scene in some way," you miss the *SS Beard* boat. She also suspects the category of restaurant counts. "We've never been a really super-high-end kind of place, or those kind of chefs," she says. She's addressing price point and attitude, but one might ask if the genre of food served (I am forced to invoke the accursed word *ethnic*[218] here, since their Border Grill empire showcases Mexican cuisine) is implicated as well. Whatever the cause(s), here's

[216] The year James Beard died.

[217] The JBF's website proclaims, "On November 1986, the James Beard Foundation officially opened the James Beard House." And then, "in 1990, the James Beard Foundation made another leap forward by establishing the James Beard Foundation Awards for excellence in the food- and beverage-related industries. The first awards were given in 1991." The site also provides some clarification for Milliken's comment about the Who's Who of Food and Beverage in America honor. It was established by *Cook's Magazine* (the publication subsequently reborn and rebranded as *Cook's Illustrated*) in 1984 and, in 1991, was folded into the James Beard Awards program. The process remains unchanged: "Each year a ballot of 20 possible candidates with bios is created and distributed to the entire Who's Who group for voting. [Five or six] inductees are announced as part of the James Beard Foundation Awards festivities in the spring."

[218] I hate this term. It reads as dated, inaccurate, and offensive. That said, we, the food-writing community, haven't found a legitimate replacement for it. When I use the word *ethnic* here, it can refer to one specific non-Western culture, or it can describe a combination of regional or cultural influences and traditions. And let's not, please, speak of "fusion" either.

my suggestion: Maybe they need to initiate a gift program—a monthly basketful of tamales to the Beard House.

If the Beardness does favor one side of the country, most of its affections lie with New York City. You can probably guess why. It's not so much that this is where the media and chez Jimbo are based; it's also where one finds the highest concentration of restaurants and (Vegas aside), more specifically, of fine-dining establishments—the expensive ones, the Beard magnets. That's why, as Cohen complained, it's that much more competitive in the Big Apple. If you're a vegetable-cooking gal with a minuscule, laid-back shop (or, really, a gal who cooks anything at all in her own or someone else's spot) in this, the city that never sleeps (because we're always eating), the award is not something to get too hopeful about.

Still, everyone primps for the "Oscars," that one evening in May when the winners' names are announced at a ceremony followed by a glitzy reception. (You find a lot of women wearing bedazzled dresses; looks like a middle-aged prom reunion. Rachel Zoe would gag if she saw these things go by on a Hollywood red carpet.) It's never a night that gives the ladies much to celebrate—until the night that celebrated the ladies. Each year, a theme is selected, and it informs the black-tie gala that follows the big announcements. At this party, chefs are invited to cook and serve grub appropriate to the chosen leitmotif. (In 2011, for example, it was "The Ultimate Melting Pot." How inclusive.) In 2009, guess what year it was? Can you? The Year of the Woman. For whatever reason, this laud-the-ladies program involved asking a number of the country's most accomplished (and mostly underappreciated by the Beardness) to stand onstage, decked out in orange chef coats, like prisoners in a lineup. My favorite part of the shebang (which I wasn't present to witness) is that only two females took that stage to receive a medal (sixteen of the ninety-six[219] of the night's nominees were skirts), and then, following that, all

---

[219] Helen Rosner, one of, in my opinion, the best (food) writers typing right now, crafted the perfect post about the ludicrousness of the charade for her (now defunct) Eat Me Daily blog on April 30, 2009, before the events took place. She updated it afterward to account for the final stats. It is from that brilliant piece that I borrow these numbers. And, for your amusement, I will offer a fragment of her musings here:

the tangerine-clad sisters prepared and served supper at the fancy fete. They came. They stood. They worked. What a year for women!

The intentions were good. I spoke to Susan Ungaro, who has been the foundation's president since 2006 and was, before that, the editor in chief of *Family Circle*, a magazine targeted to (and read by) women. She made it clear that while the institution administers the awards, it operates separately from the judging; her involvement is with the festivities. If you have a problem with the evening's theme, she's the one to speak to. If your gripe is about the measly number of women nominated and, measlier still, victorious, she can't help you there. If you're wondering how someone who's aware (and she is) of the disparity between the total male versus female honorees could organize a *celebration* of the very people who, moments earlier, were made short shrift of, she offers this: "It was a loud flag-waving of wanting to focus the spotlight on all the great women, not just in the chef or restaurant world, but the media too." Stuck between a rock and a hard place—giving the disenfranchised special attention even if it draws criticism, or ignoring them entirely—she decided it was better to do something than nothing.[220]

"Of this year's nominees for the Restaurant and Chef awards—the ones that, let's face it, are the only ones most people care about—women aren't too well represented. It's no worse than any other year, sure, but contrasted against the hot-pink announcements that this year's gala is 'celebrating Women in Food,' the asymmetry comes into sharp relief.

"Of the five nominees for Outstanding Restaurateur: **zero women**. Outstanding Chef: **one of five**. Outstanding Restaurant: **one of five**. Rising Star Chef: **one of six**. Best New Restaurant: **zero**. Outstanding Wine Service: **zero**. Outstanding Service: **zero**. In fact, of the 19 overall categories, the *only one* in which a majority of the nominees are female is—surprise, surprise—Outstanding Pastry Chef, a.k.a. 'the Ladies' category,' in which three of the five have two X chromosomes . . .

"So here's the message: The girls can look hot onstage, and they can plan the party. Heck, they can even cook for the guests. But their pretty little necks aren't strong enough to wear that James Beard medal."

[220] Ungaro had some other thoughts on women's place in the Beardness. I'll just scatter a few for your contemplation:

"James Beard, he may have been a gay man, but he loved and championed a lot of women in the food world. Some of his best friends and the people he mentored were women—Gael Greene, Alice Waters, Barbara Kafka, Julia Child . . ."

Vis-à-vis the disproportionate guys-to-girls ratio: "I think it reflects society—look at *Forbes* and *Fortune* magazines on the salary of the one hundred top American executives, all of whom are men and are paid twice as much as the women executives. I think there's a more democratic environment in our restaurants."

"There was a time [when] pastry award nominees were always women and now we have men in that category."

"[It's] not just about women, [it's] about anyone in the industry who hasn't made it. You have to toot your own horn [to] . . . get press; you have to support each other."

"In the 21 years since we've been awarding the James Beard Awards, over 350 accomplished women have received a medallion in all categories [combined] . . . When we started there weren't many women in the industry."

"Our mission is 'to support, nurture, and preserve the country's diverse culinary heritage and future.' "

When I checked in with Ungaro, it was two years after that of the Woman, and I was eager to know what impact was made. "I've done my counting, tried to see how many women are represented," she told me in the spring, before the ceremonies got under way. "This year, 2011, our [female] nominees just in the restaurant/chef [division][221] are nineteen out of ninety-five, so almost 20 percent." The real test is for the judges—and it's not merely a matter of how many (or few) biddies they put on the ballot; it's who wins that counts. Good news: In 2011, it was more than two. And of the five who carried the heavy emblem on their knockers that night, one, Gabrielle Hamilton, who won the Best Chef: New York City title, was the first female to claim it since 1999.[222] Andrea Reusing received the Best Chef: Southeast prize, and Saipin Chutima (in a tie) the Best Chef: Southwest. The other two went, respectively, to Belinda Chang for Outstanding Wine Service and Angela Pinkerton for the one and only Outstanding Pastry Chef Award. Even snail-paced progress is better than none at all. Cohen may not yet have cause to dance in the streets, but a girl can dream, can't she?

And with that, let's go back to the vegetable lady's list of grievances. The age cutoff—thirty is the oldest one can be—for the Rising Star JBA poses a serious challenge to those who strive for greatness outside of the haute-cuisine temples. I'm not sure the small date-of-birth window is at all prohibitive here; the offending variable seems to be the class of kitchen in which one is employed. It's almost silly to state, yet again, the now obvious: There ain't a lot of chicks in those precious galleys. The last time a female chef's name was called for this title on Beard night was in 2004, "Allison Vines-Rushing." She was the chef de cuisine at Alain Ducasse's eponymous four-star French boîte at the Essex House

---

[221] Those, in case you weren't certain, are the awards we've been discussing here. There's a Book, Broadcast & Journalism Awards Dinner held on a separate, earlier evening. We're not getting into that. Maybe a masochistic chef will decide to pen a tome about that and interview me for it.

[222] Sumathi Reddy, "Women Make Mark at 2011 James Beard Foundation Awards," Speakeasy blog, *The Wall Street Journal*, May 9, 2011. Note: In this article, Hamilton is quoted as saying she thought 1997 was the last time a woman won this award, but Lidia Bastianich took it home in 1999.

in Manhattan. What's more exceptional, her holding that medal or that job? It had been a decade since a girl had been dubbed Lady Rising Star at that award ceremony. Before Vines-Rushing, Chicago chef Sarah Stegner[223] took it in 1994, and two years earlier, in 1992, it went to Debra Ponzek at Montrachet.[224] In twenty-one years, three women. In 2011, of the five nominated, two were women,[225] and one of those was a pastry chef, Christina Tosi. The big deal here is not that we had two out of five, but that a pastry chef was considered in the same pool (or league) as the rest. I don't think anyone was truly surprised when neither lady's name was called.

From Cohen's problem with being a slower-to-rise, lower-hanging star to her third grouse, the insidiousness of what we might—if we're going to be crude about it—label award-financing, we're having the same conversation about how exclusion can be the impetus for independent action and how the products of that recourse are unable to receive the same recognition as those within the original, blackballing system. And, yes, apologies for the redundancy, it comes down to dollars and cents, to Restaurants (capital R) versus bistros. Do the James Beard Awards discriminate against women? Not directly. Do they discriminate against diminutive, less formal establishments that have

---

[223] While in Chicago, eating my way through that windy-but-delicious city, I had Friday lunch at Carrie Nahabedian's restaurant Naha (you've already met her in these pages), and I mapped out my intended weekend culinary itinerary for her. She told me it was imperative that I squeeze in a stop, between breakfast at Green City Market (a farmers' market you should try to visit if ever you're in town) and lunch at the Purple Pig, because Sarah Stegner's lemon ricotta pancakes were worth my trouble. If anyone else had advised me to change my schedule for lemon ricotta pancakes, I would have dismissed him or her, immediately. But Carrie, I trust. Off I went to Prairie Fire, owned by Stegner and her husband, George Bumbaris, and, for a midmorning snack, had the best, lightest, fluffiest, most ethereal pancakes of my life. The syrup was superfluous. I would tell you all to hop a plane just for a short stack but, alas, the restaurant is closed. Stegner and Bumbaris can be found at their other spot, Prairie Grass Café, in Northbrook, Illinois, where I've no doubt they're doing some damn fine cooking. However, there is no sign of those pancakes on the brunch menu there. Maybe if we all post requests on the "Contact Us" page of the Prairie Grass website, the chefs will bring the pancakes back. Do you think?

[224] More on this Manhattan treasure later, on page 241. In the meantime, Ponzek ditched New York for Connecticut in 1995. In the town of Riverside, she and her husband Gregory Addonizio opened Aux Délices, a specialty foods and pastry takeout shop. They've added two more franchises (one in Greenwich, the other in Darien) and built a commercial kitchen in Stamford where cooking classes are taught.

[225] Here's one for you: These were the only two women on the entire list of thirty-one chefs chosen as semifinalists in this category. I guess we should jump for joy because both made it onto the list of nominees (or, finalists). In 2012, there were five gals in the semifinalist pack, and the same two (Tosi and, from Gautrau's in New Orleans, Sue Zemanick) made the final(ist) cut. Faux spoiler alert: Tosi wins.

smaller budgets? Yes. Are those the kinds of venues that women are more likely to open or find jobs at? Yes.

There's no reason to rehash the conversation about how, to catch the eye of the nominating public (and subsequently of the online voting body, the regional panelists, and the Restaurant and Chef Awards Committee[226]), restaurateurs are encouraged to spend money on PR, or how, press aside, the JBAs tend to favor eateries with certain costly features, such as pastry departments. That's all part of how you capture the attention (and adoration) of the ballot-producers and ballot-casters.[227] If you fancy yourself a contender (as in, if you are Amanda Cohen's doppelgänger and have, in fact, gone on to open that second restaurant she hypothetically tossed out there—the "superfancy" one) and manage to get on the Beard radar, how do you ensure you stay on it? This too costs money. There are myriad JBF-sponsored shindigs to which chefs are graciously invited to participate (cook) and are not paid for their efforts; it's all out-of-pocket. As Mary Sue Milliken relayed, she and the other Hot Tamale, Susan Feniger, "saw the writing on the wall with the Beard House early on, and we just stopped doing any fund-raisers [for the Beard foundation], because we weren't sure, but we didn't have a good instinct about where the money was going.[228] And then it sort of became clear. And now, I think, with the

---

[226] As per the James Beard Foundation Awards Policies and Procedures (found on the institution's website) under the section header "Nominee Selection and Judging":

"Anyone can submit a chef or restaurant for consideration during the online open call for entries in the fall. There is no entry fee.

"The Restaurant and Chef Awards Committee produces a ballot with approximately 20 semifinalists in each category. This ballot is distributed online to a voting body of 308 previous James Beard Restaurant & Chef Award winners; 200 to 250 panelists divided evenly among 10 regions (see below); and 17 members of the Restaurant and Chef Award subcommittee. All votes count equally and are tabulated by the independent accounting firm Lutz & Carr.

"The finalists in each category are announced in March. A second ballot is then distributed to the same voting body. Winners are announced during the Awards Ceremony in May."

In 2012, seventeen (industry-related) authors, journalists, or editors sat on the Restaurant and Chef Awards Committee. Each year, members are listed among the foundation's aforementioned Awards Policies and Procedures.

[227] See previous footnote for a refresher or clarification.

[228] Ah, right, the scandal. In 2005, it was discovered that the (then) president of the James Beard Foundation, Len Pickell, was stealing from that institution. Big time (more than a cool mil). He was convicted (pleaded guilty) and went to jail for the crime. He died in 2007, by the way.

new people who have taken over, I think we would probably do something, but, you know, we just haven't." Cathy Whims, in the running for Best Chef: Northwest (2011), also acknowledged the pressure to participate (and pay). She shared the following anecdote about the ever-constant should-I-or-shouldn't-I event quandary. "I talked to Joyce Goldstein[229] about whether to do one recently. She said, 'If you're doing it for the goodness of your heart, yes; but, not if you're worried about saying no.' I was still scared to say no, and it's expensive and hard work." She singled out restaurant labor and oven space as two of the items that factor into the steep tally.

No matter how undemocratic or flawed you find the methods behind their madness, the Beards wield power over chefs, enough to make an otherwise outspoken candidate nervous about going on the record. Awards—the promise or custody thereof—can coerce people to do things they'd prefer not to or, alternatively, stop them from saying yes to other opportunities they'd like to have. Naomi Pomeroy, a former Best New Chef, was nominated for the Best Chef: Northwest Beard in 2010, but then snubbed a year later. Comparing them to the Screen Actors Guild awards, she values these culinary honors because she sees them as a measure of her community's respect. She worried that participating in Bravo's reality show *Top Chef Masters* could turn off her colleagues in the industry—that her peers might take her less seriously and the nominations cease. Did she go on television anyway? Hell yes.[230] And she's glad she did. It brings more people to your restaurant and makes you more visible to potential investors. One wonders which is more profitable, doing a national television program on which you're ranked as a master of your craft or receiving a JBA. One also wonders if her chances of obtaining the latter will be affected by

---

[229] A true trailblazer in the culinary industry, Goldstein has written a ton of cookbooks and is, today, a sought-after restaurant consultant and one of the country's preeminent food writers. Before that, though, she was a chef-restaurateur. She holds a Beard or two as well. In 1993, she received the Best Chef: California.

[230] A season three contestant, Pomeroy was up there with Milliken and Des Jardins; she finished strong, in fourth place.

her choice. Something tells me it won't.[231] (Being on air certainly hasn't prevented Mario Batali from raking in the Beards.)

So what does happen when you win? Emily Luchetti, who grabbed the gold for Outstanding Pastry Chef in 2004 and is currently the board chair of the James Beard Foundation, has a healthy perspective on the value of such prizes:

"Throughout my career, at times I've gotten a lot of awards, and at other times I haven't gotten a lot of awards. There are always the ones you miss . . . You can't live for the awards; you can't define your existence around them, because if you don't get them, you're going to be pretty disappointed and pretty unhappy. That being said, when you do get the award, it does feel good. Does that mean, when I got the Beard award that I thought I was the best pastry chef in the world? No. It meant that I was one of the top in the world—or the country—and people acknowledged that. It's kind of your turn for fifteen minutes. It doesn't mean you're the best ever; doesn't mean that the other people nominated with you were any worse than you or that you were any better than them. It was just your time and the stars were aligned. But you don't let it define your existence, because an award doesn't pay the rent. It can open doors that hadn't been opened before, or that were harder to open . . . It's not just about winning; it's being part of the group."

Another proud owner of a certified authentic Beard pendant, Ana Sortun was one of the people I enjoyed speaking to about all the hoopla, because she gave me a reason or two to believe in the process and its outcome. Where most women (understandably) are frustrated with the state of Bearded affairs and wary of the mysterious goings-on behind the curtain, Sortun represents the model winner (Best Chef: Northeast, 2005) and, now, voter. "The James Beard stuff, it doesn't get any better than that," she told me. "It's fantastic. It's not like it's coming from one person. It comes from everyone, and it's just such a

---

[231] The year 2012 found Pomeroy back on that James Beard list of Best Chef: Northwest nominees.

great thing . . . I think it's the coolest thing for all chefs . . . We support it; it supports us . . . It's genuine." Nice to hear a little positivity amid the negativity.

I wanted to know more about the voting, at least from Sortun's vantage point. She focuses on the practices of past clinchers, because that's where she's coming from. "Most of the people who have won a James Beard Award understand the significance behind it, myself included." She says. And then she goes into greater detail about how she decides which of the ballot's categories to concentrate on, and within those, which boxes to tick off. Ideally, you should aim to eat in the restaurant of every finalist in a region if you plan to cast a vote for its related award. Will you select a winner in one area if you haven't done the homework, I asked. "You're not supposed to . . . It's clearly stated on the ballot; you cannot vote for anyone if you've never eaten at their restaurant." She tempered that with an aside—"everybody cheats a little bit, but you're not supposed to."

Guys, is anyone thinking what I am? What if you went to the restaurant(s) of only one of the nominees in a group of five and voted for him (or her)? If the rule is that you can't select a chef whose restaurant you haven't dined at, technically, you've done nothing wrong. But how do you know that that person's restaurant was better than those you didn't go to? How does this make you an accurate judge for that category? There's no balance system in place here; it could become a popularity contest. If one chef is better known, or has the ability to put his name out there more or mingle with the other chefs, then his might be that single restaurant in a region's category to which more eligible voters are apt to go. I queried Sortun about this and realized it relies on an honor code, to which, she, for one, always tries to adhere and believes others do as well. She offers an example. "I wanted to vote for a specific chef; I had never eaten at his restaurant, but I know him, so I flew down to Philadelphia and ate in his restaurant before I had to turn in the ballot so that I could vote for him . . . I made a point so that I could do it fair.

You just do what you can do; the guys are really doing it with the heart and soul of what the James Beard is all about. So, if you're in Chicago, you really look up all the people you're supposed to be checking out." Sortun continued and brought up the voting-age factor, which is, like the honor code, simultaneously reassuring and worrisome. "There are people who have been voting for twenty-five years; so they do know what's going on. It's different if you've just won and it's your first year voting . . . Every year I vote, I get to vote for more categories, because I'm paying attention . . . People like Daniel Boulud, he knows everything that's going on, you know. He has been voting for so many years . . . When you get on the list of semifinalists, then the chefs start coming in, 'cause it's their responsibility. And I'm not talking random chefs, I'm talking Alice Waters and people who are voting. A lot of people really do take their responsibility seriously. But, again, they can't run around to every single place in the country. You have to skip some columns, or say you know three out of the five restaurants that are nominated. But still, I think it's fair."

Let me tell you what raises an eyebrow here. First off, who has the time and financial wherewithal to do all that traveling? Maybe, since, as I've already delved into, winners tend to be those with well-funded enterprises and full staffs, this is no biggie. And that's wondrous that after twenty-five years Daniel Boulud or Alice Waters are ace ballot-casters, but what about the freshmen? Finally, how do we feel about three out of five? Just asking. (When you ask yourself that, also contemplate where you're more likely to go—in the Midwest, say. Do you think people might favor larger cities?[232])

I'd like to believe (and I am optimistic, despite the arched brow) that Sortun is one of many mindful, honorable judges. Not all are from that past-winner circle. Of the 500-plus voters, 308 are such former

---

[232] I have no idea, by the way, but Sortun threw out Chicago as her example, and I notice that in 2011, the Great Lakes category included three chefs from that town, one from its suburb Western Springs, and one from Ann Arbor. If you're in Chicago, it's easy to test out the work of the three chefs based there, but how many people are getting in a car and driving out to Western Springs? And will a special trip be taken to Ann Arbor? Advantage, Chicago toques, I'd presume. There's your three out of five.

day-carriers.[233] That leaves the remaining 200 to 250 regional panelists and the 17 who sit on the subcommittee. We can only hope they do the same due diligence and care as much about the legacy they're meant to uphold. I gleaned some intel about these additional inputters because a few interviewees (a past winner or two who believed the standards were higher when her turn came, back in the day) commented on how the nomination process had changed, and I wanted to get the lowdown. Mitchell Davis, the vice president of the foundation, couldn't have been more helpful, and, just like Ungaro, he gave me the impression that a concerted effort is being made to enhance the fairness factor over there.

Here's what he conveyed, via e-mail.

> The change is that until a few years ago (maybe five?), we used to distribute a hard copy Call for Entry ballot for the Chef & Restaurant awards. This was sent to all members, everyone who cooked at the Beard House, our entire database. And anyone could request one, fill it out, and mail it in. When we went online, and the whole online food universe exploded, obviously more people could suggest possible candidates. The links to the call for entries were distributed on blogs and e-newsletters and through other means. The limiting factors of having to request and/or receive a ballot, complete it, put a stamp on it, and mail it in the old system meant we had fewer entries. But we know that people would still "stuff the ballot box" with multiple submission[s] or by organizing mail in campaigns that we weeded through with the help of our accounting firm. Now, online, similar shenanigans may also take place, but because every computer submission has a unique IP address, it's easier to prevent or sort through the irregularities in the forms.

> "Although our numbers of responses for the call to entries has jumped exponentially now that we conduct it online, the biggest difference I think is that more restaurants in more diverse

---

[233] See footnote 225, page 227, and, yes, night-carrier might be the better term here since the awards are presented at eventide.

areas have come to our attention. That's why we started to release the 'semifinalists' to the public, which are the results of the top twenty to thirty entries in each category. We used to keep this secret, only to be seen by the 400 or so judges who vote on who actually becomes the top five nominees and then vote again to pick the winners. But we were encouraged by the diversity of the entries to let people know that even though it seems like some of the same names appear from year to year in the final list of nominees, the field of semifinalists for consideration has widened tremendously."

For anyone who appreciated the former proceedings because they relied on a closed circuit of peers, a widening of the net isn't necessarily a welcome amendment. Remember, the modification applies to the nominating. As long as it doesn't interfere with the determination of semifinalists or, more important, voting on finalists, I'm not sure it's the worst change; there might be a battle to choose the lesser of two evils here. People cried "popularity contest" before; now there's just a bigger (potentially less discerning) populous involved. The 17 committee members[234] decide who's on that last ballot (the one that matters most). What the adjustment does, as Davis noted, is give some love to a greater "diversity" of venue; plus, it grants the Beards ampler exposure and, in so doing, allows the award-winner (or even nominated) sticker to have greater clout with the dining public (if not the chefs themselves).

No chef (none I've spoken to), even those on the inside, has a wholly reverent view of these awards. "I support the Beard Foundation," Atlanta chef Anne Quatrano says, "There are so many people who cook their frigging hearts out every day and it's so nice that there's something that recognizes them . . . But it's annoying that it's a big business." Not annoying enough to stop her from sitting on the board, which she

---

[234] That would be the Restaurant and Chef Awards Committee whom you learned more about via footnote 225, page 227.

does. That overseeing body, she explains, "is responsible for how it's [the foundation] funded—the schlepping and cooking we all do for the foundation is important, too, but it's really the sector of food-obsessed people with money who keep it afloat . . . We [those on the board] have nothing to do with who wins." She mentioned that her taking on that responsibility renders her eateries and the chefs who helm their respective kitchens out of the running for an award nod. "I have a chef de cuisine at each location and a co-owner at Abattoir," she says, "and they want recognition . . . to be recognized by Beard or *Food & Wine* magazine, those are very important things to my staff—probably as important as making money . . . It helps you forge your career path. It was huge for us when it happened—fantastic to get *Food & Wine* when we did.[235] It was a huge deal and made you feel like part of a community . . . I think the Beards can have that same aspect . . . They are a little too big for their britches now . . . it's such a production." Neither the cockiness nor the impediment placed in front of her team inhibits her. She has an agenda that trumps her desire to see her employees (or business) enjoy a hat tip. "My goal was to get the Beard Foundation a little more involved in giving back to the food community. I think it's unfortunate that the Beard Foundation doesn't have a conference or a meeting of food people around food-related topics."

Quatrano sees the flaws and her response is to correct them and improve the organization. Better to fix it than let it go to pot. "It would be a shame if they ever disappeared." Yes, it would; that's all they've got by way of meting out industry-sanctioned accolades. And that's where I ask, does that have to be the only option? What if, in addition to the Beards and *Food & Wine*'s Best New Chefs, there was a separate entity that zeroed in on small-scale operations? Since everyone loves Hollywoodspeak, I liken these to the annual Independent Spirit Awards parceled out by the film community to celebrate standout work. The ceremony is always held the night before the Oscars, and it's

---

[235] Quatrano and Clifford Harrison, her husband and business partner, both received *Best New Chef* shout-outs in 1995.

a dressed-down, quirky affair (John Waters has been a frequent host). This, you see, would allow the hard, innovative work of restaurateurs and chefs in less glitzy or prominent kitchens to have their day in the sun. Maybe it would be a locally operated proposition that restricts voting to numerous, concentrated communities within the industry. I haven't thought it out so much. I'm hoping to drum up some interest here. I'm pretty sure Sherry Yard the "Dough Ho" is on board. When I brought up my Independent (Restaurant) Spirit concept during our interview, she told me that her employer, Wolfgang Puck, has been talking about this very thing. (I've no idea what he envisions—we didn't get that far.)

Or maybe someone out there has an even better idea. As Charleen Badman exclaimed, "If the Beards did an award for best *woman* chef, it would set us back." No one's going thataway.[236] There's no reason to target a sex, race, or creed of any kind. What would be nice, however, would be to get to the untouted talent that populates the rather large swath of valuable eateries that the Beardness and the Besties doesn't cover.

If not, there's this final suggestion: "How about the idea of not having any awards?" Which revered contrarian said that? You're about to find out.

---

[236] In related (most disturbing) news, in 2011, S. Pellegrino's World's 50 Best Restaurants inaugurated the Veuve Clicquot World's Best Female Chef award. The winner was France's Anne-Sophie Pic. This 50 Best business comprises a list and event. As per its website, its "title sponsor" is your favorite sparkling water, San Pellegrino, and it's "published and organized by the team at *Restaurant* magazine, part of William Reed Business Media Ltd." Thank you and good night.

CHAPTER 10

Searching for Anne Rosenzweig[237]

The whole James Beard Award, [when] it was the Year of the Woman, we had done that ten years before . . . and we had to hire all the women chefs, et cetera, et cetera. . . . They had all the young women dressed as cancan girls. And I remember being a presenter, and before presenting, I said, "I hope in years to come that women won't have to dress up in cancan outfits to be taken seriously." And there was this big cheer that came out of the audience. And then I remember walking back to my seat and no one looked at me. The rest of the night, I think two people came over to me and said, "Wow, that was really gutsy. That's so cool you said that." Other than that, no one talked to me . . . When they started doing the Beard Awards, I was so embarrassed, and as it got more and more Hollywood-like, I said, "This is it. I'm not going. This is so antithetical to how I feel about the industry, why I got into the industry." . . . It became driving that whole PR machine, which became that whole Beard machine, which became the TV machine.

So is there any question why I disappeared? . . . It has changed a lot and become so much uglier . . . So who wants to talk to anybody?

—ANNE ROSENZWEIG

This chapter presented itself to me moments after the concept for the book did, before I'd ever stumbled upon Grill Bitch, even. And, as per usual, my motivation for finding Anne Rosenzweig was food-related. There were some things I'd been missing, acutely—namely, corn cakes

---

[237] Rosanna Arquette's 2002 documentary *Searching for Debra Winger* was the touchstone here, for the chapter's title and, in part, its contents. In her movie, Arquette interviews actresses of a certain age about what it's like to work in the film industry, especially as one leaves her young ingenue years behind. Debra Winger, Arquette's inspiration, is notorious for having walked out on Hollywood at forty, after receiving three Oscar nominations. She had become quite the recluse, until recently, when she resurfaced on season 3 of HBO's *In Treatment*.

with caviar and a deep dark brick of chocolate bread pudding with a lush spillover of brandied crème anglaise on top. These dream-haunting creations were born in the kitchen of a restaurant called Arcadia that holds a special place in New York City's (and my own) dining history.

My parents began taking me and my brother to restaurants when we were young'uns. I could show up at J.G. Melon's on the Upper East Side and order "the regular" and there was no question as to what that meant (hamburger, no roll—I was weird, okay—medium rare, with sautéed onions plus an order of cottage fries, well done, very). My intrepid, always-willing-to-travel-for-food folks thought nothing of zooming to the other end of the island for a meal.[238] I remember, in the early '80s, Dad drove us from Eighty-Ninth Street down to West Broadway at Thomas Street in Tribeca. The Odeon had just opened (in 1980), and people like Tom Wolfe and Andy Warhol made it their clubhouse. I knew nothing of that. My priority was, again, my burger and fries, or, as I got older, that lardon-studded country frisée salad, with goat instead of blue cheese and the additional poached egg, truffled, please.

For a while, Friday nights were sacred. And I don't mean the Shabbat kind of sacred. No one paid that any mind. Mom and Dad always went out to dinner (and were constantly trying the newest places, and then courting them like infatuated teens with a crush, until they tired of that crispy chicken they first raved about or found the tuna tartare a little fishy one night) and left us at home to watch *The Incredible Hulk*, *The Dukes of Hazzard*, *Dallas*, and, once I lingered past 10 p.m. and discovered it, *Falcon Crest*. As much as I loved that television lineup, I always wanted my parents to take me with them—I wanted to eat with the grown-ups and get dressed to go out too. Mesmerized, I'd watch my mom apply her makeup[239] in her muumuu-style, striped bathrobe

---

[238] We lived far well above what I now, that I reside downtown, refer to as my Mason-Dixon Line (Fourteenth Street, if I'm being honest; Twenty-Third Street if I don't want people to think me unreasonable).

[239] If any of you have lash-related queries, you should send them Nancy's way. She's a mascara expert and has sampled every new and improved formula known to man to find the best.

and long for the day when I could put whatever colors I chose on my eyelids. While they were painting the town, I'd sneak onto their bed to see what J.R. and Sue Ellen Ewing were up to and smell Mom's (formerly) signature Chloé Eau de Toilette scent. Between South Fork, the perfume, and my parents' outings, there appeared to be a vast world of glamour to which I wasn't granted entry. If only I could get past that red velvet rope.

And then, one Friday evening, they brought us with them. I must have been eight or nine. Uzzi's was the place; I'll never forget it. Today, if you go by that corner of Third Avenue at Eighty-Second Street, you'll find one of those generic restaurants that serves sushi, pad Thai, Szechuan crispy beef, and Malaysian sambal dishes (never a good sign, a mix like that). Uzzi's, sadly, is long gone. But that first night Mom and Dad introduced us to it will be with me for years to come. Dad promised we'd love the fried zucchini and we did; I preferred the lightly battered, crisp vegetal sticks sprinkled with lemon to French fries. When he told me to order the "straw and hay" (*paglia e fieno*) pasta with its combination of spinach (green) and plain (pale yellow) noodles, plus sweet green peas, salty prosciutto, rich heavy cream, and sharp grated Parmesan cheese, I followed, and we were both (Dad and I) thrilled to learn how much I liked it. That Uzzi's trip was a real breakthrough, because it wasn't just that we'd been accepted into the arena; it was that they started taking us to "proper" restaurants (instead of everyone's favorite WASP-magnet of a burger joint or the downtown hipster-family diner where crayons were placed on the table). We'd graduated. We weren't spoiled. I mean, we were, because we were going to places most kids our age probably weren't, and in New York City to boot; still, special-occasion spots were saved for deserving events. We always arrived wide-eyed, excited, and grateful—we thanked my dad at the end of each dinner. Still do, in fact. But, yes, we had already, at relatively tender ages, been taken to some pretty advanced locales—in our hometown and beyond.

One restaurant, however, eluded me. I knew all about it. The parentals had sung its praises, as had the *New York Times*. It was called Arcadia, its chef-owner was Anne Rosenzweig, and it was only twenty-seven blocks away from home.

Instead of large fancy-trendy places like fusion-style Vong, Indochine, or Le Colonial, Arcadia offered no gimmicks; on the other hand, unlike the old guard of imposing institutions—like Le Cirque, La Côte Basque, and the Four Seasons—it was unfussy and intimate. The walls were covered in a mural that depicted, as you followed it around the room, the year in bloom—winter, spring, summer, and fall—and lined with banquettes, so any young lady who sat in one felt cosseted as she surveyed the candlelit scene in front of her.

I'm not sure you have any idea what kind of food was being served in New York's restaurants at the end of 1984, when this love-liest of oases plopped down on the Upper East Side. It sure wasn't seasonal. You may think that's the most common of descriptions for today's menus, but back then? No way, José. It was heavy, haute French cuisine, nouvelle or *traditionel* (that's French for "traditional," but you can call it old). There were steak houses for high rollers too. Two years prior, Larry Forgione—he is thought by some to be a (if not *the*) father of New American cookery on the East Coast—erected his aptly named An American Place on Lexington Avenue and Seventy-First Street. Next, representing the West Coast arm of this element, California's Jonathan Waxman touched down on Big Apple asphalt with Jams. In '85, as Arcadia settled in—to provide you with a frame of reference—Alfred Portale took over at Gotham Bar & Grill, which had opened a year earlier and where you could sample a related brand of New American fare with its emphasis on what was ripe and its free-dom from the severity of French constraints. Portale's food was possibly more self-consciously modern in its stacked presentation and matched the open, generously sized, carefully relaxed room in which it was served. Also in that camp, a few months later, Danny Meyer placed his first restaurant, Union Square Café, which has always taken its gastronomic cues from the Greenmarket, on the city's map. Drew Nieporent set up his first shop Montrachet, another '85-er. Located in a wonderfully unlikely neighborhood, loft-filled Tribeca, and possessing an equally unexpected decor, that of a rustic, Provençal salon, Montrachet had a preciousness about it and felt closer to Paris than to downtown Manhattan.[240]

While Arcadia belonged to that cluster of mid-'80s game-changers, to some extent, it also defied the stereotype. As the *New York Times* critic Bryan Miller noted at the start of his review of the newcomer (six weeks after its first dinner was served): "Whenever a restaurant uses that overworked term 'new American cuisine,' I cringe, the way I do when a telephone solicitor offers me a 'prime acre' of south Florida real estate, sight unseen, for a 'modest' down payment. Arcadia, a delightful new place on East Sixty-Second Street, does use the term, but the restaurant's imaginative and well-conceived performance erased any skepticism on the first visit."[241] And then, for the circle-closing kicker, he ended with this: "Overall, Arcadia is the kind of comforting restaurant I could return to often, even if the food were dubbed 'new Transylvanian cuisine.' "

In that two-star write-up, Miller described dishes that would be at home on any menu in 2012. "Dinner entrees were as warm and soothing as a favorite old sweater, starting with the partly boned roast quails with kasha and cabbage. It was the first time I had seen kasha with game, and its assertive buckwheat flavor was surprisingly complementary to the moist tender quail."[242] Kasha's one of many whole grains people are giddy about today—I mean, who *isn't* all about "buckwheat flavor," I ask you. Or what about this one? "The house specialty this

---

[240] A grateful nod to Frank Bruni, whose "Critic's Notebook: The Contemporary Dining Scene, Est. 1985," in the Dining section of the *New York Times* (October 12, 2005) helped me keep this chronology straight (even if he didn't mention Arcadia).

[241] Bryan Miller, Restaurant Review: Restaurants, the *New York Times*, January 18, 1985.

[242] Ibid.

month is called chimney-smoked lobster. The lobster was smoked and grilled at the same time over a wood-fired grate and served with aromatic tarragon butter. The meat, which had the slightest hint of smoke, was precut and served in the shell, accompanied by deliciously crunchy deep-fried celery root cakes."[243] Everyone's all jazzed up about smoking these days, but back then (January 1985), this chimney jerry-rigging wasn't ubiquitous and certainly not a device employed by the average lobster-preparer. Deep-fried celery root cakes sound pretty sensational to me, and I know that earthy veg has taken hold of many a New York City chef in the past few years. It's in the same "let's roast 'em up" category as rutabagas, turnips, parsnips, salsify, or even Jerusalem artichokes, another tuberous type that Miller encountered during a meal at Arcadia (he found them, in slivers, sautéed along with onions and sitting beneath char-grilled salmon). Such was the bounty beyond my grasp.

They talked about this place, my parents did. I listened. I drooled. I pined. I begged to be granted an invitation. None came. Nancy (a.k.a. Mom) and I have argued about this, but since she's the one who keeps all of her calendars and still fills them out by hand, I have to trust her. According to these meticulous (illegible) records of hers, she and Jim (Dad) didn't accede to my plaintive wishes until the summer after my freshman year of college. My most favorite restaurant-I-have-never-been-to had, by then, been alive for *ten* years, and *finally*, I was in.

It was everything they had said it was, only better.

That evening, the first moment of bliss, as per my order, was provided by the corn cakes with caviar that I'd heard described so many times and was encouraged to select by Nance and Jim. I was, at that time—and I can't believe I'm saying this—still unsure about caviar—*gasp*—but between my swallowing that initial forkful and finishing every last crumb and glistening egg on my plate, all doubts were gone.

---

[243] Ibid.

Charlotte + Caviar Forever was indelibly inscribed on my palate. Oh, and not to mention the lightest and sweetest (in that way that only corn can be) of pancakes. These put the blini of my father's fancy, drizzled though his were with melted butter, to shame. And there was crème fraîche—its smooth cloud of gentle sourness equally refreshing and velvety. I tried everything on everyone's plate, but those first bites at Arcadia will stay with me forever. So will the final course. I'd prepped myself for it: the signature chocolate bread pudding with brandy custard sauce. And I thought I hated liqueur in my desserts, silly me. This thing was so marvelously dense, and rich, and there was nothing bready about it (that's because of its buttery brioche base).

Thank you for taking me.

Four years later, it was gone.

But not forgotten. Nancy had, in her eminent wisdom, procured the eponymous cookbook the chef had published not long after opening. One year, for Rosh Hashanah (Jewish New Year), Nance had the ingenuity to present the corn cakes (because it's the New Year, and one of the two most holy days of the Jewish calendar, you're supposed to treat it like a celebration; go all out) to our family table flanked by assorted—mostly ungrateful and unpleasant—relations. For once, they could find nothing to complain about. At the end of that meal, to ensure, as my people say on that occasion, "a sweet new year," Nance brought the house down with the chocolate bread pudding.

That cookbook, my souvenir of what was, for me, a gastronomic arcadia, remains my favorite. It's tiny and folds out like an accordion. As you open it up, you realize that very same mural, the one painted by Paul Durand for the restaurant, has been reproduced in its entirety. It suits the rest of the slender tome's content, which comprises only four menus, one for each season. (The corn cakes appear in summer, the bread pudding—along with that Miller-approved quail and cabbage and kasha—in fall.) Sadly, this skinny spine is out of print, so not an easy find. When I moved out of my parents' apartment and into my own place, it was the first cookbook I wanted on the shelf, and I managed to scare one up. In the past few years, whenever I see a copy, I buy it and save it for a kindred food spirit. Some are signed by its author, the chef herself.

"When the White House announced that it had appointed a new chef and that he was a man,[244] there were gasps in kitchens across America," wrote Miller's successor, Ruth Reichl, whose weekly reviews I pored over religiously and savored in 1994 when she rereviewed Arcadia. "Professional chefs had been convinced that the next person to take charge of the care and feeding of the First Family would be a woman. That woman, they thought, would be Anne Rosenzweig . . . An early champion of American cooking, she is a tough and articulate person who has devoted herself to the causes of small farmers and female chefs."[245] Reichl upped the "gracious flower-filled room" that lets you "leave the real world behind" to three stars, and noted, "the Clintons' loss is our gain" (our being New York's). She didn't know that our victory was to be short-lived. She singled out, along with my corn cakes and bread pudding (by the way, Miller gave a shout-out to these items as well; they were, obviously, instant classics), Rosenzweig's "famous lobster club sandwich," which, Reichl wrote, "is an aggressive combination of lobster and smoky bacon, vegetables, rich brioche, and sweet lemon mayonnaise. It is the best of America on a plate."[246]

Funny she should mention that sammie. Three years before Rosenzweig closed the door on Arcadia, she opened Lobster Club, a more casual eatery eighteen blocks north (closer to the parental figures) on Eightieth Street. "Just listen to this menu," Reichl commanded when she gave the place a quick once-over in November 1995. "Roasted clams with tomatoes on grilled bread with basil aioli.

[244] That man would be Walter S. Scheib III.

[245] Ruth Reichl, Restaurant Review: Restaurants, the *New York Times*, April 22, 1994.

[246] Ibid.

Buckwheat and sturgeon cakes with salmon roe and confetti crème fraîche. Lobster congee with deep-fried devils.[247] Mashed potato cakes filled with duck confit, pine nuts, and roasted garlic. Clafoutis of potatoes, apples, and gingerbread. Grilled short ribs with horseradish gnocchi. Wolffish with parsnip and leek brandade. Rice pudding brûlée."[248] I'll let the menu speak for itself (my stomach audibly began grumbling as I typed those gustatory phrases). The prices on that menu also had something to say—as Reichl reported, nothing, except for the dish after which the place was named, went above $16.50. In that well-oiled neighborhood, two blocks away from the Metropolitan Museum and Central Park, such a reasonable proposition was unseemly in its seeming impossibility. Living up to its name, it became the sweater set's clubhouse. My parents (Nance does like a good matching sweater duo) went on a regular basis and, when I was in town, I reaped the benefits. For a while.

In April 2001, all of a sudden, shuttered. *So, poof . . . vamoose son of a bitch.*[249]

Despair was mitigated by Inside, the space that Rosenzweig helped her protégée, Lobster Club sous chef Charleen Badman, put together on one-block-long Jones Street in Greenwich Village. Once I found out about this decamping, naturally, I decided to move downtown. Kidding. I had dreamed of living around there since the age of seven, and it was a happy coincidence that, by the time I should find my way to that neighborhood, one of the few things I might have missed from my past (uptown) life would be a stone's throw away. The snacks alone were all I needed—the bacon-wrapped, almond-stuffed dates; corn fritters (a subtle reminder of that Arcadian appetizer of yore); or radishes served with salt, sweet butter, and a toasty brioche.

---

[247] What are these? Just ask Rosenzweig. I did, and she replied, in an e-mail, "for the lobster congee we made our version of the long, very airy, savory doughnuts you see in Chinatown; sometimes you see them cut up (with scissors) in soups, etc. We loved that they were called *deep-fried devils*—named after pale white people (or at least, that's what we were always told)."

[248] Ruth Reichl, Diner's Journal, the *New York Times*, November 3, 1995.

[249] Jay-Z, "Izzo (H.O.V.A.)," 2001, Roc-A-Fella.

Ooh! There was, at suppertime, outstanding salt-and-pepper shrimp, buckwheat fried oysters, and a nectarine and goat cheese salad, too, if I recall. And who can forget the Newport steak? My parents, eager to stay in touch (and fearful the bond would be broken) now that I'd changed zip codes, would meet me at Inside for dinner, and Dad almost always got that steak, which was a special cut that came from the nook of a butcher shop, Florence Meat Market (one of the city's oldest and dearest), next door. At brunch, you could get yourself a grilled cheese sandwich with onions, mustard, and cheddar, or, a Rosenzweig classic, *matzo brei*. Inside was where you'd go for the roast chicken you craved and didn't feel like making yourself. Felt like home.

Badman kept it going while Rosenzweig quietly, and gradually, faded out of the picture. Ultimately, her disappearance was complete— she made not a peep and adhered to a Garbo-esque regime. Where did she go? Would she ever open another restaurant again? These questions persisted. My mom would see her picking up her daughter from school or shopping for groceries on their shared turf, the zone known as Carnegie Hill. Word on the street was that she was catering for private clients.

Inside held its own until 2007, when Badman packed up and returned from whence she'd come, namely, Arizona. That was a sad moment, truly, when I heard that the last vestige of what I considered a special strain of culinary glory was gone. Now, if you go to 9 Jones Street, you'll find Harold Dieterle's restaurant Perilla there. I have a horrible confession to make: I have never eaten at Perilla. It's not because I don't think he can cook—I'm borderline addicted to almost every menu item at his nearby Thai-ish joint, Kin Shop. But apparently out of some completely irrational sense of loyalty, I have thus far refused to cheat on the memory of Inside and its Rosenzweigian roots.

My preoccupation with this chef's whereabouts, however, is predicated on something quite rational and relevant. Here was someone who was recognized for her talent and business savvy and for being a pioneer (culinarily, yes; also in her capacity as a mentor). She created two successful and, each in its way, groundbreaking eateries and operated a third—that would be an unassuming, little-known place called the '21' Club, which she was recruited to revamp in 1986. She was considered one of the country's best (even if the Clintons didn't go with her for their in-house meal-fixer), and she remains, I believe, one of only three female (savory) chefs to be awarded three stars by the *New York Times* (Debra Ponzek came first in 1988. Lidia Bastianich is the other, and her receipt of those followed Rosenzweig's by a year). And she walked away from it all, of her own volition. Why?

Sure, I missed the restaurants, but my curiosity about this exeunt and its greater implications was even more pronounced than my hankering for a plate of soft-shell crabs with corn and peaches. The usual reason given for a lady chef's checking out is motherhood—either she wants to have a baby, is pregnant with one, or has an infant to raise. Rosenzweig's daughter, Lily, was already in middle school. That excuse then, was out. We weren't dealing with a young, new mum; this was a woman in her forties who, it appeared, didn't want to spend any more time working in restaurants. Maybe, I started to think, this is part of a larger issue; what do female chefs of a certain age do when they've had enough of the kitchen's physical demands, heat, and abnormal hours? This is what I wanted to discuss with the chef and, while I had her (if I could get ahold of her), the rest of her career—how she was able to accomplish all that she had and what had informed her decisions along the way.

She is notoriously press shy, and I wasn't sure I'd be able to find her or convince her to speak to me. I thought, perhaps, Amanda Hesser might be able to help because she had done a piece in 2010 on Rosenzweig's iconic corn cakes for her now defunct (and sorely missed) Recipe Redux column in the *New York Times Magazine*.[250]

---

[250] True story: Back in 2007, when Amanda Hesser and I didn't know each other, I e-mailed her and asked if she could, in fact, do a Redux on one of Rosenzweig's recipes. Three years later, my dream came true. Thank you, Amanda, for that, and for the phone number.

Hesser generously shared the chef's landline, so I left a message on the latter's home answering machine and hoped for the best. A few days (possibly a week) later, Rosenzweig phoned me. I explained this book concept of mine and she was shockingly amenable (I had expected no call returned, or maybe a curt "not interested"). We parked at Jack's Stir Brew, home of Aunt Rosie's chocolate chip cookies (I averaged one per diem while drafting this mess), where we talked for more than two hours. By the time I stopped the tape, all the questions I thought I had were answered (as were some I didn't know I had). Rosenzweig, enjoyable tangents and the rest, had shared her story and opinions and we had laughed about all of it. Instead of my paraphrasing, I think I'll try to afford you the pleasure of her company and insight. Here she is, in her own words. (Note: I have, on occasion, moved some sections around to get the chronology right, but there has been no tampering other than that.)

I didn't really go to culinary school . . . I was an apprentice—I mean, I did a couple of classes—but really, my training was as an apprentice to a chef. I was an anthropologist—and I had done fieldwork and lived in East Africa, West Africa, Nepal, and India—and it was through that experience that I got really interested in food. And, basically, [I] wanted to work in a kitchen just to satisfy that curiosity about food. Because it was a really big part—when you're studying other cultures, non-Western cultures, especially in cultural anthropology—food is a very big part of it. And as a kid growing up in New York, there was always that interest in food. So I knew that the European model was that you apprentice. So I thought, "Okay, great, I can still work"—I was working at the Museum of Natural History at that point—and I thought, "Here, I can work for free and get an education and just sort of resolve the curiosity that I had about food." And that very first day I was in a professional kitchen . . .

Well, first of all, it took me a really long time to find a kitchen that would take me, 'cause that was back when there were basically no women in kitchens. But that very first day I was in a kitchen, it was extraordinarily exciting, revealing—that giant aha moment where you go, "Wow!" I did it back then with no expectation of going into the field and from a place of great naïveté, which served me extraordinarily well . . . There were absolutely no illusions about what it was going to be, and to me that was a great fun part of it.

I came from a very academic background,[251] so I would be in a kitchen for twelve, fourteen hours a day with a chef, being screamed at, doing stuff, watching, and then at night I would go home and hit the books, because that was my training . . . To me, it was just natural. I was enthralled, and I wanted as much information as I could get . . . The process was so much fun. And I met so many people along the way who said, "I've got a five-year plan; I've got a ten-year plan." I said, "I have no plan." And it has been absolutely the best thing . . . You miss the serendipity of what might happen. If someone comes along with an offer to do X and you go, "Oh, but I've got this plan and I've got to stay in this kitchen" or "I've got to learn how to do whatever," you miss an opportunity to do something that zigs instead of zags.

Basically, I was taken on as an apprentice as sport—I didn't know that till later . . . But, again, in my naïveté—I got screamed at all the time and I thought it was a hazing that everyone went through, because I was at the bottom. I assumed everyone had gone through it, and perhaps they had, but not in quite the same way. And basically, the idea was to see how long I would last before I dissolved in tears and left. And I found it just a very exciting challenge and an amazing education. Because I

[251] Rosenzweig attended Columbia University where she received her B.A. in anthropology. Her brother is a professor of economics at Yale.

was made to do so much more, screamed at for not doing it fast enough, but built up everything I needed to build up to be what I needed to be as a chef, or as a cook.

And it wasn't that I was oblivious. It was, "Okay, fine. Let them be that way. I'll show them." And I think also, for me, I wasn't a kid—I mean, I was a kid; I was in my twenties. I had spent years—well, not years, but, you know, different periods of time—living in mud huts in Africa by myself, being, surviving, thriving, and getting that sense of self. So it [the rough treatment] really didn't matter . . . That was the other thing that was so fascinating, because [the restaurant kitchen] was this small society, and removing myself from that and observing that whole culture was just fascinating. Basically, the first kitchen I worked in, most of the guys hadn't even finished high school; but they had other great skills. The first month or so they taught me how to hot-wire a car, and [I] begrudgingly gained some respect that I could do the job.

The other thing that was very lucky or different than how most people got through it is I became a chef very quickly. Not because I wanted to, but after apprenticing for a year or so and working in kitchens, I went down to a place on Bleecker called Vanessa. I was given the task of being the pastry chef or the pastry cook (whatever) and in charge of brunch, because those were both jobs that, at their restaurant, no one wanted to do. So again, in the same sort of thing, you're taking on a job that nobody wants, but it was fine. I loved doing it and it forced me to go to a place where I didn't know stuff and work that much harder. So there were certainly parts like that where I was self-taught; there wasn't anyone there to teach me how to be a pastry chef, it was, again, go hit the books and work.

One of the things that happened when I was down at Vanessa is—I was the pastry chef, brunch chef—and Mimi Sheraton, who was the critic for the [New York] Times, reviewed the restaurant and thought it was fine, okay, and basically said, "Whoever's doing the brunch and whoever's doing the desserts, this is really spectacular." And two weeks later, they fired whoever the chef was and I was the chef . . . It was one of those things that felt like what the whole career had been like, and that was getting bumped up, each time not really being ready and just having to work that much harder to be deserving or to do a good job. So that was pretty daunting, but when you're in the thick of it, you don't have time to think about that. You're like, "Holy shit." All the things you have to do. And on top of that, the owner of the restaurant was sort of a derelict owner in the sense that he often didn't pay his bills; he had other businesses; he didn't know how to run the front of the restaurant. So a lot of that stuff fell to me, because the group in the kitchen was working so hard that I needed to protect what was happening to the food once it left the kitchen. So I learned how to do a wine list—I had one great wine purveyor who became a friend and taught me a lot of stuff. I took over some of the bookkeeping, because if my purveyors didn't get paid I wasn't going to get product, and, just by logic, [I] learned how to train a front-of-the-house staff . . . And it was great training. Other people would have gotten really angry, and it was, like, another opportunity—you look at it as another opportunity. And a necessity—what else are you going to do? You're going to let the service be shitty? I don't think so . . . I love business; I think it's fun. A lot of people don't have the head for it—men as well as women.

So being down there [at Vanessa], for whatever reason, there was a lot of press, which was very lovely. And then people started approaching me saying, "Do you want to do your own thing?" So it was another one of those opportunities . . . that you don't plan for, and when you're presented with an opportunity . . . It certainly seemed to me a better opportunity to be able to control everything, rather than be at the whim and mercy of idiots . . . So I was working with somebody and we managed to raise some money through investors—some very, very rich people. And then the rest of the money—we couldn't get a bank loan. So we had to go to . . . the closest thing to a legal loan shark, and that's when regular interest rates were 12,13 percent, so we were paying 19 percent for a loan.

One of the ideas for the restaurant [Arcadia] was—at that time, back in the mid-'80s or so, everyone was opening these huge restaurants—I really wanted to open something small and what I called "grown-up." That was my term: "I want a grown-up restaurant. I don't want these big huge barns that are really loud."

The space that was found had been a restaurant a number of times and was seen as sort of a bad-luck space, which I then grew to love—that was my thing; I always wanted to find bad-luck spaces . . . It took at least a year [once the lease was signed] and tons of money. And I took a job during it—I was working as well.

In terms of Arcadia, that was magical. Everyone seemed to get it . . . We got reviewed by the *Times* after six weeks. We were starting out and Bryan Miller was starting out, and I think he wrote subsequently—or maybe it was in the review—he didn't know whether to give it two or three [stars], but because he was new, he decided to err on the cautious side . . . which was fine, because business took off exponentially. . . So, really in a sense, when I look back and say about how wonderful it was, I didn't really have time to enjoy it for years and years and years. It was like being taken by the scruff of your neck and just thrown.

At Arcadia, I had to be such a businessperson, and it was great. It was a wonderful perspective that so few chefs have, 'cause they don't know [how to] run a business.

The question came up as to whether to have a PR person and that was when everyone had PR people . . . I had two very strong thoughts. One was I really felt what PR people did was bullshit and that, having dealt with the press down at Vanessa, I could handle the press better than PR people could, for a lot of reasons. PR people usually didn't get what your essence was . . . And so the other [reason] was, when you open a restaurant, you spend so much money, and at the end, no matter how much money you have—well, I don't know, I've only done it where you're always running out of money at the end—there was no money [left] to do it [pay for PR]. But the other [first reason] was a much bigger thing. I used that [the money] as an excuse for people who kept asking, but, for me, it was, "I totally don't want it. I can do this so much better." And I think one of the reasons that we got so much press at the beginning is that everyone who came—every kind of writer or critic or whatever—felt like they were discovering the restaurant and hadn't been bombarded by a million press releases.

Well, then there was also the '21' Club. Let's not forget the '21' Club . . . So very early on in Arcadia, there was an approach by the guy who was the head, [who had] bought the '21' Club from the original family and wanted to remake it, reenergize it. And this was an interesting time in the city when guys with lots of money, with big companies, wanted different trophies. So it was when Donald Trump bought the

Plaza Hotel, and these guys—it was Marshall Cogan—bought the '21' Club, and it was pretty funny. It was one of those male battles that you laugh at . . . So they had no idea how to do a restaurant and were big fans of Arcadia, so [they] wanted us to come over and do what they had no idea how to do. I didn't want to do it. Arcadia was my ideal. I loved it, it was completely controllable, the clientele was wonderful, spectacular, lovely, interested in the food. And I felt so simpatico. Why would I want to fuck that up? . . . But there was something very intriguing about the '21' Club. Here was this male bastion, so there was a little part of me that went, "Ooh, this could be . . ." and also that it was an interesting sort of adventure. So I said, "No—no, no, no—no," which they took as a negotiating tool, so they kept offering more money. But I really didn't want to do it. Then it got to be a ridiculous amount of money that would enable me to completely control Arcadia. So I went "okay." Again, if I'd had a five-year plan, I never would have done it . . . And there was a part of me that, having this very entrepreneurial spirit or sense of myself, I wanted to see what it was like in a corporate environment, which was truly vile, I learned. But I was happy to learn it . . . And, again, going back to this naïveté that I had, I couldn't believe how the most mediocre people were the most successful people . . . And so it was kind of interesting for a while, but really, it was eye-opening. After a good number of years at Arcadia making all my own decisions—and for the most part, they were pretty right-on—now everything had to go through a filter of a lot of stupid men . . . Because the premise that we had was to bring it to a next generation of people, so there were all these things that we started—we started a whole jazz thing and I got the most amazing jazz people to come in. And it was just extraordinary to look at these guys; to have them not get it. So I managed to disentangle myself from that . . . [after] maybe three or four years.

One of the things I always wanted to do—because Arcadia was so expensive, a lot of my friends couldn't come—was a restaurant that was less expensive, just more laid-back, just a different mold, and that was basically the impetus for that [Lobster Club]. And again [in 1995], I took over a space on the Upper East Side. Maybe another impetus in the back of my mind for Lobster Club was to have a backup . . . I called myself a serial restaurateur. Again, it was a bad-luck space, but a very cool space.

Arcadia went for fourteen years.[252] That [at Arcadia] was our lease, and a month before the lease was up, the building was sold and we had a new landlord . . . And that was the big real estate boom, and the new guy came in and said, "If you want to stay, we'd love to have you. We're tripling the rent." . . . I said, "Thank you very much, but there's no way."

In the beginning at Arcadia, it was mainly guys [in the kitchen], 'cause that was what was around. Then as the restaurant got known, more women appeared at the door. And then I went, "Oh, this is a nice idea." But still, there weren't many women around. But, I think, as time went on that I tried to mentor women.

What I did was, with Charleen [Badman] and some other women from the restaurant [Lobster Club], [I] helped her open Inside . . . [In 2001] I found someone to buy the restaurant [Lobster Club],[253] which is, in this business, really hard to do. Basically they wanted a turnkey operation . . . Charleen always had said that she wanted to do her own thing. That

[252] From 1984 to 1998.
[253] Lobster Club was open from 1995 to 2001.

was her goal. And so, for me, I was sort of interested in doing something somewhere else . . . [Later that year] I opened it [Inside], Charleen was going to be the chef . . . The clientele was lovely, 'cause it was, you know, this little block; it was so sweet; it was very fun . . . and we had the butcher next door. It was like Paris, or we could imagine it was like Paris. And the bread guy was down the street and . . . I had a lot of my old customers and a lot of people who were just interested in food.

Starting from Arcadia, I had started catering for a lot of my clientele, and when I started in the business, catering was really looked down upon. It was like being a culinary instructor. Those who really couldn't run restaurants became caterers. But I did it as a service to my clientele, and then, as well as [for] customers at Lobster Club. And then catering became hip, hop, and happening, and as you see now, every chef has a catering division. And so I started to pull out of Inside. I did a lot of the menu stuff, tried to help with business stuff, but basically put it into Charleen's hands, a lot of it, and started doing more of my own stuff—consulting, helping other people open businesses, teaching . . . I think it was a combination. I wanted to give Charleen a chance to do her thing, and a part of me said, "Okay, if I'm not there all the time, I can do all these other things that I've missed doing."

When you have this small business, in a sense it's very hard. [As] a chef-owner, no one has the vision that you have . . . Employees don't have the same stake that you have . . . so that there's really no getting away from not being there. Lucky for me, I'm a type A personality, so I loved running around like a freak . . . Maybe that was also kind of an impetus—consciously or unconsciously—when I opened downtown to kind of pull back; after having so many years of it not being a normal life, which was fun, and I loved [it]—to see what it would be like to raise a kid not running around like that . . . I think there's some sort of sacrifice . . . It's just the way it is, unless you have a househusband, and how many of us have that? I also had a husband commuting between L.A. and New York.

One of the things we did, my colleagues, this older generation of chefs, we started this so-called mentoring organization. It's called Women Chefs and Restaurateurs . . . It was mainly the women on the West Coast that were so ahead of us in a sense, and I attribute that to . . . the French paradigm. Because in New York, when you went out, the most important, serious restaurants were the French restaurants, and then the Italian restaurants. And they didn't have that same paradigm on the West Coast. So there were women cooking in kitchens before we were cooking in kitchens; and women chefs before we had women chefs . . . [The premise] was that it would nurture women (and men)—in parentheses—but also give them the skills that we basically learned on the job. But also, we were dealing with an industry that was ten, twenty years behind many other industries, so we had to think about things. We would often lose women because they wanted to have families, and it was difficult—whether you were a restaurant manager or a cook or a chef—to manage all that. No one had ever thought in this industry to do job sharing. And also, we knew that we, most of us, had to cobble together the whole idea of raising money, and to help women get the skills of how to raise money, how to go to a bank, how to approach a bank, and things like that. And then there were places, like in the Midwest, where women couldn't even get into a kitchen.

None of us has really been that involved in it [the organization] . . . It seems like the really interesting younger chefs, male or female, are going the smaller route anyway. I think that if you walk into a butcher shop—when you think about New York, [there are] all these young butchers doing stuff—and said, "I'd like to work for free," that they'd say "fine," they'd say "cool." And you could do that in so many different places now, because there's the military-industrial complex of people like Batali and stuff like that. And then [there are] all these young people who are doing really cool things in very small, artisanal sorts of ways—for lack of a better word (I wish there were better; there should be a better word). But, I know for me, when I go out to eat, that's where I like to go.

For years, people always asked me, "Where do you like to eat?" And I would always say, "Well, I like to go to small, ethnic places," because it was often a family cooking, something really important and interesting, and completely different than what I was doing, and that's why it was compelling and interesting to me. But now, there are all those sorts of places; now [there are] these young chefs doing that too.

And I've seen bunches of these kids that come out of Boulud's kitchens—and I won't say that it's not wonderful training—but I call this the French model. And unless they're smart and creative—which a lot of them aren't, 'cause not everyone's going to be really smart or creative—they hold this paradigm of how you should cook. And the French model can be, to this American, just infuriating . . . With that sense of precision, there's a tremendous amount of waste. And I've seen that from some of my younger colleagues, because when you're working at that level where he can charge so much for food, and he has so many people working for free . . . or they're working for really low wages, you're getting a really strange sense of how a regular kitchen might operate. So on the one hand, it's a great education; on the other hand, it's not really how the rest of their culinary life might be.

And the industry is so different now. I remember when I started Arcadia, that my customers would come in and say, "Oh, I want my son or daughter to come work for you," because they saw it in such a different light, and it has become so different . . . And I would say, "Sure, let me get them a job as a dishwasher, 'cause they'll really see what it's like." And that would end the discussion. Because they had no idea what the industry is like.

My daughter has decided, this week, she wants to go into food . . . She has always hated the food world; she grew up in it. She never even wanted to learn how to cook. She loved food, loved going out to eat, is a foodie, but knows just how—saw how hard I work . . . She said, "I'm going to be the Food Whisperer." And I said, "Probably someone's already done that." And she said, "Well, maybe I'll write about food." . . . Two weeks ago she was a rabbi and four weeks before that she was a doctor. And that's just the first semester of college . . . I fear she may fall into food. I don't know.

Rosenzweig's daughter might fall by association. The chef has helped a number of women if not fall into then stay in food, and make marks. Have you noticed that people are always so quick to talk about the dynasties established by male toques? Family trees are rendered to illustrate how many emerged from the kitchens of Daniel Boulud, Thomas Keller, or Tom Colicchio. Between Arcadia and Lobster Club, Rosenzweig spawned her own clan—Missy Robbins of A Voce, Rebecca Charles of Pearl Oyster Bar, Jennifer Scism, who was, until quite recently, the co-owner of Annisa,[254] and Cat Cora[255] (she interned at

---

[254] Scism opened the space with Anita Lo, and took care of the wine program and oversaw front-of-the-house duties there.

[255] Cora is the sole female Iron Chef. She partnered with the Walt Disney World Resort in Orlando to open her first spot in 2009, four years after she was given her Food Network title. She was, for the record, trained as a chef and, although not a proprietor before TV stardom came her way, had reached executive status.

Arcadia), to name a few. "I had one [line cook at Arcadia; sous chef at Lobster Club] who's now a wonderful organic farmer out on Long Island," Rosenzweig added to the list, "her name is Patty Gentry." Not a chef, okay, but this goes back to something Reichl made a point of mentioning in her review of Arcadia—Rosenzweig's championing of farmers, the kind of activity chefs engage in all the time in our current era of locavore, connect-with-the-source mania, but back in New York City circa 1984, not the "it" stunt to pull. Food writer (author of some stellar cookbooks) Andrew Dornenburg is another graduate of Rosenzweig's school, and the token guy. As Rosenzweig mentions, once Arcadia started receiving some attention, the girls came a knockin', and she came to relish the role of mentor.

"She knows how to run a business," Badman says of her. "And she's made a big point, and I can't imagine that any one of us—whether it's Rebecca, or myself, or Jennifer, or I'm thinking of Patty Gentry, as well—[who] came out of that kitchen [who] wouldn't say that she taught us how to run a business and how to make things more successful. And when we had Inside together, she sat me down enough times and was just like: 'This is about running a business and you need to run a business. And you love your food, and that's great, but if you don't learn how to run a business, you will never be able to run a restaurant; it just won't be successful.' "

This mentoring stint is one that Rosenzweig finds equally necessary again. "Just the idea of having more women in the industry," she mused at Jack's, "is so interesting, because it felt like, fifteen years ago it was sort of going in that direction. And now, it seems to have swung back, that it's just this macho thing that is unbelievable."

She remains above the testosterone-heavy fray, but keeps in touch with many of her past mentees. Badman is a close friend and visits from Phoenix, mainly to eat with her former employer-cum-sensei. They embark on food crawls around New York City. Rosenzweig might stage a dumpling tour of Flushing or a massive pig-out at the newest culinary temple on Long Island City followed by an evening of pizza. It's not so different, in a way, from their former days at work together when Rosenzweig took Badman under her wing. "I was very fortunate," says Badman, as she recalls her initial encounters with her guru. "I packed two suitcases and went to work for Anne Rosenzweig. And that's exactly what I wanted to do, and it worked out that I got to do that . . . I remember walking into Lobster Club and she was talking to the waitstaff and she was telling them what was going on for that day, and I stood there for what seemed like forever. And she finally looked over at me and was like, 'Do you need something?' and I almost walked out that door 'cause she scared the shit out of me. I said, 'I'm here to see the chef about a position?' She just pointed upstairs . . . But, as far as the nurturing part, she finally hired me and she said hello and figured out I could cook, she took me to the farmers' market—she's the first person who took me to the farmers' market. I'd have Sundays off, she'd be like, 'Meet me in Chinatown, this is the restaurant.' She'd take me to lunch, and I remember saying to her one time—she had the *matzo brei* in *Food & Wine*—'Oh, really nice article about your *matzo brei*.' She goes, 'Oh, you read those magazines?' She would be the nicest person at the same time, but she took a lot of notice that at least I was reading and I knew who she was and I wasn't just somebody who came off the street and wanted to get a job at a kitchen working in New York, that I did some due diligence and research about her."

The most established chefs still turn to Rosenzweig for guidance. I brought her and Anita Lo together for drinks to reminisce and catch up. Toward the end of our cocktail hour, Lo asked the legend before her (not me, obviously) if she could get in touch for some advice about an exit strategy. Even in stepping away, Rosenzweig has set an example. She caters for an elite (as in, only people she likes) group of clients, many of whom she fed at her eateries, and acts as a consultant for new restaurant projects. These gigs have allowed her to continue doing what she loves—working with food and developing businesses—without having to deal with anything anathema (the press, the celebrity circuit, or the "macho thing"). They also enable her to enjoy more "normal" family time.

That's one exit strategy. There are others.

Claudia Fleming didn't want out completely; she just didn't need anymore of that chaotic, stressful intensity you can't escape at a top New York City restaurant—Gramercy Tavern, in her case—and she was ready for a new challenge. Today, you'll find her on Long Island's North Fork, where there are farms and vineyards aplenty and the pace is notably (and enjoyably, if you ask me) slower. She and her husband, chef Gerry Hayden, own an inn and the restaurant contained therein; they're open for business only on long weekends in winter, and then more regularly throughout the summer. She carries on her fabled dessert-making tradition and is able to utilize the fresh produce that surrounds her; he's on savory patrol. I asked her why she abandoned the big city (and her prime gig). "There are a number of reasons," she began. "I'd been at Gramercy for quite some time and felt I'd done everything I could do there . . . There wasn't anywhere for me to go . . . I didn't want to go to another restaurant . . . I'd just gotten married . . . [I] wanted to try and have a family . . . I spent most of the time traveling and doing food events . . . I felt like I hadn't done anything new in two years . . . just turning out the same old shit and sick of myself . . . So there were several things that factored into it . . . I thought I was ready to leave the restaurant business, because, certainly, I wasn't going to open anything by myself."

Next, she explains, while at this crossroads, she was contacted by Pret a Manger, the to-go food chain that serves prepackaged, freshly prepared grub for the working public who likes its food fast but doesn't condone fast food. She'd always wanted a sandwich shop, so heading up the edible operations there sounded like a dream job. As she tells it, she got "swept off her feet" and worked for them until "they imploded." Then she left. Hayden, meanwhile, had sold his half of the partnership at a Chelsea spot called Amuse (no longer with us), and they both went the consulting route. Once they bought their second house on the Island, they decided to supplant themselves and the North Fork Table & Inn took shape. Recently, since it seems these chef types can't sit still, the duo rolled out a daily lunch truck to serve the area (guess that sandwich-shop dream never died). "If anything," she says about their collective enterprise, "I'm leaving and he's taking over."

For an alternate and prodigious detour, there's Soa Davies's career permutation. "You most definitely get tired . . . I'm very, very feminist; I'm very adamant women can do anything men can as well. But there's a physicality to cooking and being a line cook that, after a certain age of being a woman, it's just really hard to keep up with the young boys. And I am the first to admit it." And so she did, admit it. Davies had ascended to a position that any aspiring chef would envy—the saucier at Le Bernardin, Eric Ripert's four-star shrine to seafood in Manhattan. Sauce is perhaps the most important element on every plate that emerges from that kitchen. Ripert takes the sauce-making very seriously and has been known to pronounce himself as "a saucier in my heart no matter what else I do."[256] Davies had been entrusted with that most precious of stations and proven more than up to the task. What next, then? "It's really tough," she contends. "If you leave a restaurant like Le Bernardin in New York City at the top of your game, where do you go, except on your own?" And if you don't feel ready to do that or aren't sure what you want "your own" to be? Lucky for Davies, Ripert showed up at exactly the right time with the answer: "I think Eric always had the vision of, here's someone who

---

[256] Todd Kliman, " 'Our Movie Star': Eric Ripert," *Washingtonian*, May 2008.

likes to create, here's someone who has a palate that I trust; and it was his vision that I would take on a bigger role. When he approached me with the idea, it was right at the time [when] I was at the end of my tenure with Le Bernardin. So I knew that I'd learned as much as I could possibly learn; I knew I wasn't going to go anywhere further. And I think he very much sensed that and offered this opportunity, and I pretty much jumped at it."

What Ripert did was put Davies in a creative, managerial role, where she could tap into her cheffing strengths and tackle business development. She is his culinary director and oversees menus (the generation of new dishes, for example), conceives and implements food-related concepts, and makes sure the back of the house is in tip-top shape. This she does for each of his four eateries (in addition to Le B, as we like to call it, he has restaurants in Philadelphia, Grand Cayman, and Washington, D.C.). Plus, she advises on his cookbook and television projects.[257] She loves it. "Everyone asks me if I miss the kitchen," she notes, "and I can honestly tell you, I spend so much time in and around the kitchens, that I'm not really out of the kitchen. Yes, I have bankers' hours, so to speak, and I work days, and I don't do service, but I very much am focused on supporting the service part of, especially, Le Bernardin, and then beyond, all of the other restaurants I consult for. So it wasn't a conscious decision of 'I'm not going to be in the kitchen anymore,' it was more of a decision that 'I get to have more say in different things and I get to see a different side of it.' . . . I get to see the entire operations picture instead of just coming in, setting up my mise en place and doing service, because that's such a small part of each restaurant. I get to talk to our sommelier about the wine pairings and about how certain nuances of sauce would go with certain wines, and I get to talk to Eric all the time about food pairings . . . So I've gotten to evolve much more as a creative person by taking this step outside of the kitchen, because I'm not under the pressure and

[257] She took home a 2011 Daytime Emmy Award for Ripert's show *Avec Eric*, which she coproduced.

constraints of service, and having to put out dishes and having to get food out to the dining room."

I wondered if, after this experience, Davies thinks about setting up a Soa's, a place with her name on it. Not anymore. "For the longest time, even when I first took the position, I thought I would do my own thing. But the more I opened restaurants for other people, the more I realized, unless you're committed to completely giving up your life, it's a tough thing." It's easier, we discussed, to make that kind of sacrifice when you're in your twenties and thirties. As you get on in years, climbing that mountain doesn't seem as sexy.[258]

"When you've been working long hours for twenty years, while everyone is playing," says Seen Lippert, "being *outside* on the streets at dinnertime is a revelation . . . I wanted to have that. I was no less enthusiastic about my profession, but I wanted to enjoy and not be on a budget for the first time." Be advised, Lippert's departure does have a bit of fairy dust sprinkled on it. Like Cinderella (okay, not exactly), she had toiled away at Chez Panisse for eleven years, then moved to New York to open a restaurant for one of the city's well-known gastro-preneurs and then did the same for another operator. Just as she went to work on her next endeavor, launching a space with Joe Bastianich and Mario Batali, her cohorts sent her to speak to a guy about a property. Turned out she knew this fellow from her Berkeley days. Instead of finding her a business location, he invited her to a dinner party and set her up "with the most wonderful person." Lippert had no intention of getting married. She had done it before, to one of her CIA classmates, and it hadn't turned out so well. This, then, was a grand surprise. After the nuptials, she continued to help others open restaurants and

---

[258] Interesting Twist Alert! Davies has found a way to step up her game. While I was editing this sprawl, we caught up and she told me she had just (a week prior) left Ripert's offices to go into private practice. She is not opening a restaurant on her own. She is applying the consulting skills she honed with Ripert to other people's projects. That means she's a free agent instead of an in-house employee, but she gets to flex the muscles she built up at her former gig. I asked her to describe her new enterprise, Salt Hospitality, via e-mail: "The time had come to venture out on my own, and because of my love for food and respect for people striving to be the best in the food world, I have started my own creative consulting firm specializing in menu and recipe development and testing, and restaurant concepts to help restaurants and hospitality companies improve business, profitability, and brand awareness."

signed up for duty at the Yale Sustainable Food Project, established by her ex-boss Alice Waters. Dealing with the union over there grew tiresome and Lippert finally considered taking it easy for a while. For the first time, and she's aware of how lucky she is, she found herself in a position where she didn't have to work. Why not try that? So she did. Three years later, she got the itch and took to teaching cooking classes at her home in Connecticut. She misses having a project to engage in—creating something, and then seeing someone enjoy it. "I want to be involved again," she told me, "but not with the hours or the lifestyle of a restaurant—not to say I wouldn't want to be in a restaurant again . . . I struggle because I'm not in my whites, but I'm no less a chef." What's the solution to this predicament? She could try consulting, à la Rosenzweig, but Lippert has another scheme in mind. She describes a restaurant in Sicily that's owned by four friends, each of whom spends three months out of the year as the chef. This collegial model is the one she'd like to employ; it's a seasonal spin on job sharing. I like it.

Is this different for men? That question nagged me while I wrote this chapter. They're not immune to the fatigue or physical wear and tear of cheffing. I can't think of any elder statesmen who are still going at it in the galley. Where are they? The spotlighted ones like Ripert (or Colicchio, Batali, Keller, Lagasse, Boulud, and Flay) are those who build the empires. They're not bound to the kitchen either (only by choice, when they feel like being back on the line for a spell). They're industrious and mostly nonstop, but so is Rosenzweig. Building a league of (culinary) stations might actually be the ultimate semi-retirement plan. Better than a 401(k) for anybody (male or female) who has the foresight to know that he or she will want off the brigade but not out of the game. Maybe we can learn something from these guys, who aren't so much better at removing themselves from the industry, as they are at pulling back before we do and putting themselves in positions that allow for the vacations and earlier bed-times that we grow to appreciate (and require) as the number of can-dles on the cake increases. This, I believe, we too can accomplish and enjoy, if we want it.

There are very few things we might never tackle.

"I've started to really theorize about the whole molecular gas-tronomy thing . . . I read a profile of Grant Achatz in *USA Today* that my mother saved for me. It was so sweet of her. She's like, 'Do you know this chef?' I was like, 'Oh, yeah.' And he basi-cally said, 'You know, I started cooking like this because I was bored.' And I think there is a certain boredom level with male chefs that they hit and then they just want to play with those ideas, and I find nothing appealing about it. And I don't know any women who do. I know people who can do it and who have to do it; I have a friend who's executive chef at MiniBar[259] [Washington, D.C.], and she has to do it, but it would never be her choice. So I think, it's almost like, if you're not in it [the profession] for the right reasons—and I think a lot of men aren't—then you find another way to keep yourself involved. That's one theory. And then, the other theory is, making it all about you, of course."

—*Ann Cashion*

"People, when they're talking about the subject of gender, will often say, 'Do women cook differently from men?' . . . I thought about it a little bit, because a couple months ago, someone did say something like that to me, and I had to say, 'I'm not going to answer that question,' and I sounded like a jerk. I just felt

---

[259] This is one of Spanish chef José Andrés's restaurants. Some would say he's responsible for placing his country's food—both the progressive and traditional strains—in the American public eye and making that cuisine (especially the technical aspects of the avant-garde approach) part of the ongoing culinary cultural dialogue. He is also the vision behind the Bazaar (in Los Angeles), which Waylynn Lucas references.

like, 'Ugh, I've got nothing to say on this.' But I do feel, in some ways, women are less interested in manipulating food and more interested in a context . . . or more interested in making a connection, or more interested in doing something that has relevance away from that table where that food is served at that moment . . . I'm sure that there's been something written on men gravitating toward molecular gastronomy and why women aren't . . . I can't think of a woman who would decide that she wanted to dehydrate an oyster . . . I'm trying to think of a woman in the world who has a restaurant that, even if it's not molecular, is that style of restaurant [that's] like, 'Come and bow to me.' "

—*Andrea Reusing*

"I keep on going, 'What's the next new thing?' What's been the next new thing since sous vide and foam? Seriously, what else can we possibly do? My thing is bringing people together around a table. But are you going to give me a word for that? Women do that every day at home, right?"

—*Ericka Burke*

"Molecular gastronomy seems to be a competitive thing. It's like basketball; it's like sport. It's like, who can have the coolest tool—the this, the that. I mean, whose is bigger? It's very cool; it's extremely cool. I feel that I am not moved emotionally by that food . . . There's a space and a time for that . . . and when you're eating it, you're like, 'Wow, okay, that was so clever,' and I love clever. Lord knows I love clever."

—*Carla Hall*

"I think that the technical bag of tricks as it has been taken from the food processing industry and also from the pharmaceutical industries—I have to be careful how I say it—it's not that it doesn't have a place in the broad spectrum of cuisine in our contemporary time. But the problem is that there are a very, very, very few geniuses in whose hands that becomes an expression, very few. Around those people, there are many, many, many people flocking to say [who] they worked with and we can name the people—Heston Blumenthal, Ferran Adrià, you know, all the people from Spain . . . And then they [the flockers] come back to their environments and do that kind of practice, but they're not geniuses, and so in their hands it's appropriated work. It's like me sitting down with Elizabeth Bishop and then coming home and writing some poetry, you know what I mean? It's really, really not right. But our culture and the media and the way that everyone wants to rub up against something new and the way that it all makes money . . . all of that starts spreading. It's like oil on top of water and it's washing up everywhere and it's just horrible; it's just ridiculous. And it actually denigrates the few practicing geniuses. And you should ask those people what they're trying to express with their food; they'll probably give you some really extraordinarily interesting answers. But I just don't think that it's practiced in a way [that] is coherent, where it's technically beautiful. I think it's generally practiced, and it's awful."

—*Amaryll Schwertner*

"I hate that term *molecular gastronomy*;[260] it has such a bad label that goes along with it. I've thought a lot about why there [are]

---

[260] I hate this term too (and not because I'm a girl). A few years ago while working on an article for *Gastronomica*, I interviewed Hervé This, a physical chemist known by many as the "father of molecular gastronomy." He is not a chef, and he believes that you cannot be a chef and a scientist at the same time. These are two separate (albeit related) disciplines. Scientists study and generate knowledge, whereas those who cook produce food. Molecular gastronomy is a branch of science, not of cookery. Therefore, this is all according to This, molecular gastronomist is not an appropriate designation for a chef and, similarly, a chef cannot practice molecular gastronomy (and still act as a chef). Kinda seems like a semantic morass, I know, but it makes me appreciate "progressive" or "avant-garde" cuisine as happier alternatives to "molecular gastronomy."

not a lot of women chefs doing it . . . and it really puzzles me, especially being in a place[261] where I am. It's always the male cooks who are so interested in it and so excited about it, and I don't know if it's just a different mentality, if it's much more scientific . . . A lot of that style of cooking is based from ego, and it's wanting to be very showy and it's like, 'Oh, look what I can do!' or 'Oh, look at all this smoke (or nitrogen or stuff)' or 'Ooh, I figured out how and I'm the first person to be able to make this potato soufflé that stands up like this' . . .

I think that there are very few people who know it and can do it well . . . Why make a spherification[262] of watermelon if it's not going to be better than biting into a fresh, juicy piece of watermelon just freshly cut? There's no point. It doesn't make it better if it doesn't enhance it; if it loses the integrity of the natural ingredient . . . So many new young cooks I get want to know all about it, and want to play with liquid nitrogen, and want to experiment with agar and xanthan gum, and make spherifications and foams and jellies. I will never let anybody touch it unless they can make a perfect pastry cream. Unless they can make a perfect mousse, unless they have the basics down to perfection, they have no business starting to get into a new technique [when] there are only a handful of people in the world [who] can really do it correctly . . .

There are not a lot of [women] pastry chefs out there who are doing really cutting-edge, avant-garde food and desserts and cuisine. I think it's still sort of Susie Homemaker . . . Desserts are equated with celebratory cakes for birthdays or fun

---

[261] That would be the Bazaar in Los Angeles, where, at the time of our interview, Lucas was working. Like the aforementioned MiniBar, it's another product of the José Andrés brain trust. It's a stage for avant-garde cuisine and, as its pastry chef, Lucas performed accordingly.

[262] This is a technique attributed to the magical elves at mastermind Ferran Adrià's El Bulli, that famous, now-closed eatery in Spain. It relies on a chemical reaction to turn liquids into solids—they are shaped into caviar-like spheres that are coated in a thin gelatinous membrane and burst on the tongue to rerelease their liquid contents.

cupcakes or your mom's favorite sweet thing that she would make you or your favorite candy bar."

—*Waylynn Lucas*

"This actually was a topic that we brought up at Women Chefs and Restaurateurs a couple years ago when we were in New Orleans and I was on a panel with [chef] Susan [Spicer]. The person asked the question . . . 'Is this a boy's club?' And it's a very interesting question for me that does come up fairly often . . . I do sense that from a lot of female chefs, too, that [molecular gastronomy] seems like the Antichrist. I'm not sure why."

—*Elizabeth Falkner*

I'm not sure why either. Here's what provokes my befuddlement: pastry. Were you not expecting that? Go back to chapter 5, my friends, and you'll see this was coming. Let me jog your memory: "The molecular gastronomists are really savory chefs with a hard-on for pastry." (That was Shuna Lydon, in case you forgot.) Or take Sherry Yard; she sees her specialty, pastry, to be the branch of cooking that's most informed by and connected to science. Those who gravitate toward the latter will, in the kitchen, be most fulfilled by the processes integral to baking, working with chocolate, spinning sugar, making ice cream, and the like. "It appeals to our Cartesian as well as our creative mind," she says of her art. "Now that's definitely shifted with more of the molecular cooking that's much more Cartesian-minded. But when I started twenty-five years ago, there wasn't that." Had progressive cuisine existed then, would Yard have chosen that? Maybe. So how is it, someone explain, that pastry arts and Modernist cuisine can be touted as simpatico, and yet pastry gets dubbed a girlish pursuit while the sci-fi high jinks of avant-garde cookery remain reserved for boys only?

Although most of the women I spoke to had rather vehement opinions about "molecular gastronomy," with its flavored air and truffled spitballs, there were one or two of them who dabbled in it. These were pastry chefs. Waylynn Lucas, who is currently out of love with the whole thing, applied it to her desserts at the Bazaar, where an avant-garde perspective governs the entire menu, and then Elizabeth Falkner, who is the only[263] (at the moment) full supporter of the movement, was exposed to it as a pastry chef and adopted it for her segue into savory. I respect her attitude toward what many have come to see as smoke (literally) and mirrors. Falkner doesn't look at the tricks of culinary physics (another label for it) as attention-getting aids; she sees them as implements that can amplify her food and as conduits for self-expression. She also doesn't understand why people insist on an oil-and-water opposition between the ingredient worship and farm-to-table ethics of Slow Food and the devotion to equipment and lab-to-amuse-bouche-spoon operatives of Modernist cuisine. You might say she's something of a farm-to-lab-to-plate kind of girl. When she talks about her relationship to the produce of Northern California and her training there, and then about her discovery of these alternative (a euphemism for what some others might call "diabolical") methods and substances, you begin to understand that the context in which information is received can impact how it is processed and appropriated. Falkner didn't find divine (gastronomic) inspiration in Spain. She wasn't dazzled by a futuristic flight of masterfully manipulated morsels. She was studying something much more practical—why don't I let her tell you about it herself?

"And then here comes this movement from Spain, and I'm thinking, 'This is awesome!' Because, by that point, I'd been to

---

[263] The only one among those I interviewed . . .

Japan, and I'd also worked in a lab in Italy with a bunch of food scientists and bakers on giving shelf stability to some different muffins and stuff . . . But by that point, I was already interested in a lot of the different gums and emulsifiers, and then as a pastry person you're always like, 'Oh, how cool, I don't have to use gelatin in everything.' But when I went to Japan, I remember going to the agar[264] aisle [in the store], because there were so many different versions of it. It was so cool. There were bricks of it, and then so many different versions of the powders and brands. And then I brought some stuff back and started talking about it and playing with stuff. And then I was invited to this workshop weekend in Oklahoma—believe it or not—by the Bama Pie Company, because the chef used to work in New York and she knew that there were a bunch of chefs around the country who were starting to be interested in a lot of stuff that she was dealing with on a daily basis because they use all that stuff in industrial manufacturing . . .

"It's not like I'm choosing one or the other either . . . It's just more tools; it's more ingredients . . . Instead of just talking about the ingredients, let's talk about the equipment that we have . . . I have a wood-burning oven, I have a fryer, I have a grill, I have two CVap ovens that I can [use to] cook slow and low . . . (You can actually smoke in there . . . you can proof breads in there; you can make yogurt; you can bake in there, because it has browning technology. It's like, I have a lot of options just in equipment.) . . . I also just love to cook in a cast-iron pan . . . I think of it as a tightrope to walk on."

---

[264] That would be agar-agar, a natural gelling agent formed from seaweed that can act as a replacement for animal-derived gelatin. Agar, you see, because it has a vegetal base, is the choice for those who are vegetarian, follow kosher dietary laws (there's that whole problem of mixing dairy with meat items), or who, in general, don't appreciate products processed with mammalian collagen. Falkner's point is that, while in the United States these types of stabilizing agents may seem abnormal or connected to the "evil" world of mass food production, they have age-old applications in non-Western countries like Japan, where, yes, there is an entire supermarket aisle dedicated to agar.

While Falkner works on her balancing act, her female peers stay firmly planted on solid anti-molecular ground. Their stance, I fear, does little to improve gendered stereotypes or their Susie Homemaker reputations. Because, like it or not, those cryogenically freezing dudes get the "cool" vote. And us chippies, we're losing that election by a landslide. We may not care about such things, but when it comes to getting funding, driving people to restaurants, rating high on the buzz-o-meter, and attracting the media, cool counts. I'm not, by any stretch of the spherified imagination, suggesting that women chefs pretend or try to like this progressive program to get ahead. I'm suggesting two things. The first is to separate the attitude from the art or the means from the ends. They may dislike what they perceive as the *style* of avant-garde cuisine (I'm not a fan), but look at Falkner—she's focusing on the tools of the micro-trade and employing them to suit an individual agenda that's removed from the trend quotient and the blokes who buy into it. The second is to ask what can be done to let the world know that lady chefs have more than cupcakes in the oven, and that they're as much a part of the culinary zeitgeist as the guys who blow liquid nitrogen smoke up each other's asses and into our food.

CHAPTER 11

The Rebirth of Cool

There are no rock-star women chefs.

—HEATHER BERTINETTI

*Part of my theory about why you don't have more successful women chefs
and restaurateurs is women chefs don't look cool. It's just that somehow,
they don't look like partiers. They don't look rock 'n' roll. They don't seem
like, "Hey, we'd all be fun to hang out with," you know? So then you have
these investors who only hear about these male chefs, who think, "Yeah,
I'm going to live the rock 'n' roll lifestyle and invest in them and I'm going to
be able to go out and party, and we're all going to sit down at the table and
drink for hours together." And with the women chefs, I think that's a huge
problem.*

—AMANDA COHEN

Do you want your mom to be the archetype of cool?

—NANCY OAKES

During our senior year of college, my best friend Helen and I decided
we needed role models. Whom, we pondered, could we look up to and
be inspired by? Which women, I asked Helen, would you say are cool?
Like, *really* cool? What did I mean by that? I never defined it, but somehow, Hels and I knew exactly what this meant. Cool—the real deal—is
something you know when you see. It's not a costume that's donned
and it can't be packaged, or even mimicked, because it's driven by an
uncompromising sense of individualism. We started throwing names
out. There were actresses like Patricia Clarkson, Annette Bening, Susan
Sarandon, and Anjelica Huston. There was Mary Frances Berry, the
professor and social activist who taught our undergraduate course on

the History of American Law[265] and headed up the U.S. Commission on Civil Rights under the Carter administration. When President Reagan gave her the boot because she challenged his policies, she sued him and won to reclaim her position. President Clinton appointed her Chairperson of the Civil Rights Commission, and there she stayed until 2004. While performing those duties, she managed to find the time to teach students like Helen and me about the Slaughter-House Cases.

Who else did we have? I think we put our friend Evelyn Hockstein on there—or, actually, I'm not sure if we did at the time, but I know we would now. Ev always went her own way, camera in hand, stray cat at her heels, and, as soon as we graduated, was drawn to trouble, wherever it was. Gaza Strip? She was there. Tajikistan? Check. She has gone to Zambia to track the hunger crisis there, documented child prostitution in Nicaragua, visited Haiti in the wake of the quake, and snapped a few portraits of Dominique Strauss-Kahn. Our pal the photojournalist is on the list.

I've been adding to it over the years. Some of my tack-ons include: Michelle Rhee—she was the chancellor, District of Columbia Public Schools from 2007 to 2010; Sheryl Sandberg, the CEO of Facebook; Maria Cornejo, the Chilean clothing designer; Sonia Rykiel, the French fashion visionary; crooner and songwriter Neko Case; China Machado, model, fashion editor, gallerist, and then some; Judith Jamison, who, in December of 2010, twenty-one years later, stepped down from her post as the artistic director of the Alvin Ailey American Dance Theater; director, screenwriter, producer, and fashion muse Sofia Coppola; Claire Denis, a French filmmaker and professor of that medium; novelist and literary journalist Joan Didion; actress, entrepreneur, activist, and philanthropist Jane Fonda; Anna Deavere Smith, a writer, actress, social commentator

---

[265] Confession: I took the class pass-fail (it was the semester I broke my kneecap and the HandyVan wasn't so good at getting me to places on time, so I had to take some precautions of my own). Note to others: If you find yourself in a class where the professor, no matter how riveting she may be, employs the Socratic method, you should probably *not* take said course pass-fail. You should get out ASAP, or else go for a proper grade. Showing up without having done the day's reading is *not* recommended. I am still trying to define *social jurisprudence*, and I'd ask my friend Holly, who was also enrolled, but, alas, I think she might remain unclear on its meaning as well.

(of sorts), and professor; Kathy Halbreich, the former director of the Walker Art Center in Minneapolis and current associate director of New York City's Museum of Modern Art; her mother, Betty Halbreich,[266] who was the first personal shopper and still guides Manhattan's best-dressed from her headquarters at Bergdorf Goodman; and my divine cousin Fran Kessler, about whom someone (she herself, I think) should write a book.

For me, though, the ultimate in cool, gender aside, has to be Patti Smith. A true artist (if you've read her recent memoir *Just Kids*, you know she can't help but make art—it is how she exists), Smith expresses her vision in prose, poetry, drawing, photography, and music. She defies categorization, and yet, in many ways, she *is* rock 'n' roll. And like many of the women on my ever-growing roster, she is also a mother. (Whoa, since when is *that* "cool"?)

Patti Smith was the first person I thought of when presented with the current lady chef conundrum. "There's this idea of the cool chef, right?" I asked Jessica Boncutter. "And now that cheffing is really cool, and it looks basically like Anthony Bourdain or David Chang, and has usually got tattoos or rides a motorcycle (or Vespa), and—"*Yeah,*" she interjected, "he's really into whole animals . . . We call it bro'ing out on whole animals." We cracked up. But when the giggles stop, you have to put this into a less comedic context, which we did as our conversation went on. Today, we both acknowledged, in terms of pop culture, chefs are among the coolest things going. And when you think about the chefs who are waving the "cool" banner, they're male. When they're written about, words like "rock star," "rock 'n' roll," "rebel," "badass," and "innovative" are invoked to describe them. All this, by the way, starts to seem a lot less cool after you've seen it replicated everywhere. That's, unfortunately, beside the point. Cool sells. And it gets backing. The more those guys are put into the spotlight, the more money people want to invest in their futures. This got me thinking, "Well, all right then. Let them have their inked guns, their fancy gadgets, and their

---

[266] Betty, who remains my ultimate style icon, was my father's mother's best friend; her daughter, Kathy, was my dad's sandbox-mate and childhood chum.

I-don't-give-a-fuck swaggers. That's fine. What, then, do we have? Us girls? What is our brand of chef cool? Who's our representative?"

What's crucial to understand is that I'm not recommending that we imitate the guys. Girls "bro'ing out" looks ridiculous and, when taken to the extreme (by anyone), pathetic. As Ericka Burke says, "What's sad to me is you see some of these young women who are just—they want it so bad . . . And they're looking at their competition [who] are these tough-ass dudes with tattoos and piercings, and they're kind of going down the same route. And that's all cool, whatever; but I think you're badass if it's internal. You don't need to do all that other stuff to be badass. And it's not even really badass; it's just to have that passion and soul for what you do. So, I think, my advice to young women would just be to be quiet and listen to yourself and just follow through with it."

Sage advice. And still, because in order to speak to the folks out there who believe that what they're shown is "it," we need some icons, or figureheads, to put a female face (or two) on it ("it"?). It's time to celebrate the lady chefs who possess their own kind of cool. That's why I asked many of the women I interviewed the following question: Who is your industry's Patti Smith? As for the prerequisites, Burke offers the following guidelines: "Someone that men and women would look up to . . . What makes you cool is believing in yourself and being okay to be you, and not needing to emulate somebody else. I mean, that's cool. Know your strengths and know your weaknesses, and own them. To make it in this business as a female, you have to be strong, you have to be willing to take risks; it's also about having fun. If you can't get through the really rough times without laughing or smiling, you're fucked." Got that? Be strong, take risks, have fun, and as Polonius said to his son Laertes in *Hamlet* (act 1, scene 3), "This, above all: to thine own self be true."

So who's on it? Who were the outstanding nominees? There was a smattering and, which warms the heart, many of the women queried chose other interviewees encountered on these pages. Elizabeth Belkind had two contenders. "One person that came to mind is Elizabeth Falkner. She's definitely a force to contend with. I mean she's very much out-there and very much herself. There's a limit to how many people can be like her," she said. Belkind followed that with: "I think Nancy Silverton is fabulous. She's eccentric and successful and super-committed to her work. I mean, she's still serving dinner, making it with her own hands. And you don't see that many chefs who are at that point in their careers doing what she's doing . . . But she's a big personality in a very differ-ent way than Elizabeth [Falkner] is. She's, again, very much herself, and articulates that self very well in the public. And then just has a tre-mendous following." Mel Nyffeler gave Silverton a nod too. "My role model was Nancy Silverton . . . When I was baking bread, I feel like she really turned people on to a more traditional style of bread-baking, and eating naturally leavened bread, and made it more available . . . She doesn't own that [La Brea] bakery anymore, but built that business—a small neighborhood business—and sold it for millions of dollars . . . I just like her style. I like her story. You know, she had two kids while she was doing all this too."

Providing two other familiar names, Melissa Perello went with Naomi Pomeroy and Alex Raij. Cathy Whims gave a shout-out to Barbara Lynch, who, the former highlighted, born a "Southie," was saved by restaurants to emerge from her at-risk neighborhood and built an empire of eateries in her hometown. "Loretta Keller's really cool," Nancy Oakes said of the San Francisco spot Coco500's chef-owner. "She shoots robins for breakfast out of her window. I mean how cool is that? That's cool." Sarah Schafer listed Claudia Fleming, pastry chef Nicole Plue (taste her food at Cyrus in Healdsburg, California), and Anita Lo, whose name was mentioned a number of times. So was New York City's star April Bloomfield of the Spotted Pig, the Breslin, and, one of my frequent haunts, The John Dory.

Among these worthy front-runners, a clear (most-nominated) winner appeared.

"Gabrielle [Hamilton, of Prune] immediately springs to mind," Cathy Whims said. "She stuck with one restaurant; is a talented, gifted writer; raised a family in a restaurant; survived in New York City; and is tough as nails." Anne Quatrano seconded this: "Gabrielle is one of the first people who did it in New York City . . . For so long, in New York City, unless you had a few million dollars, you couldn't open anything, or certainly nothing that would be recognized in any way. She got huge national recognition for a restaurant she opened for practically nothing." And then there's Boncutter, with her enthusiastic endorsement. "I think my friend Gabrielle Hamilton at Prune is amazing . . . Gabs is great . . . She's got a great style; she has a wonderful sense of aesthetic, which is masculine and feminine at the same time, which comes through in her restaurant as well and her cooking. Her cooking is very unique, very personal. She's got a little bit of the rock 'n' roll edge to her, a little artsy, but very understated. She's a downtown girl, right? . . . She's just cool. She'll be wearing, like—instead of a chef coat—this cool chef coatdress . . . I have a lot of respect for Gabrielle. People who move to New York [who] work [at Bar Jules], I send them there, and we have girls here that worked at Prune. But I have so much respect for her, because there's not somebody [else] who has been able to stay true to herself and feminine in New York."

As luck would have it, Gabs agreed sit down for an interview. Better still, our meeting transpired at the beginning of the process— it was before she received the James Beard nomination and subsequent award for Best Chef: New York City; before I'd read her un-put-down-able memoir *Blood, Bones & Butter,*[267] whose pub date landed two months after we met; and before she'd racked up the myriad accolades from these other ladies. It was noon on January 19, 2011, to be precise. I was excited because I had always suspected she was—if somewhat intimidating—definitely cool. She seemed like the kind

---

[267] *Blood, Bones & Butter: The Inadvertent Education of a Reluctant Chef* (New York: Random House, 2011).

of girl I would have wanted to be friends with in high school but who had no time for sprightly pip-squeaks such as myself. I loved Prune (although I hadn't gone as often as I'd liked) and devoured everything she'd ever penned. She had contributed to *The New Yorker*, among other publications, and served as a judge twice (most generous, since it's an unpaid gig and requires recipe testing in addition to drafting) for the Tournament of Cookbooks I founded with Amanda Hesser and Merrill Stubbs of Food52.com.

It surprised me that Hamilton was game for the whole lady-chef book project, if only because I knew she had written a tome of her own and was probably sick of talking, thinking, or typing about what she does and who she is. But no, she was loquacious, opinionated, and, well, for that hour-plus, I actually felt like we might have been old friends who'd been stirring up trouble or laughing at the status quo since the ninth grade. She was also kind. As we chatted at the staff table downstairs, next to the Prune kitchen, lunch was being laid out, and she asked me if I was hungry, a gesture that made me feel like part of the family. And it *is* a family. You sense that from the moment you walk into the joint, and when you're around Hamilton or any of her gang, the familial vibe is heightened. I can't quite say she reads as a maternal figure or, alternatively, acts in a paternal manner; she has a gender-neutral parental presence. At the same time, as Boncutter noted, Hamilton herself possesses a femininity that she doesn't try to subdue. We discussed her style of bossing people and all of the choices she made—deliberately—while creating and running Prune.

I don't think you need a life story or even basic chronology; I'd rather you read her memoir for that. What's more resonant, in light of our hunt for cool, is her perspective on life, cheffing, restaurant management, and some less obvious topics. So, if it's all right with you, I'm going to share a bunch of Hamilton's musings, in her words:

Sometimes, I wish it would end, the whole fucking female chef thing. It's just like, are we really, really [in a whisper] going to talk about this still?

Now we have bar chefs, don't we? Yeah. I guess I understand *chef* as "the chief" . . . Yeah, the chef is the chief; they're the one in charge.

I get caught up in [the term] *chef-owner*, because I'm a chef-owner. And I'm always amazed when I read that, like, Scott Bryan is no longer at Veritas, I was like, "*Whoa!* I thought he *was* Veritas." And then I realize, "Shit, that person's an employee—an *employee*," and that is a very different category than what it is to be a chef and owner of a restaurant . . . And I think that chef-owner person . . . you are the person who is defining, and safeguarding, and maintaining the company, the corporate culture. Although in our industry, what we mean by *corporate* can be very funny. You're the one who decides how many drinks we're drinking after work and what kind of swear-words we're throwing around on the line—you're defining the taste and style of your place and you are making sure everyone has what they need to do their job in that idiom and in that location. So you have to make sure that the people are arriving on time, that they are well rested, that they are paid, that they can rely on arriving to the place, and it will be clean and well lit and well equipped, and that their schedule is reliable enough that they can also live their life in a way that makes it conducive for them to come to work and do their job really well. They have to have time to do their laundry [laughs] and make out with their girlfriend, or whatever they need to do, or else they're not going to really want to come in. Your job, as the chef, is to be able to give them everything they need to know, food-wise, expectation-wise, technically, even if you have to look it up.

CD: *There's something almost parental in that.*

It's funny; I can hear that now. If you'd said that to me, maybe even—well, for sure ten years ago—five years ago, I might have jumped across the table and taken your fucking head off . . . because it does not get said of male chefs.

CD: *But I said "parental," not maternal.*

That's right, but the only parent I'm going to be is the mother, not the father, so I can only hear *parental* as *maternal* in a way. In fact, you're right, and it's not unlike that; there are lots of parenting styles, and so that's also the chef's to define. In some ways, it's a very nice thing to say. It's like, true parenting, where you're not just siring or birthing or dropping your bomb out there or your progeny . . . I'm going to guide you, help you.

In large part, the people who make up the workforce in this industry, they're young. They still need to be told, "You're drinking too much" or "Can you stop going out and partying too hard?" and "No, I'm not going to let you work a double [shift] on Saturday." So they still make sort of young, juvenile decisions for themselves. And even though they've left home and they're living on their own, you can still see that they could benefit from a little, firm grip on the shoulder that says, "Son, it's time for you to get a fucking haircut, and I can tell you're eating dinner out too much 'cause you don't have any money left over, and it's possible to live on this salary, so what are you doing?"

[The brigade system] is a little like the parenting our parents did, so, um, I don't know for sure how our new style is working out. The results aren't in yet, and it's possible that that old system really separates wheat from chaff; it produces pretty rugged, hardworking people. Now we have a new generation, [who] if I'm making sure they wipe their ass and don't drink too much, that's pretty infantilizing—not infantilizing—it's like, "Wow, you're twenty-six years old; you should be figuring this out on your own. But when you're not, I really want you to realize I'm going to give you a nudge, and I really do want you to show up." And that's what I seem to have in the labor pool . . . As a person who grew up [being] beaten with wooden spoons and [being] put to bed without dinner, and [with] all the like hard-core shit that old parenting styles allowed, of course I'm going to be on the pendulum and swing the other way.

I don't know that what we are doing now, in contrast to the generation prior to us, is so much better. And the word *chef* is so belittled and thrown around so casually, even the customers come in and they're like, "Oh, I want you to meet my husband. He's an excellent chef." And I say [gasps], "Oh, Mr. Jones, it's so nice to meet you and where are you a chef?" "Oh no, at home, at home he's a chef" [imitating his wife], and you're just like, "Okay, that's fine . . . "

So I have a lot of negative opinions about the competitive TV chef shit, and I realized I was having a lot of those opinions unresearched, and to not be a fool, I rented a full season of *Top Chef*. I had not seen any of it. And oh! I watched it and I could not believe that, first of all, these people called themselves chefs, and what they didn't know about cooking—just about cooking . . . The Quickfire Challenge thing, there's this chick on there—and I hate to come down on the chicks, 'cause, but still—I was just like, "This girl is a chef and she is admitting in front of everyone on this television land that this is her first oyster." She'd never shucked a [whispers] fucking oyster before. And I just was deeply embarrassed. And I was like, "I'm not calling myself a chef anymore." Then, by contrast, you had this guy from Austria or Germany or I don't know, and I was like, "Now this guy's a chef; he can bake; he can make sauces; he can work with meat; he understands shellfish. I mean, he got eliminated for some attitude problem or whatever, which I totally—whatever, I understand the TV show now that I've watched it. But, anyway, the point is . . . I just couldn't believe what was passing for the word *chef* now. And really, these guys—and maybe women, I don't know—they go to these competitions, these Master Chef competitions in Switzerland or wherever, and it's mind-blowing what they can do . . . Just take Jacques Pépin. Jacques Pépin can bust out a *pâte à choux* as quickly as he can bone out a chicken. And he can also answer some questions about *poisson à la vapeur* or whatever, and come on, *that* is a chef, in terms of cooking technique, et cetera. On top of it, you know what else he can do? He knows food costs; he knows payroll; he knows workers' comp—I mean, that's when I started to call myself a chef.

When I opened Prune eleven years ago, I called myself a dishwasher, and I still struggle with the word *chef*. Albeit, I had learned on the job, and when I opened Prune I was not a chef, but I did apply myself, and I learned, and I'll take the title now—and I'm forty-five years old, and I'm eleven years in. I was a good cook when we opened, and that's it, and a little anal-retentive in cleaning. So those two things happened to carry me along through the parts that I didn't know, and now that I know, it's like, "Oh, okay, now I'm a chef."

I feel the same way about books, really. I don't know what it is about the kitchen and food and the restaurant world, that everyone feels entitled to it. You would not just call yourself a doctor—and I am not suggesting for a fucking second that me being able to bone out a chicken or properly braise a lamb shank is anything like diagnosing your spleen cancer. But still, you have a goddamn recipe for poulet in a pot, and you're going to call yourself a chef or you're going to write a cookbook? And writers used to be writers, and books used to mean something. It wasn't just like, [here are] a bunch of pages between two covers with words . . . But then I also ask myself, "Why are you so uptight about being the gatekeeper?" Like, "Okay, you're a chef, Bob Jones. You cook big breakfasts at home for your family." Like, "You can be a chef, what do I care? I know what I'm doing." And same with writing or books . . . I get caught up in the "Henny Penny, the sky is falling," like, you're a chef and I'm a chef and yet you've never shucked an oyster.

I was trying to get out of this business. I did not choose this profession. It was a sort of emergency decision a long time ago to get a job and then I've been stuck in the industry forever. And then I lived on this block and this was the space that was available. So I didn't really have a decision to make; I didn't have any money. I decided to take it on and the space told me what to do. In hindsight, maybe I could have raised money and gutted the place and turned it into something different. But what I inherited was a French bistro, and I just pared it down and cleaned it up and made it less specific. But I had to keep the bones of what was here, so I went with it. The banquette, the zinc bars, the mirrors; I kept everything, the plates. It was a super-thrift job; I didn't have any money. And I didn't have any pedigree whatsoever. I had spent, probably, twenty-something years in the industry prior to opening. But I had not been a chef; it's not like I could call on seven chomping-at-the-bit backers who were going to throw money behind me to open some restaurant. It's just a shoestring, hey-kids-let's-put-on-a-show-in-the-barn kind of story, and the barn provides its confines and so—I actually love that, in fact, if the whole world had been open to me, I would have been paralyzed by indecision. And the fact that the space told me what to do was very helpful.

And secondly, the reason I opened this restaurant was very, very much in reaction to what was going on at the time that I had terrifically wearied of. I was deep in catering and working these huge catering facilities, which, they themselves were trying to mimic and imitate what was going on in restaurants . . . Obviously, the quality in restaurants at the time was much better than what we could do in the catering world, but the attitudes were the same. So, in 1999, there was a paragraph-length description of each menu item. There was the beginning of locating your products—that kind of descriptive language was entering menus, of Farmer Bob picked this out of the leftmost quadrant of row seven or this diver scallop was handpicked by Steve Seaman—it was just starting . . . It was becoming derisive. Although, at that time, interestingly, it was still fantastic to get green-lipped mussels from New Zealand and Buddha's hand [citrus] from far away and so we were still marveling at the stuff that could be flown in and air-shipped. Now, of course, we disdain the idea that you might get your microgreens shipped in from Farmer Bob in Ohio, or whatever that guy's name is, Farmer Jones[268] . . . That's not local enough. If I can't forage it off the FDR [Drive], it's not good enough for us now.

So, at the time, those were the kinds of things I was trying to work against. In catering, everything was being turned into a torchon.[269] I don't know what is up with the Torchon Movement, but, my God, if we weren't shoving everything we possibly could find into a roll, a roulade, and submerging it into a water bath and slicing it, whatever. Anyway, I was like, "Eh, it's not what I

[268] Find him at Chefs-garden.com.

[269] A clear and thorough discourse on the process of preparing something *au torchon*, as the French say, can be found in the foreboding culinary bible that is Thomas Keller's *The French Laundry Cookbook*. Before he reveals the recipe for his Poached Moulard Duck Foie Gras *au Torchon* with Pickled Cherries, Keller, with the help of writer Michael Ruhlman, teaches the following: "*Torchon* means 'dish towel' in French, and the dish takes its name from the fact that the foie gras pieces are wrapped in a cloth (we use several layers of cheesecloth) into a thick cylinder and then quickly poached." That you'll find on page 103 of the book, published in 1999 by Artisan. Wrap it in a "towel" to form a solid round then poach it. Got it?

want to do." So I opened a restaurant. Basically, I opened the restaurant that I wished that I could go out to eat at. And at the time, really, it honestly did not exist. I wanted that quality, that high-end quality, like strong cooking technique, in a place where you didn't have to get so dressed up and feel so uptight. Like, I loved going to Vong.[270] Oh my God, I mean, the flavor shit that would go on there, I would just [gasps], you know. You had to close your eyes and understand what the hell was happening and just be like, "This is so *in-cre-di-ble*." But I always felt so uptight on the chair, and I wasn't well dressed enough and then I would put my hand on the table and be like, "Oh shit! I have some crap underneath my fingernails," and I just did not feel comfortable. And I know this is an incredibly antique idea now, in 2011. Like "Ooh, a place where you could have high-quality food but in a relaxed setting," it's almost quaint to even say so. But, in 1999, frankly, it didn't exist until, stupidly, I opened that place where I wished I could go and ended up having to work in it all the time [laughs]. But on the other hand, if you look at what's happened since, it's a dime a dozen. Any corner, and you can go to that kind of place.

I don't think it was [labeled] "a women's restaurant." . . . I don't actually think it took as strong as it might have. I feel like I shut that down, pretty fast and hard, because it was absurd for people to describe this as comfort food or anything remotely—I guess there were some attempts at calling it the *cuisine de bonne femme*[271] or *cuisine de grand-mère*[272]—'cause we did not have a roast chicken [on the menu] when we started. That was not any-where here. It was easily squelched when I said in any interview "Really, so what is comforting about monkfish liver? In what

---

[270] The second restaurant Jean-Georges Vongerichten opened in New York City. It's closed now.

[271] French, of course, it translates, literally, to "the cooking of a good wife" and is used to describe simple, home-style cuisine.

[272] "Grandma's cooking," also French (as in, same idea as above).

world do you offer it?" I mean that was there from the get-go. Or "Huh, razor clams? Is that comfort food? Really?" It was such challenging food—there was so much tripe and offal and marrow bones and innards shit that I grew up eating—that I could not let the naming [of] it as "comfort" or "women's" cuisine go for very far. But what we did cultivate, and I would say, on purpose, defiantly, or politically even, is that "You bet it's a chick place." You are going to notice, as soon as you walk in here, that it's female. So it was purposely pink. I didn't pick pink out of the ether. I did not want that Nehru jacket in midnight blue—that was also going on at the time. It was a defiant sort of "This is pussy pink. This is pink." And after all the years that I'd worked in the business, where I'd tried to shut down my gender and just adapt to the normative, which, in that case, would not be normative— it would just be male, which, of course, is the normative. [Laughs.]

So all those years of smoking the filterless cigarettes, and saying cocksucker, and getting burned as bad as everyone, and, you know, being dykey and double strong and double hard, I was, like, "I'm going to make very delicious food, and I'm going to put lipstick on every day, and I'm going to wear a dress. And I want you to see that even chicks can cook." So rather than hide the gender, I decided to flaunt it. So we had lots of women on the floor, female manager, female chef and owner, female bartenders—I mean that in itself was kind of—yeah. It's kind of incredible to walk into a restaurant and see the kind of restaurant—I don't mean Hooters where you want chicks behind the bar or Hogs & Heifers or whatever—I'm talking about fully dressed women [laughs] making a serious cocktail where there [are] little glimmers of frost on the top of your vodka martinis, but not on your gin martini, you know? That they would know the difference, that was, for me, very exciting.

My sister and I are always talking about this, how we are not the kind of women who get together for a glass of white wine; that is so not our story. It's like, "What's wrong with you women? Have a drink!" Like "You can drink bourbon" or "You can drink bitter Campari and gin" . . . In fact, I remember, later, we [the restaurant] started, actually, to get characterized as macho. So, yes, there was an attempt at the beginning to make it comfort food or blah-blah-blah, but it did quickly hit—'cause the portions were large, the food was challenging, the innards and offal, and we didn't have—and still don't— there's no Diet Coke.

I think it's fun to work with a lot of women, because then, during the prep shift, the conversation just is whatever we're talking about, and the men have to be part of it, too, so it's fun. I love that people mention their periods all the time, and, well, everyone gets them, constantly . . . always at the same time. So it's always like, "I need to step off the line [laughs]—after we get through this push? It's imperative that I step off the line for five minutes!" . . . I think just by having women in the work-force, it feminizes the workplace. And then, sartorially, yeah, we just like to—I love the chef dresses. I did *Iron Chef* in a dress; I cook here in a chef dress. It's fun . . . I would not do [*Iron Chef*] again . . . because I won [laughs], and I don't want to go back again and lose [laughs again] . . . That was fun.

I was gonna ask you who you thought my peers [in New York] were. Where do I fall? I don't know where to locate myself here . . . I think Prune started something. I mean, I don't want to be the person who said that, but I think we did. I mean, I know it, because the menu ends up on other people's menus. The light—the silver-tipped lightbulb—the soundtrack, the bread-basket, all of that stuff is now out there everywhere. So I know. But I'm like, "Who's the other. . . ?"

[Vis-à-vis David Chang and the initial press and ensuing success he enjoyed after, like Hamilton, opening a small, eccentric space in the East Village and seeing it spawn a new genre of restaurant.] "If I think about the David Chang thing, it's true.[273] No one was calling. So [back then] I did not ever get a James Beard Award or nomination. I did not ever get *Food & Wine* Best [New] Chef, I never got featured in *Gourmet* magazine with Ruth [Reichl] at the helm. And Dana Cowin [editor in chief, *Food & Wine*], every time *Food & Wine*'s Best [New] Chef stuff came up, they would ask me to write an essay and they would not nominate me—and I never knew what that was about.[274] I was like, "God, that's weird. I feel like, it's pretty good what we're doing here. I don't know." Or we were reviewed in $25 and Under in the *New York Times* and not as a [starred] restaurant.[275] So those things are not in my control. I think that might be places where you'd feel the, um, gender problem. And I didn't get caught up in it. I just was like, "I'm just going to put my head down and do my job and see how this plays out." And, ah, yeah.

Well, now when I see all the restaurants that are like what Prune was, I'm jealous. I really have restaurant envy . . . I'm like,

---

[273] A reference to the following observation Laura Shapiro made in her online article for *Gourmet* titled "Where Are the Women?" June 12, 2008: "When Gabrielle Hamilton opened a tiny, uncomfortable place called Prune in 1999, her idiosyncratic menu caught on, the restaurant became successful, and today she's a much-admired figure on the scene. When David Chang opened a tiny, uncomfortable place called Momofuku Noodle Bar in 2004, his idiosyncratic menu caught on, the restaurant became successful, and today he's a much-admired figure on the scene—with numerous awards, scads of magazine profiles, two more restaurants, and a public that worships him. However you account for the difference between these two career trajectories, it's got to include something besides the food."

[274] He's *ba-ack*. For the sake of comparison: David Chang opened Momofuku Noodle Bar in 2004, received his first James Beard nomination in 2006 for Rising Star Chef, and won that award the following year. He was twenty-nine at the time, so eligible for that 30-and-under award, which age-wise, Hamilton was not when she opened Prune in 1999. Chang has gone on to win two more Beards, so far (one for Best Chef: New York City/Momofuku Ssäm Bar in 2008 and another for Best New Restaurant/Momofuku Ko in 2009). He received the *Food & Wine* Best New Chef Award in 2006. Hamilton was first nominated for a James Beard Award in 2009 and won in 2011. She also received a James Beard Foundation Book Award nomination (Writing and Literature category) for her memoir in 2012.

[275] In 2011, days before the official release of her memoir, Frank Bruni reviewed Prune for the *New York Times* and gave it one star. That was nearly twelve years after the restaurant opened and Eric Asimov wrote it up for the $25 and Under column.

"I can't believe they have a real kitchen," or they have a waiter station. They have an actual place for waiters to do their side work and they have beautiful finishings; they have the right glass and the right gold-leaf silkscreen on their window; they're appointed. In the Brooklyn scene in particular, it's very jealous-making. It's actually enviable and maddening for me that I have a chronic bad experience where I'm walking into the most beautiful restaurant. I feel so excited, I'm like, "God! Look at this, it's so beautiful," and it's a movie set. It's a goddamned movie set. There's no substance. It is all style, and they have everything . . . They've got the brick oven; they're slicing the meat by hand; they've got the Four Barrel coffee; they've got the wine from the little—Occhipinti[276]—from Sicily; or they've got like all the right stuff, and they don't know what they're doing. It's just like, "Shit! If I had this restaurant—if I had this space and this marble countertop, I would just be so thrilled to not have to work under the conditions . . . " This place [Prune], I bought it out of bankruptcy in court; we still use the fucking dented pans that came with the place. I just replaced the plates and cups, what, three years ago or something—it's just ridiculous. It's like, "Ah, what I wouldn't do for a brand-new blah-blah."

I feel like it's only in the past couple of years that I figured out that I do not want to open another restaurant. And, in fact, I did have ideas to do other restaurants along the way, and they never came to fruition. I have a business partner here who—it's a complicated relationship and it's not a partnership. He's a 20 percent owner, and he was the guy who started the investing and got the groups of friends and family together to get this thing going in the beginning. But he doesn't have anything to do with the restaurant. Anyway, he's never been that guy for me in the way that, like [in Chicago] Donnie Madia and [chef]

---

[276] The wines of Sicilian vintner Arianna Occhipinti.

I made my commitment where it's my job to keep it fresh and committed and I'm going to take such care of this restaurant. I take the same care in year eleven as I did in year one. And I'm learning the depths of that—what it is to get deep, as opposed to broad. And sometimes I go to the restaurants, you know, of my peers who have six restaurants, and I walk in, I'm like, "God, this place has no soul." They just slapped it [on]; you could even envision the planning meeting. It's like, "Okay, let's get the light fixture from that place, and we'll put that plate in here, and get the girl at the door—oh, you know what we'll have? We'll have carts!" . . . I walk in and I think, "Somebody took the water and poured it into the soup. And what used to be fucking incredible broth is now diluted." And I don't want that to happen at Prune. I want Prune to stay superstrong and superfresh and I want to be here.

And then, what I figured out is that it's almost like taking a second job, in fact, it is. But if I have a writing career, I can make my money that way . . . Well it's hard, we'll see. Cooking and writing are really hard jobs . . . I think the next thing will be a cookbook . . . Can't I just see how this one [book] goes first?

That literary foray has gone quite well. Hamilton's published work has drawn rave reviews from chefs, food writers, and literary critics. It scored a slot on the *New York Times* bestseller list for seven weeks. She has appeared on *Charlie Rose* and received *beaucoup de* buzz from the media. Now, even if I could wander over to Prune as frequently as I'd like, there probably wouldn't be room for me and my dinnertime roasted-bone-marrow craving, or my lunch-hour bacon-and-marmalade-sammie hankering. Place is *packt like sardines in a crushd tin box*[277] (these, the fish—sans packaging—you'll find at the Prune bar, where they're placed on Triscuits smeared with mustard). I've been

[277] It's the name of a Radiohead tune, everybody! You'll find it on the 2005 *Amnesiac* album.

trying to imagine what her secret genius concept is for that "something" she's "hell-bent on doing," and wait with bated breath for its arrival. Is that because I believe Hamilton needs to have another storefront? No. I like how she thinks, and I look forward to having another place of hers to visit—whether or not food is served there is not of concern. My wish is that it combines her passions for cooking and writing; but, again, not necessary.

Pam Mazzola saw Hamilton's only having one restaurant as a possible impediment, or caveat, to the New York chef's eligibility for official cool status. "You know who's amazing? The woman who owns Prune . . . But she's only done one thing . . . that differentiates her from a man . . . There's not any male chef that only has one restaurant that's got some 'chops' (quote unquote). Name one . . . I'm not saying that's a good thing, 'cause I think there [are] a lot of great things about only having one restaurant." Mazzola wasn't saying that she found Hamilton less "cool" for sticking to a single eatery; she was suggesting that the "rock star" patina is a result of (and sustained by) expansion. My question is—and it sparked this conversation—why is there only one version of cool? Why do you have to go pop to be a rock star? I always thought there was an element of rebellion behind rock 'n' roll. So why do you have to conquer Vegas or spread your restaurant seed around town to be taken seriously as a contender, or thought of as having "chops"? Doesn't matter if you're a boy or a girl; why, if you do it your way (big or small) and stick to your guns, can't you have one way-paving culinary institution, and be lionized as a legend in your own time, huh?

Call it "female" or "pussy pink" cool; I see Hamilton's Prune-and-Prune-alone MO as cool, period. You can be as monomaniacal as you want; follow Judy Rodgers's example and stand by your Zuni. Or, like Gabs, you can use your restaurant as a base from which to launch a hyphenated career. She's a chef-writer. There are other hybrid gigs—chef-activist, for one. I wish, in the future, to see more chefs expand their roles by specializing in substantive disciplines like these, instead of blindly grasping at whatever scraps of fame or fortune lie within reach, and, too, that those who do receive more media attention, public praise, and financial backing for having made that choice.

Question: What does the future look like for women chefs?

"I think it's an astonishing time to be a cook. There is no question. Whether you are a home cook; a professional cook in a restaurant; a cook at a school that's using local produce. A lot of economic forces are overlapping . . . [There are] just so many ways to do good, important work, whether good for the planet, good for your health, good for public health. Whether it's small-scale manufacturing of something that's really satisfying and sustainable, and with a schedule that allows you to have a life; whether a combination of farming and making something; whether it's teaching in schools; or building farmers' market communities . . . Twenty, thirty years ago, you were a home cook or a weekend prodigy, or you thought you wanted to open a restaurant, or you cooked in a restaurant, but now the landscape is so varied and the world of food embraces more than restaurants."

—*Judy Rodgers*

"Well, I hope we're not having the conversation that we've been having since the beginning, about why there are not more of us. It comes up every five years in a magazine. Every three years in the *New York Times*, they'll have something about women chefs, and I just don't know if there'll ever be more of us. I think it just is what it is. How to improve it? Probably by becoming better businesspeople. I'm not saying we should have less of the nurturing, but finding that balance between running a business and being able to have both—to have it all—because I think a lot of women chefs have lost their businesses because they are too nurturing, too giving, not able to run a successful restaurant. And we can do that; you can find the middle without compromising or without giving up too much of yourself."

—*Charleen Badman*

"I hope to see more [women] . . . I would think that now—in kitchens or any careers—there are more women in the highest positions, because they're waiting longer to have kids."

—*Stephanie Izard*

"I don't know how it can be improved . . . If I look at all the girls who are down in the Bindi [now closed] kitchen right now, the one who is my chef will probably not own her own restaurant, and there's one who's a line cook who probably will . . . I'd like women to be appreciated, and I like all that, but is that going to happen? I don't know . . . but you also have to work for it, you know? There's no special treatment, and you don't get any special knowledge."

—*Marcie Turney*

"I don't ascribe any restrictions or any arbitrary sort of boundaries. I think that women should and could and will do whatever it is that they want to do. Would it be helpful if there [were] more respect ascribed to women in these positions by their male counterparts? Sure. By the media? Sure. I don't know why it exists that if you put a male and a female together doing any similar job that there might be this perception that one person is more or less competent, more or less dedicated, I really don't know. I know it exists . . . Women do have to endure a lot more and maybe they just need to take what they've had to endure, or to use a more dramatic word, suffer, in either collecting money so that they can have their own business or working their way up through a system . . . I have a lot of respect for any path, and as long as you stay on that path, you're going to get somewhere with yourself and then that's going to reflect back out into what you do with your life. And so you can get help from the media or from male mentors or from so many different places, but the fact of the matter is that when you're dedicating yourself to doing something—if this is really what you're going to do— it's probably going to take a really long time to get somewhere, and you'll be lucky if you're in an environment where you can express yourself freely, or relatively freely . . . The men may be luckier. The men may have a better support system; banks may want to lend to men more over a woman in this business. But, still, I think you can find your way . . . it may take a very long time, but I think you will find it, and your way is more internal. I think you find your way in to yourself and your talent and then the world holds in that particular way. And hopefully, there's no end to it."

—*Amaryll Schwertner*

"Maybe it would help if people became more evolved. If men became more evolved and more respectful of women . . . or they became in touch with their emotions more [giggles], then they would appreciate and respect women more and then we could be on more equal footing . . . Women, again, they've gotta fight; and they've gotta do what they feel is right; and they gotta open more restaurants; and they gotta go against the opposition for it to make the shift . . . But for now, I don't know, you look at these [cooking] shows where these women just are homemakers—and, yeah, they gotta make a buck and that's how they're making their money—but they have to stand up for what is true . . . I think people want it [more women chefs advancing and being represented]. They totally want it; they want to see it. It's just up to the women to stand up and do it."

—*Jessica Boncutter*

"For a woman to do this [work in a restaurant] it really has to be something that you really want to do above all else, because it's still hard, it's still a struggle. I think women are a little more creative about accepting what they can do with this as a career. Not all women think they need to be chefs. A lot of women go on to write, cater, and find other ways to be in the food industry. And they're happy with it. How do I think it's going to change? I can't really say, because I think the whole economics of food is changing and I'm not really sure what direction it's going to go into. It may go into a direction that offers more opportunity for women. With this big shift we've had in the last couple years, I think economics is really going to determine where restaurants are going to be in the next ten years, and I don't know where it's going to land . . . It's kind of scary."

—*Pam Mazzola*

"Well, it's interesting. In the time that I've been in the business, which is almost thirty-five years now, things have changed from women who wanted to break in to the kitchen on the line, doing everything that everybody else could do—picking up big pieces of meat and slinging 'em around. I don't see as much of that anymore and it's very disappointing to me . . . I've been in restaurants and Women Chefs and Restaurateurs for a long time—I was on the board and am still in the organization—and I have seen [it] change from an organization that was a lot about women who were in the kitchen to a lot of [women who work in] food writing and test kitchens and a little bit more nine-to-five;

not quite as much of the every night on the line, sweating. And I'm kind of disappointed . . . I think women are certainly capable of doing that—maybe a lot of them don't want to. We actually have a little bit of trouble coming across women who apply for line jobs, oddly enough. Twenty years ago, that was not a problem. Lots of women were coming in, applying for line jobs. And we don't have as many now."

—*Christine Keff*

"You know what I think would help? The expectation that chefs need to work fourteen to sixteen hours a day needs to change. I think people—the public—still have some expectation that the chef, the person who owns the restaurant, is cooking their meal. There's no chef [who] can be there 24/7."

—*Pam Mazzola*

"I guess there has to be more than one way of looking at things, making room for different types of people. That's not the easiest thing to consider. Or maybe it has to do with a woman finding a place that suits her needs—not so much an organization changing what they're doing to suit someone, but finding the right match. There are restaurants that are very sympathetic to the needs of their employees. (You want to hope that you're one of them.) And then there are others that are less so . . . There are people like the Baylesses,[278] who had a child and built a playroom in the basement of the restaurant, and I think that they were very sympathetic to their employees' children too . . . That's how they managed to have children—or a child—and still be part of that child's life."

—*Johanne Killeen*

[278] Chef Rick Bayless and his wife, Deann, own three eateries in Chicago and have developed additional restaurant concepts elsewhere—at select Macy's department stores and O'Hare International Airport.

"If I could wave a magic wand, I would love a system whereby there are lots and lots more mom-and-pop restaurants that are creating community, and we politically, governmentally set up a system where those kinds of systems are really viable . . . Those mom-and-pop restaurants can buy from mom-and-pop farmers . . . And if cities and governments could create wages, or maybe subsidize health insurance for restaurants, or in some way nurture that . . . Because it's really important that we eat healthier food and less crap food . . . I would want more hand-cooked, handmade food around—real food—and access to it in a broader way—every corner shop and school system. The restaurant industry really needs to do more . . . The chapter in the [Bourdain] book *Medium Raw*[279] that really hit home—and I've been doing it in our restaurants and in my home already for the last couple years—is the part about 80/20 [80 percent plant, 20 percent]. We have 80/20 plant-based dishes[280] on our menu, and at home we eat an 80 percent plant-based diet. I had my entire staff read that chapter at our staff meeting . . . I'd like to really harness all the creative juices we have out here in the restaurant business and create really spectacular 80/20 options and shorten the amount of time it's going to take for us to turn the tide in this country."

—*Mary Sue Milliken*

"I'd like to think that the future looks bright, and I do. I think there is a change coming. It's very, very slow, but everything happens slowly. [There are] very few overnight changes or overnight successes."

—*Amanda Cohen*

[279] Anthony Bourdain, "Meat," *Medium Raw* (New York: Ecco, an imprint of HarperCollins, 2011), 95–110.

[280] I had the pleasure of sharing one of these with Milliken during our interview at the Border Grill (downtown L.A. outpost)—the crispy potato rajas tacos. Wish I hadn't been taking notes the entire time, or else I would have been able to get a few more bites of goodness in.

"I think it looks good. I think it looks better. I think [there are] a lot more women stepping up, a lot more women realizing that they have a voice . . . Women should be feminine, yes, but I think that some women will . . . fall into that hole, and they won't just get it done, and they won't be creative . . . Because there's so much more media now with chefs—suddenly chefs have become the rock stars. The male chefs have become much more arrogant . . . I don't want [women] to become as arrogant, but I just don't want them to lose that drive . . . I don't want them to lose that focus."

—*Sarah Schafer*

"For my generation, it was a smaller group, first of all, and it seemed that women chefs at a certain level kind of recognized each other and there was a sense of community. Everything is much bigger now, but there are more outlets for younger chefs too. There are organizations to join . . . The outlets are there; it's just a matter of finding them and being able to work with somebody who maybe has similar goals or has had experiences that could help you . . . Women in general are very open to mentoring and trying to help other women."

—*Johanne Killeen*

"Well, I'm certainly positive. I can't imagine it being worse [laughs]. I mean, not that it's terrible . . . It's certainly not bad for me, but I can see, in talking about it, a lack of role models. Now with TV, I think it's better, even if it's maybe not who I would choose to put on TV, at least women are getting attention for being chefs. Is that true? I don't know. Maybe not, they're all tarted up . . ."

—*Renee Erickson*

"The more women [who] see women opening certain kinds of businesses, the more confidence they will have that they can do it."

—*Melissa Nyffeler*

"The more women who get involved in, for instance, a La Cocina,[281] or are mentored in this entrepreneurial way, you'll slowly see more women in the business. And I think you'll see it on both coasts. That was my experience back in 1987, seeing that it [women in the business] actually does exist and then feeling like I can do it . . . It's like if you see a picture of something, you kind of get this idea that you can become a part of that picture."

—*Liz Prueitt*

"Something that has been lost in this country is a legacy . . . You have to see within your ranks when people are loyal and they stay with you for a long time; there's an obligation for you to be an assistant—whether you want to call it a mentor, a facilitator, whatever it is—for them to somehow get a foothold and do something on their own . . . People are afraid of competition or duplication, but, in a sense, the best way for people to get into business is if somebody they've worked really, really hard for helps them in some way. Even if it's getting them to the right place to get money or giving them ideas about how to do it, that's really important."

—*Nancy Oakes*

---

[281] As per the San Francisco organization's website, at Lacocinasf.org: "The mission of La Cocina is to cultivate low-income food entrepreneurs as they formalize and grow their businesses by providing affordable commercial kitchen space, industry-specific technical assistance, and access to market opportunities. We focus primarily on women from communities of color and immigrant communities. Our vision is that entrepreneurs will become economically self-sufficient and contribute to a vibrant economy doing what they love to do."

"I'd like it to get to the point where it's not 'Oh, Michelle Bernstein, that's one of the best *women* chefs in the country.' "[282]

—*Stephanie Izard*

"The future looks a lot like what it's like now, in all honesty. How can it be improved? I think it's great in this country. If a woman chef wants to do it, it's up to her. I don't think anyone handed me anything because I'm a woman to give me a break."

—*Jennifer Jasinski*

"Change comes from within. So it's all how you want to perceive it and embrace it . . . It's never going to be an even playing field. It's just the nature of the beast . . . You have to accept it and never let it hold you back. I certainly don't."

—*Koren Grieveson*

"The future looks bright for female chefs, but change will still come slowly. Until everyone, male and female (and those in transition), takes a hard look at how they add to the problem, at how their thinking is dictated by inequitable gender constructs or societal norms, we can't achieve true equality. True, the mere mention of female chefs as a category is problematic and perhaps isn't up to date in modern feminist thought, but I think if we don't continue to talk about it, real change will be impaired."

—*Anita Lo*

---

[282] Early in our conversation, I brought up how enervated I was by that galoot Mike Isabella, who made it to the finals on Bravo's *Top Chef All-Stars* reality competition show only, thank goodness, to lose. Isabella, the show's token chauvinist pig, is the one who made this inane comment. Probably thought he was being all complimentary and knowledgeable-seeming too, jackass.

CHAPTER 12

Back to the Future

It's something very important, that we find a way to balance the feminine and the masculine in the kitchen. And what really interests me about the Edible Schoolyard project is that young kids have an opportunity to both accomplish something wonderful in the kitchen or in the garden and that they work together. And one day you do this and the next day you do that, and it's very empowering, and it doesn't have a sexual orientation at all, which is a beautiful thing that kids grow up that way—feeling that they can feed themselves in a delicious, wholesome way, and that both men and women can really participate in that, because it's the basing thing of life and is what you need to do for your family.

It has to do with respect that men have for women and vice versa. And so if women become more like men and men become more like women, we'll be in a very good place. And, again, that is the thesis of the Edible Schoolyard, [it] is to help kids relate differently to each other.

I was kind of a tomboy when I was a kid and always played, whether it was baseball with boys or climbing the trees. I really liked that kind of challenge—the physical challenge of that. And then they admired me, because I went along and did that. So it's a little bit standing up to it, and really being present. And once they see you can do it, then the barriers all fall away . . . and those are just barriers that have been arbitrarily set up. We just have to teach our children differently. There's a beautiful possibility there. But you also have to set up the restaurant differently so that kind of interaction can take place. You have to really almost prepare the restaurant for this to happen . . . It's a little in that place of affirmative action that you deliberately put women in places that surprise people, and put men in other positions that surprise people. And then they find

BACK TO THE FUTURE

307

out they like those things . . . But again, you don't have that pyramid that reinforces a way of thinking that whoever is there at the top—the chef and the sous chef—is running everything and the people who are at the bottom are not important to the whole thing . . . I think everybody should have an experience in all aspects of the kitchen, whether it is washing the dishes— doing the most, you know, the littlest tasks. It's about really building a kind of an awareness.

—ALICE WATERS

"What," I ask Alice Waters, who is sitting across the table from me in her office at Chez Panisse in Berkeley, "do you think the future looks like for women chefs?"

Maybe I should back up. You're probably (Tony Bourdain, you especially)[283] wondering why I'd begin a conversation about the future with a woman who started her revolution more than forty years ago. Surely, you're saying, no matter what Alice Waters has accomplished, there must be springier chickens out there better equipped to talk about the road ahead. I get it. No one was more surprised than I to find that what Waters started in 1971 and has continued to build upon could, in fact, be among the more visionary phenomena to apply to the next forty years.

I wasn't so sure what to expect at our meeting. On the one hand, as a food writer, I couldn't wait to meet Waters and was amazed, thrilled, and extremely grateful she had agreed to talk to me. On the other hand, well, I was skeptical. Think about it for a second; if you're writing a book about chefs (let's forget that they happen to be women), and you're going to talk to someone you're in awe of who has been known to decline the title *chef*, you're not so sure how this little chit-chat is going to go. (If you remember, way back to chapter 1, she did not dance around that issue—she admitted her initial reluctance to

[283] In his 2010 title *Medium Raw*, Bourdain devotes an entire chapter, " 'Go Ask Alice,' " to why he finds Alice Waters so intolerably irritating. Hers, he notes, is a situation wherein "a perfectly good message got lost with the messenger." He follows that up with: "In the same way, having Alice Waters on your side of the argument is like having Alec Baldwin or Barbra Streisand endorse your candidate . . . You may agree with everything they say, but you wish they'd just shut the fuck up." (New York: Ecco, an imprint of HarperCollins, 2010), 134.

assume the position, and her eventual acceptance of it thanks to some chiding from Jacques Pépin.[284]) In fact, someone could think my visiting Berkeley was an exercise in putting the moron in oxymoronic. I, however, was not concerned about that minor semantic discrepancy. I'd had a discussion with myself when I first requested some time with Waters. Whether or not she accepted it, I consider her a chef, and, more important than that, in a time when chefs are prone to use their profession as a means to gain fame or fortune, I felt it crucial that someone like Waters, who uses her power as a culinary figure for good, be recognized as the chef she is. We have enough chef-rockers; a chef-activist is someone worth celebrating and, if you're lucky enough to have the opportunity, someone whose brain you pick.

So I had no qualms about the is-she-or-isn't-she business. Had she demurred my classifying her a chef, I would have called her on it. What worried me was that Waters was going to insist on talking about and plugging her activist agenda—the Edible Schoolyard Project and its mission to "transform the health and values of every student by building and sharing a food curriculum for the school system."[285] This, by the way, is a cause about which I'm passionate, but *not* what I wanted to discuss with the Chevalier de la Légion d'Honneur.[286] We were supposed to focus primarily on the chef part of her hyphenated job description.

Despite this concern and the anxiety that anticipation of a face-to-face moment with a legendary figure brings, I was pretty mellow on my way from San Francisco to Idealism Central.[287] It was hard not

---

[284] See page 30.

[285] The "intention" as stated on the Edible Schoolyard Project's website (Edibleschoolyard.org).

[286] France bestowed this, its noblest decoration, on Waters in 2009.

[287] When I began sorting out my table of contents, I had planned on including and decided to forego a chapter titled "It's Always Sunnier in San Francisco. Why?" I was determined to figure out why there are so many lady chef-owners out west, especially in the Bay Area. Many pinned it on Alice Waters and her ilk. Otherwise, no one on that coast had a solid answer, except for the grande dame herself. Waters suggested that its distance from the Atlantic Ocean was what might have allowed California to be the perfect environment for a new model of restaurant to develop—one that isn't so entrenched in European tradition. While New York is busy seeking approval from France, the realm of white male toques and fine-dining airs, California's view of that world remains obstructed, which allows its residents to follow their own rhythm, soak up the sunshine, and appreciate a generous terroir. In the aftermath of Berkeley's 1960s Free Speech Movement, an eatery like Chez Panisse, which opened in 1971, seemed more like an outgrowth of an existing philosophy than a rebellious anomaly;

cont'd

to relax and feel the good vibrations; the sun was shining, sky clear and cerulean, and, you know, it's Berkeley. There's no room for stress in the land of laid-back hippies. There was also my trusty companion "ced,"[288] my iPod shuffle that carried me through the on-the-road portion (and beyond) of this whole book-writing endeavor. The little green gizmo knew just what the occasion demanded. As if on cue, Stars ("The Black House, The Blue Sky"), The Mynabirds ("Numbers Don't Lie"), Stevie Nicks ("Trouble in Shangri-La"), and Patti Smith ("Frederick") streamed smile-generating refrains and gypsy magic into my ears. Those ditties set the tone for the following hour.

Everyone who works on the Chez Panisse premises is kind, upbeat, and genuinely glad to be on board. And, once you're there, even if only for a morning, they treat you as though you're one of them—part of their clan. Associate Justice of the Supreme Court Sonia Sotomayor was slated to lunch there that afternoon, and, although they were excited, no one was freaking out. "So *this*," I said to myself, "is why people never leave." It was as though I was being glamoured[289] by vampires—except, instead of blood, these grounded mortals live off of kishus and dates. Yes, these are Waters's signature snacks. She keeps a bowlful of them near (as long as they're in season, of course). They sat between us on the table during the interview. (The whole time, I wanted so badly to reach out and grab one. There was an internal debate taking place in my mind as I scrawled notes, asked Alice questions, and avidly listened to her responses. *Am I supposed to help myself? Isn't it always more polite*

the same goes for the fact that a woman was in charge. Overall, both the relaxed nature of that region's dining establishments and its preponderance of female chefs are by-products of the same ethos. Once I'd reached that conclusion, the initial question, the why, became less relevant than the what. It's because of that state's particular cultural climate that Barbara Tropp, Joyce Goldstein, and Waters were able to set up the kinds of shops they did, and, subsequently, yes, it's thanks to them that other women in that zone followed in their footsteps. That's what happens when something is presented as a norm; it's not perceived as a big deal, and carries on. I think that's why the chefs who live in that idyllic enclave had little more than a shrug to offer by way of explanation for their relatively high numbers—the younger ones, especially, hadn't given much thought to the matter.

[288] My initials etched, in lowercase, on the back. Dear "ced," in fact, died only a week before I began this final chapter. RIP, little buddy. No one could have asked for a better inanimate companion.

[289] Those who watch the HBO show *True Blood* already know what this means. In that context, it refers to a vampire's ability to hypnotize humans vocally and via eye contact. It's a form of bewitching, you might say.

to wait for someone to offer something to you? Is this a test? Will I seem more assertive if I grab one of these tiny clementines? Or, will I look like a greedy, easily distracted hack? Are they even clementines? What are they?) Or else if it's not the citrus and sweet dried fruit that's fueling these angels of sustainability, maybe it's the tisane they're sipping. Waters has it brewed, by the pot, with fresh mint leaves, throughout the day. It's like the best Moroccan tea ever, without the sugar.

At the end of the interview, not only had I tried one of these marvelous tiny, seedless mandarins (that's what they are, I subsequently learned from Waters, who did indeed ask if I'd like one, and they taste like candy, I swear), but I had also realized that her raison d'être was much farther-reaching than I'd imagined. It isn't simply a plan to feed children righteous grub (noble in its own right, that endeavor). It's about making them better citizens and building strong, supportive communities. This impacts everyone—male and female—in every profession, but particularly speaks to those who are or might be involved in the food industry on any level.

Reader, I drank the tisane.

Imagine home ec, that arcane academic rubric of a bygone era, in a new guise—one that, by including boys and girls, becomes genderless. Instead of a flock of aproned young ladies standing at ovens while they wait for their tester cakes to rise, there are kids raking garden soil together, watering their tiny crops together, picking the fruits from their vines together, baking them into a pie together, and then eating slices of that pie together. Each little dude or princess learns every task. There's no sex assigned to any step along the way. If that could start in kindergarten for every child in every school (or at least in the public schools, where such things can be implemented through legislation), you'd build a foundation for different behavior in the workplace and at home. It might seem frivolous to some, giving children access to a plot of arable land or a scholastic kitchen of their own. Not to me. Alice can expound on how the experience will enrich their relationship with farming and will make them better, healthier, more mindful eaters. What matters within these pages is the ideological nourishment that this kind of project delivers.

And so, as our forty-five minutes ran out, I asked Alice, although, in a way, she had already offered her answer, "What do you think the future looks like for women chefs (or chefs, in general)? How much can be improved from within the industry and which external forces need to change?"

"I think we need to talk about all of these issues on a national level . . . We need to recognize that one in two families in this country is divorced; that we're talking about two households. We're talking about shifting kids from one place to another. It makes the situation of school very, very important for a child. And I think food is about care, so we have a real opportunity in the restaurants to sort of lead the way. And I think that is what's happening with Michelle Obama, that she's helping us see how to balance our lives . . . There's no question that's [the media] a place that can help educate us all and we need to be thinking about this, and that's why I want a program in the school that begins in kindergarten, and maybe the kids can bring the messages home to the parents—they're so good at doing that."

When I left Alice's Wonderland, well before Sonia showed up for her repast, I was left with two things: hope and, on my hands, the lingering scent of kishu. I wanted both to stay with me forever. They have, more or less. For the latter, I've been forced to improvise. We don't see kishus in these parts. I'm going have to find out who grows the little suckers and ships them to the Northeast (Waters will know)—carbon footprint, my foot. What I have found is an overpriced liquid hand soap naturally fragranced with *Citrus nobilis* (mandarin orange) peel oil.[290] The former—that would be hope—has been easier to maintain; no artificial substitute required.

---

[290] Made by that Aussie company Aesop, my bottle of Resurrection Aromatique Hand Wash includes the following quote from Carl Jung, "Often the hands will solve a mystery that the intellect has struggled with in vain." I'm wondering if the specific mystery referred to here would be why I pay $37 for soap. The answer, indeed, is offered by my lovely-smelling hands.

I've kept in touch with as many of the chefs I interviewed as possible, and I've followed their achievements and career developments. It has been a privilege and joy to get to know them all and to have them share their opinions and stories with me. While writing, my goal was to represent each point of view in a way that would do justice to its owner and, also, to create an on-page community of voices. Now that my twelve chapters are up and El Lappers[291] is weary, what remains is that army of seventy-three cohorts. In my vision of the future, this legion lives on, as a unified collective, beyond these pages. And it grows. There is strength in numbers, yes, but only if those numbers stand (the heat) and stay in the kitchen together.

[291] How quickly we forget. El Lappers is my laptop. You were introduced at the outset.

To my folks—**Nancy** & **Jim**; Mom, I'm starting with you because you're the one person who has, consistently, throughout the years, encouraged me to write and always believed and told me, without fail, that I could do anything I put my mind to. (And let's not forget those Thursday sessions at the mixing bowl. They're responsible for this too.) Dad, Voice of Reason, Father of Us All, you are that rarest and most exemplary of patriarchs. Thank you for making sure I was eating along the way (the surprise Sunday Barney Greengrass care packages never got tired; feel free to keep them coming), but, more important, for being such a present father and "old fashioned" (endearingly chauvinistic) enough to give me something to get angry about in the first place.

To the **73** women who agreed to be part of this, the Skirt Steak project and (most of the time), without knowing me at all, imparting your trust. I hope you don't regret that. You have inspired me with your candor, strength, humor, insight, bravery, generosity, and myriad talents. A special nod to **Anita Lo**, who, by allowing me to co-write her cookbook, gave me the confidence to pen my own book—thank you for putting in your wise two cents whenever asked and for connecting me with so many of the women in these pages; another to **Anne Rosenzweig**, who first agreed to be interviewed, and then became an honorary family member.

Christine, you remain my hay-mentor; your support (anything from letting me write the stories of my dreams to sharing pastry-related musings) is an endless source of pride and delight. Merci. **Pavia**, my editorial big sister, ever since you welcomed me into your fantastic world, the effects of your accumulative cheerleading (a decade's worth) and regular check-ins have been, in their beneficent magnitude, unfathomable, or, at least, immeasurable. **Lock**, many thanks for your motivating advice dispensed through our marathon IM sessions. **BL**, steadfast friend who's always up for a debate or there to put in a good word, is there a "new black" version of thank you? It's yours, a million times over. To a few friends who helped me get through all this in ways that only they could—**Sara**, **Cam** & **FMG**—you have no idea how much it meant to have you on the other end of the phone, a nearby barstool, or whatever city sidewalks we covered on our power walks (or lazy strolls). **Amanda & Merrill**, a proverbial bottomless City Bakery stash to you for picking up the slack when the inevitable Tournament of Cookbooks onslaught hit and always having a sense of humor about the bracket-building. Piglet Forever.

Don't Stop Believin'. That's your theme song, **Laura Nolan**. You didn't—in me, or this project—even when I had.

TEAM CHRONICLE

Leigh Haber, somehow you saw something here. And you made me think that something was worth it, the whole way through.

Lorena Jones & Sarah Billingsley, the ladies who kept everything on track and held down the fort even when it seemed as though it might all cave in, I salute you.

Vanessa Dina, how, from that sprawl of a first draft you were able to envision the perfect cover, and on the first try, I'll never know. I remain forever grateful and in awe.

Jane Tunks, when I first saw your name on the manuscript you so painstakingly copy edited, all I could think of was the madcap wizard Tonks from the Harry Potter books (she's the one who's always changing her hair color). We've never met in person, but, in my mind, your locks change hue regularly, and yes, you are a wizard. Thanks for making sure all my i's were dotted and t's crossed—or, for minding my p's, q's, and accents. Now, when can we have lunch at Chez Panisse?

David Hawk, for you, one more smørrebrød (and glass of the Jolie Laide) at Bar Tartine for the road, and kisses.

Jeff Levine at the Culinary Institute of Art, you couldn't have been more helpful and accommodating if you tried; ditto, **Susan Ungaro** and **Mitchell Davis** at the James Beard Foundation, who were so generously willing to answer any and all questions. And **Willie Norkin**, if you hadn't been on the other end of that initial e-mail exchange, the latter dialogue might not have been possible. Thanks, all of you.

SECURITY
Rosie Pawstein, you have my heart, cuteness monster, and although your barking didn't help much when things got stressful, your tenacious attempts to instigate fetch cracked me up every time.

TECH SUPPORT, A COLLECTIVE ROLL CALL OF APPRECIATION
El Lappers, that blue light shining in the darkest or latest of hours.

ced/ced 2, the DJ that knows exactly which song to play in any situation.

Gmail with its nifty custom auto-responder vacation reply; fare thee well, outgoing LOCKDOWN message (for now). You will NOT be missed.

PROVISIONS
Aunt Rosie's chocolate chip cookies at **Jack's Stir Brew** on West 10th Street the matcha lattes at **Bosie Tea Parlor** on Morton Street, and the Magic Bars at **Milk & Cookies** on Commerce that fueled the writing process . . . couldn't have done it without the sustenance your habit-forming treats provided.

Finally, thank you to anyone who read[1] or bought the book, or, ideally, both.

[1] Bonus thx to anyone who read the footnotes.